Walking
Patagonia

Walking Patagonia
The Way

Caspian Ray

ARCHWAY
PUBLISHING

Archway Publishing books may be ordered through booksellers or by contacting:

Archway Publishing
1663 Liberty Drive
Bloomington, IN 47403
www.archwaypublishing.com
1 (888) 242-5904

Scripture taken from the King James Version of the Bible.

ISBN: 978-1-4808-4045-4 (sc)
ISBN: 978-1-4808-4044-7 (hc)
ISBN: 978-1-4808-4046-1 (e)

Library of Congress Control Number: 2016920344

Print information available on the last page.

Archway Publishing rev. date: 1/16/2017

For Solomon

To every thing there is a season, and a time
to every purpose under the heaven.

—Ecclesiastes 3:1

Contents

Acknowledgments

To the people of Argentina and Chile. I would not have lasted a week without you.

Author Note

The walk of Patagonia began in September 2012.
I was twenty-five.
This is the way, *más o menos.*

Preface
The Life Before Patagonia

As a kid, I would spin the globe and close my eyes. Wherever my finger landed was the destination. Again and again I would spin the globe until I arrived on the Americas below me. Throughout my life, I felt an unescapable pull toward Latin America. Like a conquistador drawn to gold, glory, and God, the magnetic pull on my spirit was perpetual. Anytime I had the chance, I would visit her. Back to the small remote pueblos I went—to the thousands of unseen faces. I don't know why I loved her; I just know I spent many sleepless nights looking at pictures of her.

I visited Cuba long before it was legal, when I was only eighteen. Later I snuck into Evo Morales's inauguration with a fake press pass. He was the first indigenous president elected in the Americas, and I needed to be there. I was always searching out adventure to the South, and all of my traveling was able to occur at such a young age because my mom worked seventy-hour weeks and owned a small business with about twenty employees, myself included. She paid me substantially more than I deserved and let me take off whenever a spontaneous burst of passion struck. My conscience tried to not let me take advantage of the situation, but in Latin America, I always found justification. An obsession would come over me.

My entire life had been without want. We weren't wealthy; everyone I knew worked, but as a family we did and had essentially whatever we wanted. This had a profound effect on my formative years. I felt opposing feelings of enjoying the life and feeling profoundly guilty for it, for I had arguably done nothing to deserve an ounce of it. The birth of the Internet allowed these thoughts to fester inside my soul. I could see the whole world and the extremes of its grossly rich and horridly poor. It depressed me, mainly because I preferred this life. Every day, I chose it.

I wanted to relate with the rest of the world and not just see it on the Internet. I needed to, if only for a moment in time, truly experience something different. I needed to feel pains of true hunger. What was thirst, and what did water taste like when that thirst was quenched? How did people sleep under bridges, and in places where excrement was not rightly disposed of? What was pain, and how did the feet ache after a brutal day? How did a beer taste when it was not purchased but truly earned as only a gift can be, as a reward for the hardship of life?

This is what travel must be about. I could discover no new lands. The days of being an explorer were over. I wasn't smart enough to be an astronaut. In a world so big with seven billion people it felt nearly impossible to be special. All I could do was walk, and experience the in between. The whole trip would have to be mapped out. Routes needed to be selected, and I knew where point A would be.

Point A was the southern tip of Tierra del Fuego and the region known as Patagonia. At the time, while I was omnipotently manipulating the globe of Google Earth, it seemed feasible I could walk across the entire continent of South America. My elevated imagination put point B at the extremes of Colombia.

What the trip needed was a couple companions, and I asked everyone, but walking endlessly didn't appeal to many people.

"But dude, think of the freedom!" I was trying hard to sell it.

Two friends from childhood bought in. The first to sign on was Devin. At the time, he lived in Macau, teaching English. He wanted to get outside the city. He wanted pure Patagonian air and he wanted freedom. The second was Jackson. He was in Egypt, working with a nonprofit, and I told him we would be legends.

As departure neared, it became difficult to think about the lands north of Patagonia. The region is shared, though historically not amicably, between Argentina and Chile. Patagonia is a fairy-tale land, and defining Patagonia is impossible with any word other than "adventure."

Tierra del Fuego—Fireland—is the huge island at the extreme bottom of the Americas and Patagonia. This is a land of constantly-changing weather patterns. The four seasons often occur daily. Here the natives had huge fires that Darwin and sailors could see for miles, thus giving the island its name.

In southern Chile, imposing mountains peaks protrude from the waters of the Magellan Strait and along the innumerable fjords of Patagonia. Mythical creatures like the towering ground sloth, the mylodon, lived there. Torres del Paine can hardly be described with words. So dramatically, the earth's crust is crushed upwards to the sky by the most powerful tectonic forces on the planet. The world's largest earthquake occurred in Chile's northern reaches of Patagonia at the vibrant city of Validivia. Here is the Chilean Patagonia rainforest where seemingly ever plant is endemic.

Patagonia is also the land of the southern glaciers. Glaciers like the Perito Moreno and Viedma feed enormous cold blue lakes. The ice melts down the Rio Santa Cruz through the flat desert lands. This is the land of the *corderos* (sheep) and gauchos. The land of the screaming westerly wind whipping up from Antarctica. The Andes form a rain shadow over most of Argentine Patagonia. It is a vast shrubland with views that are perpetual. There are thousands of rock formations, each one a geologist's dream. Here the dry night sky makes belief in the stars possible. Here is solitude.

Mount Fitz Roy is Patagonia, and it has inspired much more than just a clothing company. This is the mountain from every fairy tale—the one with the princess waiting at the top. The rocky and frighteningly steep peak is so dangerous to climb that only a handful do so every year. The unpredictability of the Patagonian weather often proves fatal for climbers on the three-thousand-foot granite wall.

The only trees in the Patagonian Desert are on estancias, and they are tall and thin poplars. Here is the least populated place on the South

American continent, with fewer people here than in the Amazon rainforest. Gas is never a guarantee, and I passed stranded motorcyclists debating whether to pour their vodka into the tank or drink it and wait.

Patagonia follows the Andes north. Parque Nacional Alerces is the land where, legend says, Walt Disney was inspired to make *Bambi*. The huemul deer are endangered, and seeing one is rare. Many trees in this forest were born before Christ.

El Cholilo is a wild, dusty town that celebrates the festival of the *Asado*—the festival of grilling. Thousands of cows and lambs are put on crosses, and they fill the entire length of a football field. Every man gazes at the affair with supreme satisfaction, knowing that he is indeed the greatest creation. This is a place a Texan might call heaven. Butch Cassidy did.

Further north in Patagonia is the town of El Bolson, where there are more dreadlocks than at a Phish show. Microbreweries are abundant, and deep into the Andes, up the steep sides, and surrounded by big trees, Mapuche natives have resettled and are regaining territory by using squatters' rights. Patagonia is where celebrities own small countries.

This is the land of volcanoes and rivers formed by the lava—a place that feels prehistoric. Mythic tales of Patagonian dinosaurs existed for centuries. Legend has it that if you eat the calafate berry, you will return to Patagonia, and I would soon be eating them. Now it was the end of September, and spring had just arrived to the Southern Hemisphere here in Argentina.

1 Arrival

A journey is like marriage.
The certain way to be wrong is to think you control it.
— John Steinbeck

I arrived at Ezeiza International Airport in Buenos Aires at 10:00 a.m. There wasn't any public transportation from the airport, and taxis into town cost forty bucks so I decided to wait here the ten hours for Devin. I didn't want to share a room in a hostel on our first night, so I found us a cheap hotel online.

I had more time to kill, and after drinking a few cups of coffee, I walked into the bathroom. I sat down to pee. I just sat there in the stall, not even looking at the graffiti. I could only see inside my mind. My elbows were on my knees, and the palms of my hands were pressed against my closed eyes. My fingers curled against my forehead.

"You can do this," my spirit said to my mind.

I left the stall and walked to the mirror. My thick umber-brown hair, recently cut short, was under a baseball cap, as always. I had light green eyes and a single dimple in my left cheek that often allowed me to get away with mischief.

After a few more hours, the plane arrived, and passengers aboard Devin's flight started exiting. I had a small level of apprehension that he wasn't going to show, but soon the crowd separated, and I could see him smiling. The adrenaline came over me. Devin was here, and it felt awesome. It felt real. We jumped up and down, grunted, and cheered.

"Yeah, YES ... YEEEESS!"

Devin was slightly taller than I was at around five foot ten, with a slender Asian frame and light skin that would soon turn dark. He didn't weigh 130 pounds wet, and I barely weighed 140. We were two adventurers who certainly didn't look the part. He was smart and excited and liked burning plant matter. Finally a pipe dream of ours had become reality.

The cabdriver drove us to the hotel. It was in Plaza Miserere. With noticeable worry, the driver told me to hide my watch and hurry inside. It was a Suunto watch with altimeter, temperature, compass, and everything else that caused it to rapidly digest batteries. I had not considered this ahead of time. The valuable watch would soon be worthless. The cabdriver put his hand on my shoulder and said that we weren't in Patagonia yet. This was *El Capital*.

"This is a dangerous part of town." The driver was shaking his head, seeming to know for certain we were doomed. I didn't feel his worry. Nothing bad ever happened to me.

At 11:00 p.m., we knocked on the door to the hotel. The receptionist said it was *todo ocupado,* and with no backup plan, walked into the plaza of misery. We breathed deeply and took in our surroundings. This was our first adventure. All the old cement and stone buildings had gates on their windows. On the corner, under the awning of a large building, a couple was having sex on cardboard boxes.

Another hotel was near, and it was sixty dollars a night. The first thing we wanted to do was unpack everything and look at it in order to imagine the adventure through our gear. We had two tents, one of them a Hilleberg. We also had Hilleberg bivouacs—essentially, waterproof bags to sleep in. Hilleberg produces the greatest four-season backpacking equipment on earth. Each piece is made, start to finish, by one man's *manos.*

Here it was warm in the Capital, but in the South we would need big hats, jackets, gloves, and boots. We had a compass, stove, gas, and Nalgene bottles. We had boots when we needed, and Vibram FiveFingers when we didn't. There was an American flag, playing cards, cameras, and sleeping bags. In case of an emergency, I had an Iridium satellite phone. We had knives, medical equipment, and a chessboard. We emptied every sack, spreading out even our fishing lures. Most important was the water purifier with ceramic filter that could be easily wiped clean. Together it was a mountain of clothes and equipment on the bed. All the bright colors of adventure were before us. Both of the packs would weigh around forty-five pounds when full.

We went out to drink beer on the corner. The couple was finished and lay passed out together. I felt like a hard-ass even though I still hadn't done anything hard.

Devin had some contacts in the city, and the next day, we met up with Simon and Belen. Simon was twenty with hair past his shoulders. He liked talking about conspiracy theories, and I wanted to listen. They took us to one of the most iconic restaurants in the city. Siga la Vaca, or "follow the cow," is a meat factory, and on our way there, Simon passed a cop and asked for directions. When he did, I noticed he called the cop *che*. He said it in the same way we would say "Sir, excuse me." Simon said *"Che, disculpa."*

"It's okay, man. Everyone is che here," Simon said to me when I acted surprised. When I heard "che" I thought of Che Guevara. I thought of revolution and anti-police sentiment. I thought Simon was being aggressive.

As it turns out, "che" is a wonderful word. It is uniquely Argentine and is used beautifully by them. It comes from the natives of Patagonia named the Tehuelche and Mapuche. It means "person" or "human." Simon was right; for the next year, I listened to the word "che" repeatedly. They called women che. Gays were che. Friends and enemies were che. They would say che when they were being sincere, and they would say che when spitting insults. Here you are che.

Belen was Simon's sister and worked with Devin in Macau. She taught Spanish where Devin taught English. Her face was quite round, and her eyes were big and dark. She cut her bangs high above her eyebrows, and her hair was long and straight in the back. She wore Converse high tops, and tight jeans pulled up high around her waist.

"You didn't know her dad was a fucking foreign diplomat? How could you not have known that?" I asked Devin. It was exciting thinking about all the laws we could break.

"She never talked about it, man; I knew he worked for the government."

They wanted us to stay at their apartment in the middle of the city, two blocks away from the monumental Obelisco.

They decided to tell their mom that Devin and I got robbed at the bus station. I told them to just tell her the truth.

"No, no way bro, we can't do that," Simon said. Lying to their mother was much more fun.

Devin and I waited outside the door but were quickly let in. Upon entering the apartment, my eyes soon lost a focal point. I didn't know what to look at. There were so many trinkets—so many wild, exotic things gifted to the diplomat over the years.

"You don't know the half of what we've had stolen!" their mother would tell me months later.

I didn't want to be rude, but I also wanted to see and touch everything. This was a museum, and it was cluttered with priceless items. I sat my drink on a coffee table made with wood from a European castle. The walls were covered in paintings, old books, and a one-hundred-year-old liquor from China with a cobra inside. The father had been a diplomat for decades and in many important places.

Their mother was Mirta, and she was delighted to have company. Mirta was a woman of character and force, and she was so smart it scared me. She had been quite beautiful and proper when younger, but illness had quickly aged her. She smoked like a soldier and knew more languages than I could count on my hands. Everything about this woman was diplomatic. Mirta was never wrong, and after the four of us listened to her talk for an hour, we left to have a drink. I still had not seen the diplomat.

There was a bar full of gringos nearby where nearly everyone understood English. It was called the Rhino and felt like a frat party. The beer was cheap and sold by the liter. After drinking twelve liters, we went back to the apartment, and I cried when I saw their mother. The alcohol caused me to hug her longer than customary and to put my head on her shoulder, in tears, as I lamented about being "the luckiest guy on earth."

The next morning I woke up not really sure where I was or how I got there.

The trip could not have started better, and there was no hangover. During adventures hangovers rarely occur, no matter how much alcohol is consumed. Still, I was feeling unsure about the adventure I had gotten myself into.

We spent the third day in Buenos Aires drinking and walking the city streets. We explored the famous graveyard of Recoleta while Devin kept asking people on the street for plants. Simon and Belen enjoyed the two days of partying as much as we did, and they waved good-bye to us at the bus station in Retiro. From here buses go to the farthest reaches of the continent. We were going to the southern limit. The journey would take fifty hours.

We boarded the bus and started on our way south. As we were exiting the city, the bus stopped on the highway. A guy got out and looked in the back, but ten minutes later we were back on the road. Buenos Aires is huge, stretching out to house 12 million people, and it took time to escape its reach.

The first stop out of Buenos Aires is Mar del Plata, the second largest city in the Buenos Aires province. Here is where people from the capital go to vacation and wear thong bikinis. We had no interest in it. The bus let a few people off and drove on.

A few hours later, we reached the last port town in the province of Buenos Aires. Bahia Blanca was named for its salt-covered beaches. It has always been a transport hub for the products of the pampa. The Pampa is Argentina's version of North America's Great Plains, where soybeans and cows seem to outnumber even the ants.

Many hours later, the bus crossed the Rio Negro and we were finally in Patagonia. Everything was separated by tremendous distances in Patagonia, and currently we were four hours from the nearest town in either direction. The bus pulled over and came to a halt. The engine problem had returned.

The bus driver went to try fixing it again, and I opened a window to feel the cold Patagonian wind for the first time. It was exciting—our first introduction to her. She wasn't happy though, and the excitement quickly wore off as my mind soon wondered how I would live with this beast for the foreseeable future. After two hours, the driver came back to the bus defeated.

"Anyone have a cell phone?" he asked with no shame in his voice.

He had still not called for help. A tractor had towed us off the road, and there we waited while the wind smashed into, squeezed through, and shook the bus. Four hours later, we were picked up by another.

Finally we passed Puerto Madryn. Founded by Welsh immigrants in 1865, the main tourist attraction here are the Right whales, which come to mate and bear calves in these waters. They are normally out swimming here from June to December, and they love showing off for boats. Here they are dying in great numbers—not from pollution or from fishing nets, but from seagulls. This predator-prey relationship is a relatively recent occurrence, and every year more beached babies appear, their backs with oozing wounds. The seagulls are learning. Whales are an easier meal than fish, and the gulls are quickly removing Madryn's next generation of cetaceans and killing the spirit of the world's happiest whale.

The last stop before Rio Gallegos was Comodoro Rivadavia, the largest town in Chubut, an oil boomtown that has been prosperous ever since. Years ago, when oil reserves began to diminish, Rivadavia began to invest in the wind and harvest Patagonia's most obvious energy source. Here the bus let more people off.

A few hours later, we arrived in Rio Gallegos, the capital of Provincia Santa Cruz. This is the least densely populated place in South America. This province is home to only 1.1 persons per square kilometer. Devin and I had to find a place to stay. The long ride ended here. We needed to board another bus the next day.

We chose to explore the big Carrefour grocery store and spent an hour trying to figure out which of the one hundred different *yerba mates* to buy. We freestyled about "the yerba, the yerba, the yerba" (pronounced jerba). Mate is the drink of Argentina. It is often compared to green tea, but it has a distinctively robust and bitter flavor. It is brewed from the leaves of two-year-old yerba plants. The Guarani of Paraguay and Northern Argentina have chewed the leaves since the beginning of time and have been drinking the tea for almost as long. Yerba was almost always a wild plant; not a soul could make the seeds germinate, but after much trial and error, the Jesuit missionaries realized the seeds needed to travel through the digestive system of a bird to germinate. Soon yerba became a local cash crop and a cultural phenomenon.

The next morning, we got on the bus and headed toward the Magellan Strait and into Tierra del Fuego. Winds created whitecaps in the sea. In the Southern Hemisphere, there is very little land to slow down the southern westerly trade winds. They are stronger here than anywhere else on earth. Tierra del Fuego sits at a southern latitude of approximately 55 degrees—an area known to sailors as the furious fifties. Here, next to the ocean I saw old wooden ships alive in a world of historic adventures. Magellan was here. Before the construction of the Panama Canal, this was the only way around the Americas. The journey was often a death sentence for even the most experienced mariners. The weather, so seemingly unpredictable, had caused Capitan Fitz Roy, the man responsible for taking Darwin around the world, to become the world's first non-shamanic weather forecaster, so intriguing was this relatively new invention called a barometer.

Devin and I went outside and stood on the deep blue ferry. The large ramp that allowed eighteen-wheelers to board was lifted. The engines roared like a train and began pushing a tremendous amount of water backward and us forward. The shore of Tierra del Fuego was visible ahead, and it appeared almost fluid, as if it were flattened dough being constantly worked by the divine baker. Here I hoped to be greeted by the famous white-and-black Commerson's dolphins, but they never came.

Back on land, the road goes through the Chilean side of Tierra del Fuego. Just a small fraction of tourists go to Tierra del Fuego for the Chilean side, and there seemed to be a level of resentment from the carabineros—the Chilean border agents.

From here it was still six hours to Ushuaia, and the bus broke down in no-man's-land. This was a twelve-kilometer stretch of land between the borders filled with sheep, guanaco (essentially wild llamas), and land mines. At the time, I knew very little of the two countries' tumultuous history.

Devin and I got outside to stretch and admire the vista. The wind was strong, but the air was crisp and clean. There were rolling valleys carpeted in vibrant green. In this brief season of mild temperatures and longer days, the landscape had blossomed to life. Undulating hills and valleys were covered in exceptionally thick grasses with tiny flowers.

There were no trees. The land is under ice and snow nearly eight months out of the year. The ground was soft and seemed to be made entirely of humus—dark, fresh, and fertile—that expanded and contracted with any added pressure. Freeze, thaw, life, death, wind, rain—the baker's fingers were at work. Clouds were jockeying for position in the sky, each trying to record a new personal best, and stretching out to the finish line of site. After an hour, we got on a replacement bus, and we soon passed Rio Grande. This is home to the biggest trout in the world and is filled with people flicking their fly rods with target-practice precision.

Farther south, the subpolar forests appeared. They are gnarly old man forests, and the trees here are covered in a white and orange mushroom known as the Pan de Indio, or Indian bread. This was often the only substance consumed by the natives that wasn't meat.

Suddenly the starting point of the Andes appeared—giant mountains of granite and andesite undressed entirely by the wind, all their cracks and scars visible. Only snow managed to hang on at the top. The bus crawled around Lago Fagnano and over Paso Garibaldi. Reaching Garibaldi is a triumphant moment for adventure bikers who make the journey south from Alaska. Why is this pass so important to the bikers? From here it is all downhill. Here was the last pedal of an epic journey.

The bus pulled into Ushuaia after dark, and a lady approached. She was offering a free taxi ride to a hostel. It was twelve bucks a night and the cheapest place. Earlier we had told Jackson a different location, and he had arrived a few hours earlier by plane. From the hostel, I e-mailed him the new coordinates. Jackson got in a cab, and when I saw it pull up, I started dancing circles around the car. I shouted words like "vida," while flapping my arms in the air, and jumping.

"You are definitely in for an adventure," the cabdriver said to Jackson driving off.

Jackson is tall, skinny, and ginger. His entire body is covered in freckles. To see the world he loves so much, he has blue eyes that invite strangers to him like a spring picnic. His hair was just long enough to form a ponytail. Jackson loves everyone, and is almost always too nice.

He lives to socialize and can speak six languages. This means he can flirt with nearly anyone, and he does.

Jackson's bags had gotten lost, and we would have to wait an extra two days in the hostel for them. I didn't mind. This gave us time to put off the inevitable, and two more days to have fun in Ushuaia.

2 The Walk Begins

A good traveler has no fixed plans, and is not intent on arriving.
— Lao Tzu

Jackson's backpacks arrived, but we still put off leaving as long as we could. For hours we sat around drinking yerba mate and playing with our thumbs.

"Well." I said.

We looked at each other and back down at the floor.

"All right." Jackson responded first and Devin followed.

Knowing our fates were sealed, we were filled with apprehension.

We said good-bye to the other guests and walked a few hundred yards to a spot to hitchhike from. There we put our thumbs out for the first time.

"How long do you think it will take to get a ride?" I posed.

We are all three very competitive; Jackson said twelve minutes, Devin quickly shot in with fifteen, and I said eight. I was the spirit, Jackson was the heart, and Devin was the mind.

Two cars passed. The third was a medium-sized cargo van, and barely thirty seconds had passed before we were climbing into the back. We started beating our chests.

We hitched all the way to *Ruta* J, a dirt road running east–west at the bottom of Tierra del Fuego. This road goes to Estancia Harberton and ends at Paso Moat. Estancia Harberton was the first nonindigenous and nonreligious settlement on Tierra del Fuego. It is now a museum.

Very little traffic was taking the road, and now that the adventure had begun, we weren't going to sit around a second longer waiting for another ride. This meant walking south, and in the wrong direction. Enthusiasm had caused us to already engage in, what some would consider, cheating. These were first miles that counted to me, and it was all so exciting and easy.

Every moment was new, and everything was saturated with water. Green eating moss growing over fallen logs. The island floated on rafts of thick peat bogs that had attached to the protruding mountains. We were surrounded with trees covered in edible orange spotted globe mushrooms. The southern beech forest of old man trees with wrinkled and randomly twisting branches kept the road shaded. We saw many beavers. People here like to kill the beavers. They are an introduced species and are damaging to the also introduced, but profitable, trout spawn.

Some people from Ushuaia have weekend houses here on Ruta J. Each house has ten or more dogs that bark at all things moving. A few kilometers into the walk, one of the dogs began to follow us. She was white and weighed thirty pounds or so, and her nose was pointing to the ground. Her tail was wagging. She was willing to submit for adventure.

We crossed a small creek and set up camp after only ten kilometers. We had walked for only a few hours, but we didn't care. We wanted to camp outside. We were ready to build a fire and to cook meat on that fire. We were ready to sleep in the wilderness of Tierra del Fuego.

The next morning, I woke up and the dog was still outside my tent, waiting. Jackson and Devin got up a little later, and we started packing. As we were doing so, a short, tough man approached us. Jackson spoke with him in Spanish, and the ginger's fluency impressed the man, and it impressed me too. I have long dreamed of having fluent conversations like this—to have another language so easily accessible for my mind to use. My past travels had never brought me the Spanish language, but only people who wanted to practice English with a native speaker. Jackson said my struggles with fluency resulted from one problem and one problem only—I had never slept with a Latina.

"It is the *only* way to learn a language," Jackson said, and he relished making this argument because he was a polyglot, and it inferred much more than Devin and I thought he had been capable of.

"You didn't fuck an Arab girl, you asshole!" Devin said to him.

"Yeah, but I fucked enough French women to make up for it," Jackson said, causing us all to holler in celebration of loose women. The machismo, the feeling of greatness, encountered at the beginning of an epic adventure is unmatched and unforgettable.

We started walking down Ruta J with the rough-looking caretaker. His job was to look after the houses during winter, when no one else was around. Winters at the bottom of the world are unimaginably hard, and he told us about an old haunted estancia where twelve people had died from starvation. It was called Estancia *Hambrienta* (hungry ranch). He was from Chile and seemed happy and to have obtained the freedom that comes with a peaceful mind and working body.

"*Puta Santa* won't go any further than this," he said. "She is scared of the dogs up ahead."

My little white mutt was known as the holy slut. Everyone "knew" her. The dog stopped right here, and a little farther down the road, the man stopped too. We continued.

The road followed a stream, making water a nonissue. We had planned on camping twenty-five kilometers ahead, but when we reached our mark, it was too exposed. The wind was too atrocious to set up a tent, and the ocean too near. A sign on the road mentioned a camp spot eight kilometers ahead, and we decided to keep going.

In the forests, there had been little wind. We had only heard her shaking the treetops. Now we were on the coast of the Beagle Channel, and the wind was unrelenting. We saw what we thought was Estancia Harberton in the distance. The founder, Thomas Bridges, an English orphan, wrote the only dictionary of the Yaghan language. The Yaghan lived on the coast eating sea lions and crustaceans almost exclusively. Off they went paddling into the treacherous ocean in small animal skin canoes, naked, covered in sea lion fat. Had they worn clothes, hypothermia would have set in immediately. The sea lion fat made the water whisk off their bodies and kept them dry. While on the canoe, the kid would maintain a fire while the adult, most likely a female, dove for crustaceans. Deep into the cold, dark sea, they hunted.

The Yaghan had traveled farther from the cradle of civilization than any other race of human. Four Yaghan traveled even farther. Captain Fitz Roy took them to England to show them civilized life. During their adventure, Fitz Roy is said to have treated them well and even to have fed them before anyone else on the ship. In England, the Yaghan even met the Queen, but Fitz Roy returned them a year later, and they lived wild. This was at their request and at the personal expense of Fitz Roy. Were the Yaghan the outcasts of mankind sent to live farther and farther away as our species traveled the earth? Or were the Yaghan the true adventurers of mankind, always searching for something more—something just beyond their view? At the time of European contact, the "uncivilized" people of Tierra del Feugo had one of the longest life expectancies on earth, despite eating no fruits or veggies, and living in one of the harshest environments. What life forgotten they must have lived.

Darwin, who was hand-picked by Captain Fitz Roy to join the Beagle, said they were the most uncivilized people he had ever met. The Captain battled the wind, but his biggest battles were in his mind. On earlier voyages, the Captain had experienced the difficulty of leading an expedition. Mutiny was always a risk—especially here, a place so inhospitable. Two of Magellan's ships mutinied in Patagonia and returned home. Fitz Roy decided, on his next voyage, that he must have another educated mind to talk to—someone to reason with and to trade ideas, and these ideas developed by Darwin during the Beagle's trip led to his publication of *On the Origin of Species* and the foundations for evolution. What is often forgotten is the idea of scientific racism that evolved from these works, an idea which certainly gave many people a falsified mental justification to "exterminate, and replace, the savage races throughout the world. At the same time the anthropomorphous apes ... will no doubt be exterminated," as Darwin said in *The Descent of Man*. These ideas certainly weighed on the soul of the forward-thinking Christian Fitz Roy, who compared the Yaghan to the Britons during the

Roman conquest nearly two millennia earlier. Capitan Fitz Roy lost the battle with his mind, and took his own life.

Today we were next to the thunderous ocean, and we decided to leave the road and walk the coast. We wanted to stand on the edge of the continent. The rocks were covered in a mustard colored lichen that glowed vibrantly. The sign said, "8 km," and we thought we could make it shorter. The road went back inland, off to the left. Estancia Harberton was to the right and appeared not far in the distance, directly east. We all agreed it was time to do some exploring. The famous ocean had washed away our tired muscles.

After the first moments of excitement wore off, we were back at work. The ground went from rock to sand, and we were high-kneeing over tufts of grass. Everything was wet, and soon we were too. We kept going forward, but we could no longer see Harberton; the small valleys were lower than we thought.

Every step was becoming a challenge, deeper into the ground each foot went, a few steps further and we were knee deep in bog. Without realizing it we had entered, and now surrounded ourselves, in a giant peat bog and there was no turning back. Thick, luxurious green mosses covered the black peat below. Fallen trees surrounded us and were starting to decompose again, thawing after the long winter. It was exhaustingly dirty, hard work. Jackson, who had been so proud of his five-year-old New Balances, was suffering the worst. The peat bogs were dangerous—thick, and at times waist deep: thousands and thousands of years deep. A serious ankle injury could easily have occurred, and we had to work as a team numerous times, pulling each other out. We were all filthy when we reached the other side.

When we got back to the road, a car stopped, and the driver told us the campsite was only two kilometers away. Devin and Jackson wanted to rest. I left, too tired to stop and wanting to be alone.

No one was in a good mood after bogging, but the camp spot was perfect. There was a meandering river with ankle high grasses, the line of snow mountains to the north, and sinking in front of me was the bog. We were under a flag tree. Named for the foliage growing in complete accordance to the wind. Every branch exclusively extending eastward. Here I was, alone in perfection at the bottom of the Americas. Green and blue were all around. The sounds of life were everywhere. The rest of the trio arrived, and we all agreed on the wonder of Tierra del Fuego.

The next morning, the orange sun rose and we packed up. In under an hour we made it to Estancia Harberton and paid an entry fee we could not negotiate our way out of. The estancia was spread out, and the first building we came to was an old but perfectly maintained three-room structure turned whale museum. The bases of its white wooden walls were stone, and the roof was a freshly painted red. There was another barn next to the museum for drying out dead, rotting whale carcasses.

The museum was filled with bones from the ocean. We were allowed to touch the *huesos*, and the experience was much cooler because of this. The girl giving the tour was a couple years younger, and had caused Jackson's eyes to light up with exuberance at the opportunity to flirt in Spanish. After the museum, she took us to the lesser barn of decomposing whales.

I walked in and quickly saw all that I needed. The putrid smell was overwhelming, and I didn't care about knowing the details. Devin left too. Jackson stayed, listening to how they removed flesh from bone.

We left the cute guide, and headed farther into the estancia. There was a tour, and we got to see where the sheep were sheared and wool was stored. There was also a quality restaurant, and the old Bridge's residence was beautifully maintained with manicured flowers, trees, and a large vegetable garden.

We quickly returned to the whale museum. There were six interns, and all of them were *chicas,* and we sat down in the back room. Jackson was dictating and orchestrating the conversation, and I inquired about yerba mate. The thermos the girls used had just broken. The lid was no longer functioning, and Devin took the opportunity to show off his mind. In just a few moments, he had taken apart the lid and fiddled with a few pieces, and it was like new again. Everyone gathered around, and I pulled out the mate from my backpack. The chicas all started laughing at the brand. It was La Cumbrecita, and they had Rosamonte. They had the high-class yerba.

Here the way to Argentina began as the mate gourd is filled with the yerba, its stems, the bits of leaves, and the green powder—a powder which is removed when the *cebadora* places her hand over the gourd— and while covering the gourd's large mouth entirely she shakes it, and when the shaking stops her dusted hand is lifted and slapped against her thigh removing the green dust, but once is not enough and she repeats the process a second time, and it is at this moment the maker inserts the metal filtering straw—here known as the *bombilla*—she gently nudges that bombilla into the yerba at an angle, and with the bombilla's metal shaft resting on the rim of the mate gourd, the maker can finally go for the tea pot and remove it from the stove before pouring a dribble onto her forearm, and if the temperature is just hot enough, then the maker pours the water into her prized thermos, turning the lid and trapping this precise temperature; she can now pour the water onto the yerba, delicately pouring in only one spot, and keeping a fine layer of yerba dry at the top; here the maker takes the very first slurps downing the entire gourd before spitting out a mouthful of dark bitter green; the drink session could now begin.

Sharing the mate gourd and the bombilla straw opens people up and helps to ease tension. Conversations seem to flow more easily. With mate, people form a circle and pass around the gourd, in a fashion very similar to how we enjoy other plants.

"Oh, so you are from Colombia; Colombian girls are dangerous," Jackson said to one of them.

"So you already know," the *Colombiana* responded, her eyes staring at Jackson like a black panther's.

The girls convinced a couple tourists to give us a lift to *Paso Moat*. The driver didn't want to give us a ride, but the chicas pleaded, and he needed to look like a man in front of his lady. He couldn't say no. Paso Moat is where the road ended.

There was a small military base at Paso Moat with a blue roof. The officers were nice and unimposing. Neither was in uniform; instead they wore white T-shirts. They let us look through their scope, and from here, all the ships passing through the Beagle are seen. We started drinking mate with the officers too.

We got to look at big maps of the area to better find the location of *Cabo San Pio.* This is the southernmost point of Tierra del Fuego and, essentially, the South American continent. They told us there was an abandoned shack we could sleep in thirty minutes away. We told them we would be back in a few days. They were going to look for us if we weren't.

We started walking and came across a deep, fast-flowing creek. It went directly into the ocean. There was no way around. Crossing it would be damn cold, and we were standing right where it met the Beagle. We found driftwood and put it across, but it would not stay in place. It was narrow but still too wide for anyone to jump across, so we took turns stripping down and walking across. The trekking poles shook against the water as we used them for support. I went across first, and the ice-cold water made me feel alive.

"The worst thing that could happen is you swim in the ocean for a while," I yelled at the others excitedly.

We made it across without swimming but never found the cabin, and now it was time to start looking for a place to camp. Near a big pool of salty ocean water were some bushes, and we set up camp behind them. We tried to get out of the wind as much as possible, but she blew hard all night. It rained for a couple hours and began snowing in the morning.

We got started in the snow, and it wasn't long before we met a man on horseback with a bunch of dogs following him. They were a pack of ten. He was short, made of iron, and had a dark mustache and thick eyebrows. He was ready to talk to someone with two legs. He told us how to reach Cabo San Pio. He said we had only a few more hours to go, *"más o menos."* He had a house near, and it was the most southern house on Fireland.

"If the weather gets bad, you can stay in mi casa … it's open," he told us. A few hours later when we arrived, huge pieces of guanaco meat were hanging on the porch. The whole world was his refrigerator.

We continued walking along the coast. Each time we arrived at a point, there always seemed to be another, just farther out. We walked for hours, uncertain and full of second guesses. At a large bluff two hundred feet over the water, we decided this was our Cabo San Pio, not really sure if it was. A small rock island was across from us. There was a cliff to our left. Beyond that were the last trees on the continent—a small forest of them. It was a forest we wouldn't explore.

We celebrated for a few minutes, and Jackson wanted us to take a picture with our shirts off at the bottom of the world. It was cold, and the wind blew with such force we had to stand at an angle just to stay level. We had just reached the southern tip of South America, and now we turned to go north.

Here the Beagle Channel was filled with seagulls and numerous pairs of mating kelp geese, and on our way back Devin decided to take aim at one of them with a rock. After he threw the rock, the birds flew away, only to land thirty feet farther down the beach. Soon we were all launching rocks at any bird we got close to. Our food was running low, and nobody wanted to ration. We were walking around the corner of a rock ledge, and just ahead were two large kelp geese standing at the water, maybe 15 yards away. One was pure white, the other was smaller and brown, but both were fat from the plunder of pure wilderness. I took aim, took a silent breath, extended my left arm back before whipping it forward. The tips of my guiding fingers gave the final touch, and I shot the rock directly into the suddenly warped face of a dying, bewildered white kelp goose.

"I got one! I got one!" I screamed as the white husband tried to regain balance. The brown wife stayed beside him.

"Well go get it!" Jackson yelled at me.

I ran up to the bird, and grabbed a large rock to smash its head on the coast of the Beagle Channel. His wife stayed till the last moment and then flew to a ledge in the distance. She forever watched us with sadness while I paced like a lunatic, my hands raised in front of me not in celebration but in questioning who they belonged to. I was horrified to have just obliterated the skull and life of a magnificent male goose, killing it in such a barbaric fashion. *Real.* Jackson ran up to the bird and immediately slit the throat, and bled it out on the shore. Then the three of us began to pluck the bird frantically. We knew we were going to eat kelp goose, and we knew we must say a prayer.

After we prayed and plucked him, Jackson ran the blade down his underside and pulled out the guts. In a few minutes, the bird was clean and we had removed all the meat. It was perfect meat—so white, pure, and healthy. We filled up an entire Nalgene with the kelp goose and stuffed the heart in last.

It began to hail, and we took off running back to the tents. Fifteen minutes later, it was snowing, and raining when we got back. The tents were barely standing. Jackson and I started cooking the goose.

"You going to eat it without me?" Devin asked angrily from the other tent. Devin was the trip cook, but this was my kill.

This meat had a very thin layer of fat, which made it nice and crisp on the outside while cooking in melted butter. Then I added salt, and all agreed this was the best food to ever enter our bodies. Food—when camping—always tastes great, but when camping at the bottom of the Americas, and when just having barbarically dominated a kelp goose, dominated with a skill acquired through years of little league baseball, and when having just made an adventure kill, and when the meal was, only hours ago, flapping his wings with thrill, the taste of this meal is the same for every person on earth, no matter the ingredients; and it only happens once, the meal that lives forever. The taste of a moment.

The next day, we were back at Paso Moat to check in with the naval officers, making sure not to mention anything about the goose heart in my backpack. From here it would take two days to get back to Estancia Harberton. We slept on the side of the dirt road where construction had cleared out some dirt.

The following morning, we approached a small house with a bunch of dogs barking at us. The owner walked out, growled at the dogs, and invited us in. There we drank mate, and I looked around at his life. His one-room shack was filled with oddities. There were old calendars on the walls, beaver skins flattened out and hanging next to them, tin cans repurposed in every way, and bullets ready to be refilled with powder. Here was a hunter and trapper.

"Do you have any books?" he asked us.

Jackson had one in Spanish, and he offered us his three-kilo sack of Argentine fry bread in exchange. Fry bread is a staple among the gauchos and poor people of Argentina. It is essentially flour that is left to rise and then fried in animal fat. We wanted all of his fry bread and offered him money, but he wouldn't take our money.

"You got extra socks"

We continued walking and eating fry bread with pieces of kelp goose, and raping about *pan* for socks. Wild horses were everywhere, and the trapper had told us, "If you can catch one, it's yours." That's how he got his, but most of the horses were intimidating with the dads looking aggressively ready to charge, and the moms ready to turn and kick us for nearing their spring babies.

When we reached Estancia Harberton, the girls at the museum again had to beg people to give us a ride. This time we split up, and I went solo. A few hours later, the three of us were back in Ushuaia.

3 Spirits of the Island

These poor wretches were stunted in their growth, their hideous
faces bedaubed with white paint, their skins filthy and greasy, their
hair entangled, their voices discordant and their gestures violent.
Viewing such men, one can hardly make oneself believe that they
are fellow-creatures, and inhabitants of the same world.
—Charles Darwin

We needed more food to continue, and soon we were back in Ushuaia
and at the same hostal. Inside were many of the same people all excited
to see us—except the manager. He didn't like anyone outshining him.
He was in his 40's and had life stories he wanted to repeat to the young
soul-searching girls who spent their traveling evenings reading. The
three Americanos came in with a magnetic celebration, all the books
were closed, and not a soul was solo, except the brooding manager's.

It felt good. It seemed like we had already gained some credibility.
We still had kelp goose, and we mixed it with rice. I had also saved
the heart for this very moment, a moment inside this hostel kitchen
and dining room, a room filled with travelers from every country on
earth, and in Ushuaia the heart of goose was shared by all. The world
became crazy, and drinking was heavy as languages flew around the
instant construction of Babel, but it could not stand. The manager came
crashing in saying we could not stay, and the room went silent. The
three Americanos found an empty lot between two buildings and slept
under the stars, laughing at the angry manager who had been unable

to enter the tower. He possessed neither of the two keys. The manager lacked English, and the manager lacked confidence.

We stayed in our empty lot one more night and then took public transportation to our hitching spot. When we got off the bus, Devin realized he had left his jacket in the seat. We waited for the bus to make its loop, but there was no jacket when it returned. Devin wouldn't survive without one, so we walked back into town to buy another.

Tierra del Fuego is a *zona franca*, meaning there is no tax. That, however, does not mean things are cheap, being so far from the production of the world and no longer on anyone's trade routes. We ran into two incredibly tall and blonde Danish girls from the hostel. They had eaten heart with us.

What are you still doing here?" they asked.

Jackson and I looked at Devin, feeling satisfied that he was receiving some embarrassment for losing the jacket. We sat down to have one last coffee. Gaddafi was being dragged across the streets on the television. I ordered a mocha.

Before long we were back on the road, hiking up the steep winding road to Garibaldi Pass. There were creeks everywhere from the mountains' melting snow, and we took many breaks. Looking north from the pass, you can see the island's two great lakes, Lago Escondido and Lago Fagnano, and that night we slept on the shore of Escondido. Our campsite was secluded in the forest, about one hundred yards from the crystal-clear lake. The ground was soft with moss. In the morning, Devin and I walked down to the lake and were able to see the clouds and mountains reflecting in the sunrise water. The fishing line I had set overnight had neither fish nor bait on it.

We walked toward and around the east side of Lago Fagnano. Waves were cresting on the shore as if it were the ocean, and we could not see the other side. We needed to reach the town of Tolhuin. My knees and joints ached from the hard pavement. I started singing a song in which I mainly shouted *"Dolor,"* the Spanish word for "pain": *"Dolor, perpetuo, dolor, siempre, dolor, todo el dia, dolor, fucking dolor."*

"I didn't know you knew the word *'perpetuo'*; that's good, man," Jackson responded positively, trying to make me feel good.

"Shut up, dude; you are such an asshole. Of course I know that word!"

We arrived in Tolhuin late in the afternoon, completely beat. It had been a ten-hour day of walking in forty-mile-per-hour winds—the most difficult day of the trip. I slept on the floor of the supermarket while Devin and Jackson shopped. We found a place to camp that was hidden from the road, surrounded by small trees. It was a spot for homeless people. We made steaks and cooked them with lots of butter.

The small town of Tolhuin is home to the Panaderia La Union—Tierra del Fuego's most famous bakery. We accidentally used their back entrance, and we were welcomed by all the surprised bakers with faces covered in flour. They started showing us around right away.

"Hola! Entra! Por favor! Entra, Entra!"

We got free samples of anything they saw us looking at. The

churros filled with *dulce de leche*—sticks of fried dough filled with thick caramel—were everyone's favorite. We didn't have to ask for anything; Panaderia Tolhuin gives free food to adventurers, and we stayed there all afternoon, drinking mate and using their WiFi. A short chubby woman stuffed extra churros in our bag when we left.

Now we were walking down main street when we heard some loud music and people making noise from inside a nondescript building. We went over to see what was going on. Inside was a revival, and a man there told us we should return that evening. We went to the homeless camp and sat around the fire. I wanted to go.

"What else are we going to do?"

A goal I had during the trip was to read the entire New Testament from start to finish. I did not expect to reach revelations, but I hoped to reach purgatory instead of my most likely destination if it were all true.

It was still early, but we could hear music coming from inside. People were shouting. We hesitantly approached. The inside was filled with nearly sixty people. Instantly projected on the billboard in English was "You are in a good place." People of all ages were singing, jumping, and crying. We were drinking the wine and sharing our individual pieces of bread with as many people as possible, each bite getting smaller until we were pulling off crumbs. Initially I had eaten my entire piece of bread on accident and to everyone's delight.

Someone touched my shoulder from behind; it was the lady from the *panaderia*—Natu. She wanted us to come stay with her family. Her husband wanted to cook for us, and we obliged.

At their small A-frame house, Ezequiel started cooking a huge roast with three chickens. He was large with a body shaped like an egg. The whole family, except for the youngest boy, was round, and it was obvious they ate well. Ezequiel slow-cooked the meat in their wood-burning stove for three hours. During this time, we shared pictures with the family and I danced with their five-year-old daughter. At nearly 2:00 a.m. that morning, we ate. The outside of the enormous roast had a thick layer of gristle that was curled, juicy, and black at the edges. It swam in an inch of grease. This made the inside of the encyclopedia-sized roast so soft that its texture resembled homemade mashed potatoes more so than meat.

We stayed with their family the next day and rode their horses. They would have let us stay forever, but we had to keep moving. We were already a few days behind schedule. After we were able to say good-bye, we covered only nineteen kilometers that day. There was a forest on the left side of the road, in which we opted to set up camp. It was a rare peaceful night, and we cooked the last of the meat. Liters of coffee were drunk, and we sang improvised campfire songs. We promised to make a YouTube video in the future called Campfire Musical. We rehearsed everyday, and every step that was not spent arguing was spent singing. We were the walking boy band.

The next morning, I woke up really early and really horny. Dreams are always so vivid in nature, and all that meat had gone straight to my testes. At the beginning of the trip, we had made a nonmasturbation pact, but this morning it would be broken. I climbed up a struggling tree looking out on the rolling hills of the Tierra del Fuegan sunrise and relieved myself to nature. The wind made it difficult to stay clean.

Later that morning, about twenty minutes into the day's walk, a car stopped behind us. It was Ezequiel and his father. Devin had left his inflatable pillow at their house, and they were looking for us.

"We drove fifty kilometers down the road and turned around. You guys have only walked twenty-two kilometers. This trip will take you a lifetime," Ezequel said, grinning, clearly pleased to know we were just regular guys, and just what he expected.

Everyone laughed and shared warm embraces. The grandfather hugged Jackson and handed him money. The three of us kindly but strongly refused.

"The money is not mine; it is God's," he said. "Buy some bread with it."

We kept walking, and soon a group of bicycles came upon us from behind. They were on their way to Alaska. Their bikes looked heavy, and they looked greener than we did. This we agreed to pridefully while inside, each of us felt a touch of jealously at the freedom the wheel provides.

Here, many days south of Rio Grande, my Achilles tendon was giving me problems, and we decided to stop at an abandoned house in the distance. Jackson was feeling strong and wanted to keep walking. Perhaps he sensed something.

The house was about six hundred meters off the road to the left. It was gray, one story, and raised off the ground about a foot. We had to cross an *arroyo* to get to it. The bridge and direct route had been washed away a long time ago. The water was a few feet deep—more so in other places. We managed to find a narrow spot to jump across and get only a little wet.

We all arrived at the house optimistic and ready to look around. It was only four in the afternoon, so we had plenty of time to explore. The house was eerie and aged. A little green on the windowsills was the only color. It had a tin roof. The door was latched shut with a strap of hardened leather.

Inside the house, the floor, the ceiling, and every wall was drunkenly warped, like an optical illusion. There were five rooms—two on either side and one in the middle. Nothing hung on the walls, and there was only a little trash. The kitchen had a few shelves. In the back left room, we noticed something strange—eight bed frames without mattresses. All of them were small and had been for children. Out the back door, the roof overhung. Just at face level, a nail was jutting out.

"Watch out for this," I said to the others.

Jackson and Devin went to inspect the barn. They soon returned and told me that all the chicken coops had children's bed frames in them too.

"How many kids did this guy have?" I wondered aloud, and we continued to wonder, eventing stories and looking for the evidence.

The barn didn't have any bed frames in it, but it did contain hundreds of dried sheepskins hanging from the rafters and piles of moldy fur six feet heigh. We went to sleep in the front left room of the house.

The moon-filled night made the sky glow purple through the window-less frame. With no light from the inside, the window appeared to float. Hours passed sleeping under the floating window.

Then Jackson woke me frantically.

"Did you hear that? Did …you …hear …that?" he whispered intently.

"No man, what?" I asked, waking quickly because of his obvious terror. He was looking directly into my eyes and then back at the window. He was nearly in tears, unable to believe it.

"A scream … first on that side of the house, and then on the other."

I sat up and grabbed the headlamp. We both looked out the window.

"Maybe it was just a guanaco, man; those things make weird sounds."

"It wasn't an animal, but … I don't know; it wasn't really human. I mean, it was human …a tortured human… shit, man." His voice trembled and was ready to break.

I looked at him, not sure what to do but ready for anything.

"It was like nothing I have ever heard before," he said again and again.

There are many ghost stories in Tierra del Fuego—stories of the screams. Everyone hears them. Everyone knows where they come from. These screams are said to be from the Selk'nam people being hunted and having their ears removed by Julio Popper and his men. Legends said the natives could outrun a horse for hours.

"I think this dude hunted Indians," I posited.

"I think so too, man." Jackson shuddered, fully believing that the unbelievable was occurring, and now I was really scared. My heart was racing. It was hard to breathe quietly. My eyes had been fixated on the floating window, waiting for whatever might come through it. The wind was blowing under the house and through all the cracks in the floor and walls, through the sleeping bags, and through the fingers of a closed fist. The spirits of the island were all around us; I could feel the energy—the loneliness and its anger. I thought about winter in this house a hundred years ago. Holed up, unable to escape because of the weather. Painted natives, immune to the cold, surrounding the house with screams. Guanacos screaming. Kids screaming. Dogs barking. No electricity. No shower—ever.

"What would that do to your mind?" Jackson and I asked each other.

We closed our eyes and tried to go back to sleep. It wasn't long until I was startled. Devin was moving, climbing out of the window.

"Devin!" I whispered at him, but he just left.

A few moments later, he came back inside. He was a zombie. His body carried him back to where he was sleeping.

"Hey. Devin. Devin. Dude, what's going on?" Jackson said with increasing fright.

Jackson grabbed his shirt shaking him.

"Hey, sorry, my earplugs were in. What?"

The situation eased, and I was able to slow my breathing, but me and Jackson, we couldn't stop talking about the spirits and about murder.

Devin had enough of our sleep-interrupting behavior and went to the next room. I drifted back to the dream world, and the Fuegian ghosts had followed me. Behind my sleeping eyes, and inside my sleepless mind, I was standing in front of the same house, only many years earlier—a time when it was occupied. A thin layer of snow lay on the ground dotted with the tracks of children and chickens. Standing outside the house was a young girl—mild, shy, and blonde. She was around eight years old, with very pale skin, empty blue eyes, and wearing old clothes. The pale girl waved for me to come with her inside. A boy was there, and he was looking at the floor, nervous and chalk white. He looked like a boy orphaned in war and all were dressed in wool. Behind me, another kid came running up, upset.

"I didn't get enough; I didn't get enough." He had eggs in his hands. "Daddy is going to be mad."

The little girl was still at my side. She looked up at me excitedly, as if she knew something big was about to happen. She tugged at my shirt and said, "Daddy's here." I looked up and out the window, and when I did, my eyes made contact with Daddy. He was walking quick and hunched over. His barrel chest approached the house like a powder keg, and inside the black void of his eyes, a lit fuse existed. Fire rage inside him. He was on a mission from hell and was melting the snow around him. Everyone went into the living room and waited for the explosion. The children were afraid, one hiding behind the other.

"He is not coming," one of them said.

Another child whispered it. "He is not coming."

The room was now full of pale-skinned orphan kids whispering, "He is not coming"—not in unison, but repeatedly.

"You can never leave," the little girl said as she began to squeeze me.

"Make him stay," all the kids said to her. "Dad won't come inside. Make him stay; make him stay."

She gripped me hard, looking straight into my eyes. Her soul was going inside me. Again she whispered, "You can never leave."

I woke with my chest tight and my skin drenched in sweat. I nudged Jackson.

"We've got to go, man."

He had been waiting for me to say this, and we went to get Devin.

Devin woke up and immediately mentioned his dream about ghost children.

Never had I actually believed in ghostlike spirits, and a few hundred yards away from the house I started getting pissed off about it.

"That house is really haunted," I grumbled, hoping to forget the event, discredit the event, and stop believing the event.

It was more difficult to find a place to cross the creek coming from this direction without getting wet. Devin didn't care and just cut straight through. Jack and I kept walking and continued to look for a better spot. The creek ran alongside the road, so it didn't really matter where we walked. Devin went directly to the road.

After twenty minutes, Jack and I found a narrow spot and went across. We were now farther from the road and couldn't see it. The beech trees had returned, and we took a diagonal approach through the forest. Jack was getting worried we weren't going to find the road. He walked faster and faster. I told him to chill, but uncertainty ate at him. It wasn't long before we were back, and Jackson rushed to look for Devin.

From here we could see a long distance to the north, where we expected Devin. The road was straight and increased in elevation in the distance. A few sections of trees flanked the road. Devin was not there. We sat, waiting and eating food. After fifteen minutes, we saw him approaching in the distance. He was mad.

"I went back down to the creek and have been looking for you guys."

"Why?" Jackson asked.

"That's how people get lost," I added.

We had prepared for whatever he might say.

"Y'all are just pussies who don't want to get your feet wet, scared of fucking ghosts."

4   A Real Man

Who am I to judge? If someone is gay and he
searches for the Lord and has good will.
—Pope Francis

When Ruta 3 reached the Pacific Coast, there were big, beautiful estancias and a few restaurants along the way. They seemed to rarely be open, however. We found a large empty one and sat against the wall to escape the wind, which was always at its worst near the ocean. We ate a few slices of salami a passing motorist had given us, and drank water.

After ten minutes, a man walked around the corner and told us that we couldn't stay there and needed to go. We finished eating and slowly got our bags together. A few minutes later, as we were walking away, the owner pulled up in his car and apologized to us for his overzealous employee.

"Do you need a ride anywhere?" he asked.

It wasn't till we were about twenty kilometers outside of Rio Grande that we wanted a ride, and put our thumbs out. There was not a tree in sight, and we begged for a break from the wind's harassment. Soon a silver Toyota Hilux—South America's version of the Tacoma— was approaching.

"It's a truck!"

We began to jump up and dance, pointing and flagging him in. We hopped in the back, and he raced into Rio Grande.

The city has little to speak of. Owing to the lack of taxes in this zone franca, it has had a mini manufacturing boom, but most travelers coming to fly-fish stay at the beautiful estancias tucked away in unseen valleys. Approximately seventy thousand people call it home, making Rio Grande the largest city in Tierra del Fuego.

The next day, we took a taxi twenty kilometers outside of town and started walking back. We had to make up those kilometers we had hitched earlier. A small *kiosco* corner store was watching our backpacks, and I couldn't believe how nice it felt walking free of one. I ran. I jumped, and I actually enjoyed walking. It didn't feel like work. Jackson translated his conversation with the cabdriver to us as we walked. "I have never heard anyone talk more about fucking women and loving God in my life."

We stopped at the big river the town was named after. It was wide and moved fast. There were no rapids, but it was powerful. Here we pulled out the fishing pole and tried catching the famed thirty-pound brown trout.

After only a short amount of time, we were zero bites into the endeavor and had lost plenty of lures, when the police came up and asked if we had a permit. We of course did not, and they told us it was lucky we hadn't caught any fish. They laughed at our attempts and walked away without issuing a ticket.

We went back into town but couldn't find a bank that was open. In Argentina, banks have miserable hours, and there are long lines when they are open. We got money changed elsewhere and were standing on the corner. We didn't know what to do. We thought perhaps we should leave Rio Grande and keep moving, but a guy walked up and saw the shoes that Devin and I were wearing—the Vibram FiveFingers. He stopped.

"Oh my, I just love your shoes. How is my English? Is it okay? Oh, I would just love to have you three for dinner, and I can practice my English." The man exclaimed, not overly flamboyant but enough to make us assume. He might have been fifty and was happy we were smiling back at him. His name was Manuel.

"Yeah, your English is great." Jackson said.

"Where did you learn?" I asked.

He told us that he had taught himself and that he spoke a number of languages decently.

"And your Spanish," he said to Jackson, "it is good, but you talk like a Mexican."

I burst out laughing while Devin covered his mouth with surprised delight, and Jackson turned even redder. We walked away with instructions to meet Manuel at the bus stop at 7:00 p.m.

"Now, just so you know, I am not a rich man; I don't have much," he told us as we walked away.

"I think he is harmless" Devin said. "He might try to touch you, Casp, but that would be it."

That evening, we met up with Manuel, and he paid our bus fare to the barrios. Then we entered the poor part of town. We got there by crossing a large bridge and walking down a dirt road to his house. The whole way, he kept reminding us he was poor. He didn't want us to be surprised. If we had been surprised, it would have embarrassed him.

The houses were wood framed with sheet metal siding. Each had a small lot. Many of these small houses engaged in some form of commerce, whether they sold eggs, fruit and cigarettes, or whether they fixed things, welded things, or baked things. Every house had dogs.

Manuel's place was a one-room cabin he had built himself. There were at least ten dogs, but only one was allowed inside. This small, fat yorki mutt called Piojo, the flea, and Piojo was the happiest dog on earth when Manuel shooed the other dogs away. The house shack had probably thirty different species of plants growing in crowded little pots. His niece also lived with him, and he had hung some sheets to make a small room for her.

Her name was Lorena, and she was a friendly *gordita* who seemed lonely. When she realized how good Jack was at speaking Spanish, she latched onto him. She showed him every single picture on her camera. Each photo had a story, and this was the only moment I had ever been glad my language skills were subpar.

Manuel was a sensitive man. He stood about six feet tall and was well built, with light brown hair and soft, welcoming features. He told us his life story almost immediately.

"I am gay." He told us. "Well, I was gay ... I don't know."

We didn't act surprised. He could see we didn't care, and he opened up more.

"I always felt like a woman. My mom told me she knew I was a girl the whole time she was pregnant. I traded my action figures for dolls. But... When I was eight, some older 'straight' guys took me into to the woods and raped me. They called me 'fag' while they were doing it... I had ten brothers and sisters; my oldest was an alcoholic. He used to get drunk and beat me."

When Manuel was older, he had worked in Europe and picked up some French and Italian. After Europe, he returned home to Argentina and became more feminine.

"I took all the ladies' hormones—those things," he told us. "I wore the heels, the dresses, all the jewelry."

Transvestites are prevalent in Argentina. Most *Argentinos* seem to find transvestites amusing if not entertaining. There was a popular morning show hosted by Flor de la V, and she is the Argentine version of our *Ru Paul*. Every city in Argentina has a street, or five, where the transvestites work.

Manuel used to be an alcoholic, and we had unknowingly showed up with wine. We felt bad for the temptation, but it didn't bother him. He now preferred a type of Patagonian herbal cure-all that tasted a lot like a mixed drink. His favorite brand was Terma, which he proudly told us was also the most expensive. He seemed so happy. I thought at any time Ramon would rise to his toes, and spin like a ballerina.

That night he cooked a chicken *guiso* with lentils. It was delicious, and we felt good eating so much hot food. We ate on the floor laughing, and we slept on the floor trying not to laugh.

Manuel woke up at five and very quietly got dressed for work. Manuel worked at a factory that assembled various types of microwaves, TVs, and cellphones. The pay was pretty good in tax-free Tierra del Fuego, and he was making the equivalent of $1,800 a month. He told us that when he first started working, the guys gave him a hard time. He had to earn their respect. To do so, he kept bringing them candies. This morning he stuffed a few chocolates in his pocket and walked out the door.

When we woke up, the three of us decided to stay longer. We wanted to live in a poor shantytown community at the bottom of the world. We wanted to shit more in his shed out back. It was filled with guinea pigs, and they went, "qwee-qwee" when we sat down over the deep hole. We played with his dogs. I know Manuel felt cool that the three Americans were staying with the gay guy everyone turned their nose up to.

"A lot of them don't like me," he told us.

We sensed a slight unease because of Manuel's obvious vulnerability. The response time on a police call is eternity, and Manuel had told us about some of his bad neighbors. The three of us jumped.

"Let's go talk to them. We will kick their ass!" We yelled knowing it would never happen.

Manuel got flustered, saying we couldn't, but it was clear from his smile that he liked having people stick up for him. He wasn't used to it, and we already loved Manuel.

While Manuel was at work, we went to the *supermercado*. This time we were going to cook for him and Lorena. After we purchased the food, we left out a side exit. We were in a concrete alley that was occasionally used for unloading trucks. Graffitied concrete surrounded us, and we sat there eating bread and cheese. An employee came out of the supermarket and waved Jackson over to her. She took him into the bathroom.

"Are these yours?" she asked.

"No, *no tengo ni idea*," Jackson responded.

He walked back to us carrying two big sacks.

"Guys, this is so weird, the lady takes me into the bathroom and shows me all of this meat. There was meat in the girls' bathroom too. She wanted me to take it."

We tried to figure out what could have happened. There was over eighty dollars' worth of good cuts in the bags, and we decided the right thing to do would be to wait there and see if someone had forgotten it. We were too gringo to realize something criminal had occurred.

About twenty minutes later, two guys walked up and asked if we had their meat. We told them yes, we had been waiting for them. The bigger was in his early twenties, fat, and wearing baggy jean shorts. The other was probably sixteen. He was a skinny, wild kid. They didn't look like great human beings, but we weren't ready to judge just yet.

"Do you want to go have an *asado* and smoke *porro*?" the *gordo* asked ("porro" being the Argentine word for elevatory plants).

Devin and I immediately got excited that our generosity would soon result in flight.

We crossed the street with the *ladrones*, following them to their car. There was a female cop on the street, and we walked right past her. I heard the word *"cola,"* which means "ass," but not much else. Jackson was listening intently. He was nervous and wanted to hear their entire conversation. We got in a hatchback green Peugeot.

The younger kid, Flaco, was texting on his phone, and the tension in the air was rising. I started feeling uneasy too. Who was this kid texting? Was he telling his friends to be ready—that they had some rich gringos to rob? Devin was sitting behind the passenger and still grinning about the prospect of smoking plants. Flaco seemed to fear nothing, holding a beer in his other hand. He didn't try to conceal it. The windows were rolled down. They owned this town.

Gordo was driving and laughing too much. Jackson was in the middle, almost leaning between the front seats to catch every word. Gordo stopped the car next to a kiosco and got out. He went inside to go buy Quilmes beer. I stepped out of the car, claiming to need fresh air. Jackson and Devin followed.

"We have got to leave now; they stole that meat, and they wanted to steal a car." Jackson implored.

"We could get easily outnumbered soon; the kid was all over his cell phone," I said affirmatively.

"Yeah, okay, I am fine with leaving then," Devin said with

disappointment. In his mind, he had already burned plants and was high off imagination.

Jack told Gordo we were headed around the corner to buy *puchos*. Gordo said they had cigarettes here.

"No, they don't have the type we like here," Jackson yelled out in Spanish.

We ran two blocks, and then went into another kiosco to hide.

"Can we stay here for a few minutes?" Jackson asked. "A guy robbed a grocery store, and we think he wants to rob us."

The man behind the counter was in his upper forties and didn't seemed pleased with the trouble being brought to his store. He said we could stay, but he didn't seem to believe us. A few moments later, the green Peugeot crept by the front door. The three of us went to the corner of the store so we couldn't be seen. Then Gordo walked in and looked at each one of us independently.

"You're not coming?" he asked when his glare finally arrived on Jackson.

"No," Jackson responded, "we actually have to meet a friend soon; we don't have time."

Gordo walked up to the counter and grabbed an *alfajor*. While paying for it, he said something to the owner and said something to Jackson. Then he walked out. The owner angrily followed behind and made sure Gordo left. He no longer doubted our story, and was the only one who knew what Gordo had said.

We decided to tell the supermercado they had been robbed. That was the right thing to do, and we wanted to make those guys pay. We didn't have anything else to do.

Jack went inside and first talked to the security guard for a few minutes, but the guard didn't seem to care. He then talked to the girl who had given him the meat, but she no longer remembered giving him anything. Jackson tried talking to the butcher, but he cared even less, and we left defeated and disappointed.

Manuel was full of energy when he got off work. He had been gossiping all day about how three *yankis* were staying at his house.

That is what Argentinos call people from the United States; the word is pronounced "janky." Devin cooked a yellow curry, but it was too spicy for Lorena. Manuel said he liked it, but the spiciest food in Argentina is normally garlic.

The meal's disappointment ended immediately, when Manuel pulled out his collection of dance songs; Whitney Houston was his favorite, and we had a party in the living room, everyone dancing together, except for Lorena who was too embarrassed. Manuel was filming it, and he kept repeating gleefully, "This has really happened ... I will have it forever."

He also told us that we could stay here forever and buy a plot of land next to his.

"They are trying to get people to move here. You can have your own place here; we will build it!"

The next day, Manuel went to work and we started walking again. Our bags stayed, so we only carried water and snack food. We started northward to San Sebastion, the border with Chile. The houses overlooking the beach were quite nice, with a Mediterranean style. They became fewer the farther we got from the city. Large rock outcroppings were everywhere. There were cows and sheep but no trees.

Devin and Jackson immediately started one of their long-winded conversations about economics. These always ended in fights, and without the weight of backpack, arguing was now easier. I tried my best to keep quiet and imagine the time when I would be alone. There was a dead cow in a field whose decomposing body had caused the grass to grow taller than anywhere else.

We made really good distance that day. There were a few gauchos on horses. Next to them, the border collies were tracking the sheep and were hardly focused. The sheep moved forward, rarely saying "baa." Everyone knew this routine. Silently they battled the wind together.

We stopped to pump for water under a small bridge. The stream was clear and snaked across the land without a single tree to obstruct the view of its slithering body. We weren't there for ten minutes when a lady drove up in a nice Mercedes SUV. She looked at us for a moment, walked around, and got back into her car and left. The *trucha* (trout) is big industry here, and she was making sure we weren't fishing on her river. People protect their fish in Patagonia.

The weather started to change, and Devin and Jackson couldn't continue their conversation without screaming. We decided to call it quits for the day and put out our thumbs to hitch back into Rio Grande. No one stopped, though. The cars were filled with people making apologetic hand signals as they passed. Then it started to rain, which made the hitching even more difficult. No one wanted to pick up a wet guy, much less three wet guys. A truck pulled over, and we got in the back. A miserably cold front had blown in. My feet went numb from the wind but the rain didn't hit us because he was driving so fast.

That night we had decided to make Manuel some real American food. We got *carne picada*, onions, and cheese. The three of us started preparing the meal; I was molding the hamburger patties. Devin watched me, and then asked if I knew what I was doing.

"What the fuck, man? Of course I know what I am doing." I was furious. He seemed to know exactly how to push my buttons.

"I don't know; some people just buy the preformed ones," he responded.

Devin was in charge of cooking and set to putting the patties I had made into Manuel's propane-fed stove. All the plates were prepared, and soon he served us individually. The burgers were rare, and I was so pleased when he had to put them back on the stove.

"We like our burgers thick in the South!" I said victoriously.

Manuel's *vecino* from next door came over. The man seemed nice, and he sat in the chair with his elbows on his knees, leaning forward. He ate with us, smiling and being quite engaging, though he spoke no English. He said it was hard having kids here. He fought with his wife constantly. The boredom of poverty was a deadly poison. Manuel's cure was finding tourists and growing exotic plants. Tomorrow would be our last day in Rio Grande. Manuel promised to cook cordero and send us off right.

The next morning, on the outskirts of town, we stood near the

Malvinas War memorial and waited for a ride. Only thirty years prior, in the midst of an economic recession, the drunk military junta of Argentina decided to stir up nationalism and reclaim the Falkland Islands. The war started when Argentina invaded the British islands with a bunch of poorly armed teenagers in April. This was right before the southern winter. They didn't expect a British response, and they didn't expect Chile to allow British pilots to station on their territory. They didn't expect France to renege on a missile delivery. Peru gave them a plane, but Argentina had no idea how to fly it. US satellites gave away Argentine positions to the British Navy. The belligerent junta had never considered defeat. There was a total of 902 casualties in the war. Argentina suffered 649, and they surrendered 74 days into the conflict. The residents of the Falkland Islands never wanted Argentine rule, and this memorial marks the young lives lost in vain. I was told by some that the Argentine military has only enough bullets for a four minute war.

We stood near the memorial next to a *semaforo* (traffic light) and stuck our thumbs out. Things weren't looking good for a ride on the edge of town. When a hitchhiker isn't walking, he appears lazy and undeserving of a ride. To combat this stereotype, I turned on Grover Washington, and had the idea of employing a new method. This became the dance-and-hitch. Together we showed no shame while shaking everything we had. Our thumbs were out and bouncing with the music. Six thumbs hitched were raising the roof. The light turned red, and a couple cars pulled up next to us. The second car was a minivan filled with kids pointing and laughing. In the first car was a middle-aged guy, alone. He was trying not to look at us. We were breaking it down while staring straight into his window. Our heads were bobbing like chickens. We were pointing at him singing, "Yeah, you know you want it." The light held, and the man finally gave in. His previously rigid neck slowly turned in our direction. We made eye contact, and I broke his will. He waved us inside. He had to hear our story. The juvenile detention center where he worked was only eight kilometers away, and he let us off there. It looked like a prison.

Contrasting the detention center, a hundred or so yards north was a giant Catholic school with an organic farm. Happy schoolchildren gave us a tour of the huge farm they maintained. Enormous hoop houses ran for hundreds of yards, growing substantially more than what subsistence required. Back on the road, no one would pick us up. It was mostly truckers, and truckers never picked up a group of three.

That day, we made no progress north and walked back into town. We met Manuel at the veterinary clinic. He had given me a puppy. She was only eight weeks old, and she needed some shots to cross the border. Normally it took a few days for the paperwork, but the vet did it on the spot and for free. I named her after the first brand of mate we ever bought, a name that means "little summit."

Cumbrecita was so little. She was a mutt with German shepherd blood and blue eyes. I wished he had given me one of the older dogs, but I wasn't in a position to pick. After the vet, we went to the supermarket together. Jackson and I stayed outside with the dog. Devin and Manuel went inside.

When they came out of the supermercado, their bags were full. Devin told me under his breath, "He spent almost a hundred dollars on food for tonight. When he saw me looking at a candy, he bought six of them."

When we got to his house, Manuel gave each of us an alfajor. This is an Argentine three-layered chocolate candy. One was dark chocolate, and the other white. Then Manuel started cooking. Devin was tired and organized his things to take a nap. The house was crowded with us and our backpacks, and Devin very carefully placed each of his things in a specific location. Last, before getting in Lorena's bed, he put the chocolate on top of his backpack and looked at Jackson.

"Can you try not to eat this?"

"It is yours, man; why would I eat it?" Jackson blurted out defensively, surprised by the aggression.

"Okay, I am just making sure," Devin responded, satisfied.

Then he hopped into Lorena's bed, and he was sleeping shortly.

I looked at Jackson. "We have to hide his chocolate, man; that was bullshit,"

Manuel continued cooking, and I stuffed the chocolate inside Devin's sleeping bag at the bottom of his backpack. Jackson and I sat around playing cards.

Three hours later, Manuel was finishing his stew and lamb steaks. The whole house smelled of greasy meat. Devin woke up just in time for the food. Jackson and I were already sitting on the floor with our legs crossed. Manuel was beginning to serve us, and Devin immediately went over to his backpack.

"Where is my chocolate?" he said, looking first at Jackson and then drilling his eyes into me.

"I have no idea, man—wherever you put it," Jackson again said defensively, and I stayed silent.

"I put it right here! Right here!" Devin exclaimed while gesturing with his finger.

He started looking everywhere and in everything. He was not going to stop until the chocolate was recovered.

Jackson started yelling, "Stay out of my bag, man. I didn't steal your chocolate!" as Devin dived headfirst inside his backpack to inspect.

Manuel realized something was wrong and tried to calm the situation.

"Maybe it is this one, over here on the table," he hoped.

"No, that is black chocolate; you gave me the white chocolate," Devin said with certainty.

All the food Manuel had cooked was sitting in front of us. The steam was rising from the bowls, and the whole house smelled like lamb. Still Devin continued searching—under the beds, behind the TV, in the kitchen. The situation had reached levels I had not anticipated. Rage was filling the cabin. I kept my head down, knowing that if I looked up, laughter would overtake me and I would probably get punched.

The three of us, were starting to hate each other. Each person was going uniquely insane. The twenty-four-hours-a-day constant companionship, the wind, the walking, the wind, the cold, the wind, the hunger, the wind—it was all affecting the mental stability of everyone.

Who were these two people walking with me? Each of us had different beliefs and desires, and these often clashed. Devin and Jackson were barely speaking. Jackson had told me a couple days ago he thought Devin had Asperger's or some mild form of autism.

"Really, dude? I think he is just an asshole," I said, fully confident that Devin's actions resulted, like mine, from choice.

"No, that is just it; he doesn't realize it. He doesn't understand. He is like a child socially."

Jackson went on and on about Devin's lack of awareness. It was true that Devin and I had our problems. To start, he spent his money only on whiskey and candy, but that did mean we had whiskey and candy. I tried to be an asshole back, but regrettably Devin's comments could live inside my mind for days. Too many of my steps came with an internal anger that often clouded my perceptions of the natural world. Perhaps the anger was necessary to distract me from the wind, or perhaps the wind was what really made me angry. Still, I was much too intimidated to walk alone. I needed him. Devin made me push harder.

When Jackson wasn't arguing with Devin he talked only about home and family. The monotony of the road cemented things in our minds and, with each step, Jackson was laying the foundation for a surprise, he would surprise his mom for thanksgiving. Here in Rio Grande, Jackson bought a return flight. Inside I was revolting with even more anger.

"You have to finish Tierra del Fuego," I told him, it was still over 200 kilometers.

His new flight left from Punta Arenas in two weeks.

5 Crossing a Border on Foot

"The love of one's country is a splendid thing. But
why should love stop at the border?"
—Pablo Casals

Everyone was sad leaving Rio Grande. I knew we would most likely never
see Manuel again, but everyone promised that there would be a next
time. Now we had the dog with us, and Cumbrecita had to be carried
most of the way. She was too young to keep up. We took turns, and
she liked it. Her ears would balance on the wind like wings on a plane.
At night we let her sleep in the tent, and she always wanted to cuddle
with someone.

There weren't any trees in this part of the island; it was all rolling
grasslands. On the side of the road, Jackson found four seagull eggs nes-
tled in the ground. We cooked them immediately. The baby birds were
already formed. Cumbrecita didn't mind, though, and with enough
chimichurri, we didn't either. Chimichurri is an Argentine sauce that
makes everything taste better; it is made mostly Italian parsley, garlic,
and olive oil.

That night, the water dance was invented, and it rained the rest
of the trip. Devin had the idea to stand on the side of the road while
shaking an empty bottle and jumping. While doing so, he would point
at the bottle like a dehydrated lunatic. He held the bottle upside down
and pretended to savor the last drops. It was a genius idea, to get water,
we would ask for it. The first trucker stopped and gave us two liters

of mineral water. We had a bottle of whiskey, and we started drinking while we relished how we easy it was to quench our thirst. We had been spending so much time and energy pumping water from the creeks.

The next day, the dog woke us up early with her crying. We immediately took a shortcut. The road was visible for miles, and the ground was soft with short bright green grass. This was much nicer than the road for walking. The vast property had no end in sight. The barbed wire fence forever in the distance.

We were only a few hundred meters from the road. The dog was being carried in hour-long shifts. Encouraging her to walk was a waste of time. She would just sit on the ground looking at us. About four hours into the day, a Tacoma pulled up to the fence and waved us over.

"What are you doing on these lands?" The gaucho asked in the deepest voice I had ever heard. A wagging-tailed border collie was in the bed of his truck.

"*Caminando para el norte*," Jackson responded.

"Don't touch the animals," he gruffed back.

The gaucho drove off after having given us permission to walk the lands. He made it clear, though, that he was the boss.

"He thought we were stealing a baby lamb!" Jackson said, looking at Cumbrecita.

It was our first encounter with a true gaucho and not a trapper; this was Argentina's version of the cowboy.

We didn't walk much after the encounter. It was an impossibly windy day, and without a shrub in sight, there was no way to escape her force. We had trouble setting up the tents, exposed as we were, and they almost blew away. Jackson's jacket did blow away, and he had to go chase it hundreds of yards. That night felt like a hurricane, and we drank the rest of the whiskey, preparing to be taken by the thunder.

After just a few days, Cumbrecita was walking more. On the third day, she walked five of the thirty kilometers. We were her pack, and now she followed us.

We came upon a red estancia and headed that way. A larger estate was farther off. It looked to be nearly one hundred years old and had the biggest trees around. It was brick and quite beautiful. We didn't go there, it was too far away. Closer were the smaller houses. They were organized in two rows and were for the workers of the estancia. It was like a little town. Tall thin poplar trees shielded the houses from the wind. New trees reinforced with multiple supports were growing slowly. In front of the best kept *casita* was the same Tacoma from a couple days earlier.

"That's the gaucho! Let's go ask him for water," I said excitedly.

Jack knocked on the door, and we stood there waiting. It took a moment for the gaucho to answer. The grin on my face was huge—the dimple on my left cheek beaming. We were grinning like people who needed straitjackets.

"Hola!" The three us of shouted at once, and trying hard not to laugh.

The gaucho cracked a small smile, not expecting to see us, but he quickly erased it and looked at us seriously. He nodded and said nothing, waiting for our inquiry. We asked him for water, and he pointed in the direction of a hose.

"Agua potable," he barked.

Cumbrecita was at the entrance, tied to a fence post, and was sleeping when we returned.

There were beautiful rolling hills approaching San Sebastian. Guanacos were everywhere, and so were foxes. The grass was a vibrant *Super Mario Land* green, and corderos ran loose. There were few fences. The vista was a dramatic separation between the blue sky and the video-game green land. Packs of moving sheep often stopped cars.

A older Frenchman on a bicycle passed us heading south. He told us we were close to the border. He had started his journey in Rio de Janeiro. Now he had only a week of adventure left, and we were excited to be so close to Chile.

Reaching the border on foot was invigorating, we were chest bumping and fist pumping, though no one else seemed to care. Still, we felt like celebrities. There was a small convenience store, and we stopped to drink mate. Once we had the yerba, more people came and talked to us.

We were sitting at a picnic table on the border, dividing out the snacks. Devin, the trip's designated cook, had been aggravating us. At each meal, he appeared to take a liberal amount of "test" bites to make sure the food was just right. Now I was secretly handing extra food to Jackson under the table.

We were entering no-man's-land between the two border checkpoints. It was about twelve kilometers across and took all our strength. A few eighteen-wheelers drove by and kicked up dirt that the wind blew directly into our faces. The excitement of crossing the border was over. Nobody was in a good mood. We had expected to be in Chile by now, and we couldn't sleep here between the borders. The dog was tired too and was pissing us off. We saw two more foxes, which slightly lifted our morale.

The border was now just a kilometer away. We were hungry, and once we could see the small buildings, we limped quicker. At the Chilean side of the border, we sat down and ate some food at the small convenience store. It was literally a hole in the sheet metal wall of the border patrol building. A Colombian woman was working and gave us a bunch of free food. Her skin and features were dark, seductive, and curved. She had arrived three months ago, saying the pay was better here. She was all alone and told us more than once, "The hotel I stay at is only twenty-five pesos a night." She wanted us to kiss her cheek, and we did more than once.

Inside we got our bags checked for Argentine foods, and they confiscated our honey and other soon-to-be-eaten food items. Jackson had decided to declare everything we had, though Devin and I had objected to his honesty, and how could he not have tried? Sneaking harmless items by border patrol agents provided all the thrill of a real crime. Still, we had finally completed the border crossing on foot, and carrying a puppy. The border patrol wouldn't let us sleep there, so we decided to walk a little farther past the town's few buildings.

We passed the hotel that the Colombiana had told us about. There was a small line of cargo trucks waiting to cross the border parked outside. We steered clear of that action. The road forked, and we followed the sign pointing to Porvenir, which was 126 kilometers away.

The wind was at a magnitude we had not experienced. We had never imagined it could get worse. Our path now ran west for days, directly into battle. Every step was a challenge and a fraction of the length of a normal one. It was impossible to talk. The wind made it impossible to even think. The straps on our backpacks whipped our faces. The noise was deafening; it sounded like a thousand rockets launched in an instant. Feeling trapped by a sickness that wouldn't subside, I shed tears of impotence.

After thirty minutes battling this onslaught, we were still in clear sight of the border town. We kept walking until we found a spot that could shield us. The sun was starting to set, and we walked down a long driveway. The drive was slightly raised about a foot and a half above the ground. We lay down on the southeast side of it. We were out of the wind as long as we kept our heads down. There was a dead fox next to us. The gauchos shoot them for eating corderos.

None of us had ever used a bivouac before, and I was excited to finally do so. The tent was not an option in this wind; we were too exposed. As Jackson was unpacking, his sleeping pad blew away, and he took off running. The wind blew harder and didn't stop. It blew the pad for nearly a kilometer before he could get to it. Devin and I laughed and talked bad about him while he was away. The next morning, we got up early and started walking. It was easy not having to take down the tent.

The wind had not let up all night, and it was blowing just as hard in the morning. Intuitively, and without speaking, we took the bird approach and formed a line. Jackson and I were taking turns going to the front. Devin was standing third, slightly off to the left.

It continued this way for what felt like an hour, with Jack and me in constant rotation. We challenged each other, pushing ourselves hard. Each time we rotated, the other got more pissed, and we pushed harder with boiling aggression. By the end of the hour, we were nearing a pace that can be achieved only through rage. Devin hustled to keep up.

"Yo, Devin, you should draft with us," I said mildly, attempting to provide him a friendly invitation.

"I am catching some draft back here," he responded despondently.

"Then why the fuck haven't you gone to the front!" I exploded at him.

"Nobody asked me to," he argued.

Jackson could no longer control himself.

"We shouldn't have to ask!" He said forcibly, taking a step into Devin. Jackson was staring at him with eyes of fire. Devin looked at the ground, knowing he would need to tackle Jackson if he were to have a chance. Jackson raised his arms to his chest in order to shove Devin, and then paused for a second before throwing his hands in the air and turning around. Jack sat down, and Devin walked off to pee, and I sat with Jackson.

"He doesn't understand … remember," I said, cracking a smile.

"I know; it's the Aspergers. That's what stopped me from hitting him; I wanted to so bad." Jack was bitterly shaken from the event for hours.

We all started taking turns fighting the wind, but soon there was a shack on the side of the road with metal siding. A sign said we had walked only two kilometers from the border. It was humiliating, and we looked down at our rations.

"We gotta hitch, man; we will never make it at this speed."

Everyone was looking for a way out of the wind. Porvenir was 125 kilometers away. Jackson would miss his flight if we didn't move faster. We all agreed Fireland was destroying us. The only way to walk was with the wind at our backs. Since the wind always came from the West, we would too.

We sat in the shack, waiting for cars to drive by. Earlier experience had taught us how difficult it was to get a car to stop for three. I went out by the road alone. Jackson and Devin stayed hiding in the shed. They would come out if I was successful and try to make the driver feel guilty. There weren't many cars; only a few passed in the first hour. Each driver was pointing in some random direction. "No, I am going that way," they told me with their fingers.

Eventually a white cargo van pulled up and two men within offered me a ride. I asked them if Jack and Devin could get in the back. However, that was filled with trash, and there was no room. They needed to find another ride. I would send an e-mail telling them my location when I arrived. I took Cumbrecita. Leaving them in the wind gave me cruel satisfaction. The driver and his friend talked the whole way into Porvenir, laughing each time one of them remembered something in English. When they did, they would shout it.

"MADONNA! A ha ha haaa."

"BEAL CLINTON! Huhuhooo!"

"DIE HARD!"

This continued the whole way, and they didn't even smell like alcohol. They gave me a sandwich and tea. We made a lot of stops, each time adding more trash in the back. They repeated to me that trash collection was volunteer; it was not their job. They just wanted to get away from their wives.

The few people we passed on the side of the road were all friends, and we stopped to chat with each one. The men were always laughing and making jokes with the people. We stopped by one man building a fence on the side of a steep embankment. The driver put his hand on the fence builder's shoulder and told me, "This man has the deep pockets."

The wind blew the tall white volunteer trash van all over the road.

"Be careful with Chileans; there are some good ones, but there are some really bad ones too." The driver said when dropping me off at a restaurant in Porvenir around 3:00 p.m. The ride had lasted nearly four hours. Now I was in Porvenir alone. Would Devin and Jackson make it tonight?

Porvenir was filled with run-down buildings and old Victorian houses falling victim to climate and neglect. Many ruins from the glory days of commerce were everywhere. There had been a gold rush nearly two centuries ago. Before the Panama Canal existed, this place was thriving. Many things were traded from this port, including the gold from just up the mountains and large quantities of wool. Now it consisted mainly of Chilean military—protection from the occasionally land hungry Argentina.

I didn't have any Chilean currency, and I exchanged some pesos at a restaurant. I found a *locutorio* (Internet café), caught up with the world, and sent Jackson an e-mail with my address.

Many hours ticked by. Cumbrecita was tied up outside to a street sign, and we were both getting bored. The days are long at the bottom of the world, so it wasn't dark although it was nearly 9:00 p.m. I decided it was time to find a hotel. Jackson showed up as I was leaving. He was alone, panting for breath, and he seemed stressed.

"I split up with Devin. He wouldn't look anymore. I am going to kill him ... You know, there are like thirty locutorios in this town, and we have been to all of them."

"I told you which one, man. You didn't read the e-mail then."

It had taken hours for them to get their first ride. Then they only went a quarter of the distance. The second ride got them to Porvenir, but they still had a problem. I was the one responsible for holding many of the important documents, and this included the cash. They had credit cards, but no way to pay for Internet usage to check their e-mail.

"A guy at this hotel offered to let me use the computer for free, but I felt so bad and tried to go so fast, I guess I didn't read it all."

They had been in Porvenir for two hours searching for me.

"Devin stopped looking and said we would never find you and that he was going to sleep in the park. I am going to beat his ass."

We found Devin a few blocks down the road, and our tensions subsided.

The lodging was decent in Porvenir, but the town was mostly dead. Tourism rarely touched it. The economy seemed to survive only because thousands of carabineros were stationed there, playing cards while protecting the country from Argentina. The military seemed to outnumber citizens, but they made me feel less safe.

We found a decent place to stay. It was two stories, had twenty rooms, and was right on the coast. It was white with a wooden roof and had a nice wooden sign hanging in front. Jackson went inside to talk prices. This would be the nicest place we had slept at in nearly a month, and he got us a room on the first floor.

"Okay, go get the dog," I said to Jackson.

Cumbrecita was tied up on the corner, barking at strays who were trying to sniff her. She was pulling at her leash, trying to escape. Jack grabbed her and passed her through the window into the hotel. We were just down the hall from the front desk—too close for her to bark. We put her in the bathroom and turned on the shower.

After we got settled in the room, which had only a queen-size bed, the day's defeat sank in. Spirits were low. The Antarctic westerlies had defeated us. Everyone was sore; our faces were burned red, and our bodies chapped by the wind. The shoulder straps and shifting packs had made our shoulders raw. The bottoms of my feet had pain in the bones. I could sense the group's downward spiral, and I tried to *cambiar la onda* or change the mood.

"You know we haven't had any *pisco* yet."

Pisco is the national drink of both Chile and Peru. It is a strong liqueur of 35–50 percent alcohol that is made from grapes. Both countries have a champagne-style battle over naming rights. Chile has even changed the name of a town to Pisco just because of this. The original town, Pisco, Peru, is where the drink actually originated. Pisco is said to bring out the animal within, and we got hammered quickly. Our bodies were emaciated and ready to easily succumb to the beast. *Blood Diamond* was on TV in Spanish, and all of us wished we were Leonardo DiCaprio, and I am not sure who said what.

"Iffin iya wuz fuckin' Leo, I'da …"

"Wut a fuckin' dominatur hees. Name sumon beder. Tell me sumon beda."

"Shiiiiiiiiiiiiiiiiiit."

We cooked in the rooms, and the pot kept boiling over on the carpet. Cumbrecita peed, everywhere. We spent the next morning getting the stains out, and then we sneaked Cumbrecita back through the window and asked the ladies at the front desk if we could leave our bags there.

"We will be back in five or six days," I told them.

6 Hunger Pains

Pisco is perfectly colorless, quite fragrant, very seductive, terribly strong, and has the flavor somewhat resembling that of a scotch whiskey, but much more delicate, with a marked fruity taste.
—Herbert Ausbury

The walk back to the San Sebastion border was approximately 126 kilometers. In the hotel room we had come together over the pisco and agreed on walking 42 kilometers three days in a row. It was exciting, and we didn't want to carry anything extra. Now only one person had a pack. We were 25 kilometers along before our first stop. Tierra del Fuego had made us strong.

There was a road through the mountains where people mine for gold using century-old techniques. We didn't take it. We wanted to, but extra walking was never an option. It lay to our north.

Very few cars passed. It felt deserted—post apocalyptic. Tumbleweeds were rolling across the road. The ocean to our south was cold, dark, and violent; the straight dirt road, lifeless. Two sheepskins were hanging on the barbed wire fence. I remembered how back home my dogs loved pigs' ears, and I took out my knife to cut off an ear. Cumbrecita went wild. Her eyes became bloodshot, and she appeared to be possessed. She gnawed away at it, growling—or what almost seemed to be purring. The rest of the day, she was stupid and refused to walk. She was willing to give up on the adventure for food.

Devin told me sometime later that he, too, would have given up on the adventure for food. It was during these next few days that he had prayed, and Devin never prayed. Here Devin promised the devil he would kill me, he would kill the dog, and he would slit Jackson's fucking throat if a steak were to magically appear.

We were forty-two kilometers from town and had just passed an estancia. We decided to keep walking so they couldn't see us camping. There were no trees, so we decided to walk to the ocean. The road went straight to it, and we walked until we reached a rocky outcropping along the Magellan Strait. There was some driftwood, and we built a large fire against a rock ledge twenty feet tall. We heated powdered milk, and were passing the pot around, taking sips of the warm liquid, while the cold waves crashed into the rocks. A mist surrounded us. Food would be rationed hard for this trip. We had twenty-four hot dogs, a bag of chocolates, and instant milk. Six cans of tuna had been emptied into a Nalgene, nearly filling it. There were also three bags of peanuts, and it drizzled that night, but I didn't mind. We were sleeping on the Magellan Strait in bivouacs with a wet dog. My two buddies were on either side of me. It was the coolest thing I had ever done. The ocean was loud, and I wondered if high tide would reach us.

The next morning, we ate the peanuts and heated water on the fire. Everything was cold and wet. We walked across a few rolling hills and by a small fishing cove with houses made from different colors of sheet metal. It was all surprisingly vibrant and artistic.

A fisherman walked with us for a short distance and said he'd be going on the boat tomorrow. He told us we could join him. He was carrying a dirty bucket and walked with a limp. This was causing him to form a hunchback, and his Spanish was hard to understand. A nearly toothless smile attempted to disguise a life that was so damn hard.

Eventually the road turned east, and the wind picked up. The day before it had been miraculously missing, but now it had returned with hurricane status. I was carrying the backpack and couldn't stand up. The wind was throwing me around and into the ground. We sat down in a roadside ditch and got in our bivouacs. It rained hard, but we all managed to fall asleep and awoke to blue skies.

The rationing was really picking at us, and we talked about killing any mammal or bird we saw, describing how each animal would taste. We imagined roasting lamb and killing another bird. A couple sheep were loose and couldn't get back through the fence. They ran back and forth along the road in front of us.

"I will smash your head, sheep; I will smash your stupid head!" was one of the many phrases Devin and I liked to scream.

We knew there was a line, and we wouldn't actually kill someone's sheep, but we kept yelling at them.

"Kill yourself, dammit!" was my favorite.

We imagined a scenario in which a car would hit a cordero and we would eat. If we could just orchestrate it. Up ahead we saw a big fox go into a drainpipe under the road. I dashed to the other side and waited for it with a rock. Jackson and Devin ran to the other side. We had the fox trapped. I said I wanted to kill it. Jackson pleaded with me.

"It is a fox, man."

"Yeah, I want to eat a fox."

"It won't taste good."

"I don't care."

"It might have rabies."

"It doesn't have rabies, dude."

As we walked on, I began to wonder why a part of me had actually wanted to kill the fox. Part of me had wanted to grab large rocks and throw them into the tunnel to injure and eventually kill the animal. If someone else had started throwing rocks, I would have too, and I was ashamed.

My head got cold, and I realized I had left my hat two kilometers back, with the fox.

The rage inside me began to overflow. Not only was I a wannabe fox-killing sociopath, but worse, I now had to retrace steps that had already been walked. Nothing was more depressing. I wanted to curl up in a ball, I wanted to cry, and to curse myself for trying to walk across Tierra del Fuego. Here was karma.

Unbelievably, the hat had not been blown away by the wind. Once

I retrieved it, I turned around and met back up with the others. The hat was sheepskin leather, and though it was falling apart, I was so glad not to lose it.

We passed a road sign that said "Porvenir 57 km away." Half a kilometer later, we passed another sign that said it was fifty-nine kilometers away.

"The road signs are shit," I said. "We must have walked more than two kilometers the day we hitched." I said.

The others agreed, giving a boost to morale.

Rains came and then passed, and they always brought rainbows. Rainbows are near daily occurrence on Fire Island, though I never got used to them. They always made me feel better. There were mountains, oceans, rivers, and rainbows when I opened my eyes, but it was hard to notice the beauty of Tierra del Fuego. The hunger and wind wouldn't allow it. These rainbows always caused us to pause and take note of where we actually were, and what we were doing. Rainbows reminded us to give thanks.

We found a good spot to camp. It was behind bushes on the eastern side of a slope, out of the wind. There was a pond we could get water from, and we passed around the last of the tuna. We had just eighteen hot dogs for tomorrow. Three were for Cumbrecita. The night was dark purple, and the Milky Way flowed across the sky.

We woke up cold and hungry. Jackson had it the worst. He looked more like a prisoner of war than an adventurer. His cheeks were hollowed out, and his eyes had sunk into his skull. It was hard to be happy and hungry at the same time, but Jackson tried the hardest.

We crossed a couple of rivers and drank a lot of water. We kept trying to hit birds with rocks but never got any. We came across another seagull nest in the ground and examined the four eggs. They were ready to hatch, but it didn't matter. Cumbrecita could eat the fetuses. We would each get an extra hot dog.

We walked mostly in silence that day, having decided to press on and walk however long it took to reach the shack. It was nearly nightfall when we arrived. We had walked for more than twelve hours. We got a fire going but saw only three cars that night. None of them wanted to pick up three dirty strangers. It was okay, though, the shack had enough room for us to sleep. An old metal barrel had been cut in half and was used for fires. We cooked the hot dogs, and a fight quickly started.

"I have only eaten five; I should have one more hot dog." Devin said.

"I don't know, Devin; there aren't any left," I said mumbling with my mouthful, stuffing the last bits of the hot dog down my throat, lest he think he would get some of mine.

"That's *fine*," Devin fired back. "That is just fine. I guess I just shouldn't be honest next time. I guess I should steal first!"

Jackson stayed silent, deciding to continue reading instead of engage. Jackson read *Zorba The Greek,* and I began to try to think about how many hotdogs I had eaten, now feeling unsure. Did I eat an extra? I hoped that I did, but my stomach didn't think so.

The following morning, we attempted to hitchhike back to Porvenir. We knew it would be hard, and after four hours of rejection, we walked the extra kilometers to the border for better luck.

There were some bicyclists, but Devin and I kept walking without saying anything. We were not in the mood to be friendly. Jackson stayed and talked to them. A few minutes later, a big RV pulled up with Jackson inside. Devin and I got in.

The couple was from Germany. They had shipped their RV to Canada and driven all the way south. They were friendly and hated the cities. The Germans dropped us off at the border.

The curvy Colombian woman working at the kiosco was really happy to see us again, and she gave us french fries and empanadas. We were there for a couple hours and still hadn't gotten a ride. People didn't want to give hitchhikers a lift this close to border control agents. Most truckers told us they had company policies against picking up hikers.

We walked to the small yellow hotel the Colombiana was staying at and laid down beside the road. If we had to stay the night here we would. A big truck had just made it through customs, and Devin ran to the road with his thumb out.

"Put some soul power in it!" I shouted

was shaking his ham bone, he was getting funky, and he got une trucker's attention. The randomness of a dirty, a dirty-dancing, a dirty-dancing Asian, a starving human, this was the way to hitchhiking success, and anyone can do it with soul power. The trucker stopped, and in a flash the three of us were packed, running for the truck. In twenty seconds we were gone, almost forgetting Cumbrecita. It was quite a sight for all the tourists who had seen us chilling on our sleeping bags a moment earlier. There are many ways to travel.

Another truck stopped, and the two drivers chatted. Devin and Jackson got in the second one. Cumbrecita and I were in the first.

"She isn't going to pee in my truck, is she?"

"No, *no te precupes*. Don't worry; I will hold her the whole time."

The drivers continued to talk as their engines shook. I couldn't understand what they were saying. The truck started moving, and immediately we took a turn leading in the wrong direction. I looked back to make sure Jackson and Devin were still following us.

"This road will take us closer to Porvenir," he told me.

It was a long dirt road, and we were going slow. It was my first time inside a big eighteen-wheeler, and I could see for days so high above the road. The cabin was spacious. There were a number of pious items in it, and a fold-out bed lay behind us. The driver shipped textiles to Buenos Aires, and on the return trips, he picked up fruits.

Four hours into the journey, the truck stopped and let me out. A sign said 120 kilometers to Porvenir. I saw more rolling treeless hills of nothing. The trip had netted only 6 kilometers. I told the driver thanks, though inside I regretted all the nice things I had said to him. Here I sat on the side of the road, waiting in the wind.

The duo arrived about twenty minutes later. Hitching a ride from here would be almost impossible. No one was heading in the direction of Porvenir. Everyone goes to Ushuaia. Devin was going to stay with the dog. Jackson and I walked in the direction of the small town of Cerro Sombrero, looking for a ride.

"We'll be back in a few hours, man."

Devin huddled up in his bivouac and put his head down next to a street sign with Cumbrecita cuddled up next to him. Jackson and I stopped at the small store at the exit to Cerro Sombrero. It had few things other than alcohol, and we drank some pisco, relaxing.

Cerro Sombrero was twelve kilometers away. It was a small village but surprisingly clean and pleasant. Some of the last remaining Selk'nam people were said to live here. Selk'nam is what the natives called themselves, meaning "we are all equal." A giant-sized chessboard is in the park ready to prove it.

We went to the supermercado and started asking people for rides. When it became known we were willing to pay for a ride, the manger got on his phone, and he came back smiling.

"The *intendente* said he would give you two a ride."

The mayor pulled up ten minutes later and wanted to negotiate.

"He wants you to give him an offer," Jackson said.

"The road is entirely gravel. It is tough on a car. How much do you have?" The mayor looked at me, waiting.

I offered him twenty-five thousand pesos *chilenos*, about fifty dollars.

"Gas would cost me nearly that much!" he said, laughing fully.

I raised the offer a little, and he laughed more. He wanted sixty thousand pesos. I opened my wallet and showed him the contents.

"I have fifty-two thousand five hundred pesos. Es todo."

It wasn't all, but the mayor did not see the greenbacks.

"Okay, give me a few minutes," he said.

He strutted off having just dominated the gringos. He needed to get gas and tell his family he would be back later. We got in his Pathfinder and headed to Porvenir. Devin was still waiting with Cumbrecita. He saw the Pathfinder in the distance and got up to put his thumb out. He didn't know we were inside.

"I could have gotten a ride forty kilometers down the road with some construction workers, but I thought that would be worse," he said when he got in.

The mayor put his foot on the accelerator. The road had big rocks in it, and he somehow managed to dodge most of them. It was just getting dark, and the guanacos were like deer in Arkansas. Eyes of one guanaco flashing in the headlights just before the other, the hidden guanaco, leaps over the hood of the car. The mayor barely missed a few of them, and there was an explosion. The car started bouncing.

The right rear tire was barely hanging on to the rim. The intendente said a few cuss words under his breath and started to jack up the car. Jackson felt bad and immediately started assisting. Devin and I stayed out of the way.

I whispered to Devin, "You know, every ride we have paid for has broken down." We both laughed, and felt bad for doing so. The mayor wasn't in a bad mood, though. He wanted to talk about boxing.

"I hope Cotto kills Mayweather. *Odio* Mayweather! I hate Mayweather." We all did too.

The mayor dropped us off at a well-maintained park in the center of town and exchanged contact information. We went to the store and bought ice cream and more pisco. Then we went back to the hotel. The receptionist at the hotel was not happy to see us.

"We had to wash the towels twice!" she said with a curl of her lip and a nostril flare, indicating our presence disgusted her.

We were strictly forbidden to eat in the rooms. She took us up to the second floor, and from the window, we looked down to Devin. He would have to stuff Cumbrecita in his backpack. I walked back outside, passing the receptionist who looked at me suspiciously. I gave Cumbrecita a hot dog, and we stuffed her in the backpack.

Tomorrow the boat was leaving for Punta Arenas. It would be our last night on Tierra del Fuego. After dinner, we drank a liter of pisco and started to feel good about our accomplishment. There was a computer in the hallway, and no one slept. At nearly four in the morning, Jackson spilled mate on the floor and left it.

"It will dry up; I am going to bed."

I spent a good portion of the next hour trying to use whatever I could to soak it up. The sun was about to rise. The owners would surely see it. The owners had, in fact, seen everything. At checkout, the ladies laughed, saying they had watched us on camera. Devin immediately started blushing. No doubt he was thinking about the night he spent in boxer briefs doing the "suck it" motion anytime we talked about our achievement.

Leaving the hotel was going to be a challenge. Our backpacks were now full with everything that had previously been stored. Stuffing Cumbrecita inside wasn't an option. The only thing we could do was drop her out of the second-story window. Jackson went outside and stood under the window. Devin was at the door, guarding the entrance. I leaned out the window and let her fall. She wasn't scared and didn't even seem to notice the fall. She was used to having dumb things done to her. Jackson caught her gently and took off around the corner.

The ferry boarded six kilometers outside of the town. These would be the last kilometers we had to walk on the island. There was a large group of carabineros jogging by us. They were in civilian clothes, and we talked about how we could kick their asses, and how we owned the island as only a handful of people ever had. Fireland was ours. We could go anywhere we wanted. Nothing was off limits. Our story would get us anywhere.

It was only in our minds though. It didn't mean anything to anyone other than us. Outside I glowed with bravado, but inside I knew we hadn't done it right. The walk hadn't been continuous. We hadn't walked the same direction. We had covered every inch of Tierra del Fuego on foot, but not the way we should have. I could feel the idea of walking the entire continent already fading. Had I allowed the dream to die? Had I given myself a way out? I wanted to blame Devin and Jackson for it, for no reason other than to give my conscience a rest. Inside, my mind came to an honest realization that walking Argentina might be more realistic, though I would not yet admit this to my soul.

We arrived at the port, which was just large enough for the blue ferry to anchor. Inside the long building was a man with a backpack that had a Nazi symbol drawn on it. He was looking out the big windows to the sea. We looked hard at him. Legends say the last remaining Nazi war criminals live lavishly, hidden in the Patagonia. Some legends say Hitler was among them. Here in Patagonia, legend is reality.

Next we bought our tickets. It was cheap boarding without a car, but there was no boarding with pets. We walked over to the school playground nearby to devise a plan.

"What are we going to do?" I asked and we pondered, swinging like children. Bending our legs at an angle, pushing with all our strength to reach the sky, before laying straight back and allowing gravity to take control.

"They store the bags belooooow." Jackson said flying, "We can't put her in the backpack,"

We decided the best approach was time. We would wait until the last moment. Right when the boat was leaving, we would hurry past security and board. Jackson was the tallest, so he stood in front. I was in the middle, and my rain jacket was zipped up tight, and I was sucking in my stomach and trying to puff out my chest. Cumbrecita was inside.

"You just look like a really skinny dude with a huge beer belly." Devin said over my shoulder.

We laughed nervously and hurried forward.

Jackson had all the tickets, and we bunched together. There wasn't a crowd, but there were plenty of people capable of noticing my bulge. I kept looking down so I wouldn't make eye contact with anyone. We boarded, and there was a small line for storing the bags underneath. Cumbrecita was moving and crying, and I couldn't stay there. Devin went with me, shielding my stomach, and we left the bags with Jackson. We had planned to board the ship arm in arm, completing Tierra del Fuego together, and it didn't even cross my mind until after we boarded that this had not occurred.

"Jack is such an asshole! He boarded first!" I said, having just realized my defeat. Devin and I always talked bad about Jackson behind his back, but only half the time to his face.

The dog was still moving and was becoming increasingly agitated by the situation. We were in the cabin, and there were only a handful of people around. In total there were about fifty people on board, and the boat was still docked. The risk was not over.

"We have got to go up top, man; she is making too much noise," I whispered to Devin.

Only a few people were on our side of the deck, and I could put my bulbous dog-containing stomach outside the rails. Devin and Jackson stood on either side of me. The wind was brisk, but we were used to it. It felt awesome being on the massive ship, leaving an island we had just walked across. It was much better than being inside. The sky was light blue, and the few clouds moved quickly. Finally the anchor was lifted and we were free from shore. The adventure of Fireland was out.

7   The Mainland

"You think I can? I think I can. They won't go back to land over a puppy," I said, feeling sure.

I unzipped my coat, and Cumbrecita popped her head out, glad to be free. As the boat distanced itself from the island, it began to feel real.

"You motherfucker, you boarded the boat first; you are the first Arkansan to walk across Tierra del Fuego!" I pushed Jack with celebration. We began to cheer like people who had just walked across Tierra del Fuego.

I pulled out a flask of whiskey. There was a lone French bicyclist named Stefan who we had seen twice on the road. He wanted to feel cool like us, and the burn of the whiskey heightened the moment and the camaraderie. We were pounding whiskey and foaming at the mouth while crossing the Magellan Strait. I wanted the moment to be with me forever—the powerful engines pushing us across the bumpy seas, the beginnings of the Andes mountains jutting out of the water, snow on every one of them, appearing and disappearing peaks covered with passing clouds.

Stefan, the Frenchman, started eating almonds, and continued to drink our whiskey. Devin looked at me, and I looked at Devin. We both turned and looked at the bag of almonds, and we stopped talking, but Jackson never did. Devin and I were mugging the inebriated Frenchman

with our unblinking stares. When he finished the almonds, he went inside the ship, saying he was cold.

"That bastard drinks our whiskey and then eats right in front of
us!" Devin said.

"I know, man; I thought he was cool. I hate that dude now. We are
on a fucking ship in the Magellan Strait, and all he did was talk about
his girlfriend … fucking loser."

Stefan came back up about fifteen minutes later. We were talking
to a cute girl with long brown hair and round eyes, and now Stefan was
attempting to flirt with her. She had come over to see Cumbrecita. She
knew a few words in English and liked saying them. Stefan was eating
a banana. Devin and I turned our backs to him for the rest of the ride.
The boat landed thirty minutes later.

We reached Punta Arenas and were still feeling strongheaded from
the whiskey. It was four kilometers to the center of the largest city for
hundreds of miles in any direction. Well over one hundred thousand
people call it home, and many kids from southern Patagonia come here
for college and stay. We walked by all the taxis, feeling above their
services. In el centro we found a locutorio. The Internet was expensive,
and I left them, they could find the place to sleep. I missed home and
wanted to make some phone calls, mainly to brag about walking across
Tierra del Fuego.

When I came back, Jackson had talked to the owner of a locutorio
who had found us a place for thirty bucks. It wasn't a real hotel, but the
owner said the man who had the extra room was his friend. There were
a couple of real hotels that we wanted to check out first. Everything
seemed overpriced though, and we finally arrived at the house with
the extra room. It was an old frightening house two blocks away from
dark-corner sex clubs. This house was actually a shared apartment, and
a man came down to greet us. His polo-style shirt was tucked into his
jeans. He was short, bald, and looked unhappy to see us. His inspecting
eyes looked through circular-framed glasses.

Jackson begin to converse with the man, and I kept hearing the
Chilean nerd repeat, "Mi tiempo es mi tiempo, and your time is your

time." He was complaining that we were late, he had been waiting on us.

The conversation was going nowhere, and Jackson pleaded with the nerd. We were tired.

"Come on, Jack, we don't want to stay here anyway," I said, ready to leave.

"He is right; you don't!" The nerd snapped at Jackson, seeming to understand my English, and we walked away furious.

"He was talking so much shit to you, Jack," I said.

"Wait, what? I was being so nice to him."

"Yeah, I know, man."

It was the first time I had understood the situation better than Jackson, and this gave me confidence. My Spanish still wasn't great, but I was beginning to hear the words independently of each other. It was no longer a mixture of sounds running together.

Exhausted, and now caring little, we went back to the very first place we had thought was overpriced. There was a nice old lady who ran it. This was her *hospedaje* (bed and breakfast), and it was sixty dollars a night cash for the three of us. No dogs allowed.

The old lady was very pleasant and liked giving hugs. She was of Croatian descent, and she led us to a house out back. I was beginning to notice a preponderance of Eastern European–looking people. Many Croatians emigrated here in the early nineteenth century looking for gold, and a place to raise sheep. Very few returned, and nearly 50 percent of the population now claims Croatian descent—more than any city in the world outside of Croatia.

The floor was tile, and I was happy Cumbrecita couldn't do damage. There was also a bathtub, and Devin got in immediately. We rested for two days. My body was hurting. In the garden out front there were flowers and trees I had never seen. I let myself do nothing. Jackson was leaving, and we didn't know what to do other than wait. I thought about the ginger, and how much he loved people, how much good spirit he had brought to the trip, and how he was leaving the trip, and how hard the trip was. I worried about losing his good spirit. He was always ready to work harder, always ready to build and blow on the fire. He always came to life when the fire raged. Here we were losing the group's good influence—the guy whose morals were restrictively expansive.

Tonight would be our last night at the hospedaje, and we decided to have a party. I really wanted to get Jackson so drunk he puked. He hadn't the whole trip, and this pissed me off. We bought straight pisco and cooked cordero on the stove.

The night began like most nights. Devin and Jackson were arguing about intelligent life in outer space and whether our generation would be able to live forever. I stayed silent and let them go. It would be the last time they had a drunken argument. I just smiled and kept feeding Jackson alcohol.

"No, yeah. I mean, yeah man, yeah for sure. The universe is so big. No doubt. I am with you on that man. Yep." These phatic phrases were sufficient for Jackson who turned back to Devin.

"You see man!"

When Jackson looked away, I made his drink stronger. The night continued, however, and I became quite drunk myself; Jackson appeared to have withstood the attack, and we fell asleep before midnight.

A few hours later though, I woke up. Jackson was getting out of his bed and moaning. He made a couple drunk angry grumbles while maneuvering in the dark, knocking a glass on the floor, shattering it, but not noticing. He stumbled into the bathroom, using his left arm and head to balance while hobbling. His knees buckled while his forearms and forehead impacted the toilet.

"Bluuuuuuuuu, uuuuyyyuuuuyuyuyu ooooh."

Devin was sitting up in the bed next to mine.

"You hear that dumbass?" he asked.

"We got him!" I cheered.

Jackson was really hungover the next morning, and it pleased me beyond content. He deserved it for leaving, and I told him that. We ate as much continental breakfast as possible.

The airport was twenty kilometers away, and we stopped next to an abandoned building. It was about an hour from the airport. We cooked *salchichas* (hot dogs), and we set up the tents for the last time. They were going home. The bivouacs were lighter. The stove was going too. We would make fires every night. We never had enough energy to use the fishing pole. The boots were too heavy. Devin and I wore only FiveFingers now. Nearly everything went home. My pack weight was cut in half and now weighed only twenty pounds without water and food.

The items that remained were one pair of boxers and long underwear, navy-blue shorts, and two long-sleeve shirts—one red and the other blue. I had a small heavily patched down jacket to be used with a half-bodied extra light Feathered Friends green sleeping bag and thin pad. A very loud yellow Marmot raincoat and black waterproof pants kept me dry. The water purifier and satellite phone kept me safe.

Our plan was to leave Jackson the next day and continue walking. The airport was mainly for tourists visiting Torres del Paine. There is a restaurant on the second level where we drank yerba mate. The waitress was very friendly; she was another Croatian Chilean. She had a big nose and blonde hair, and kept bringing us hot water for the yerba, so we kept tipping her. A Russian came over and bought us some Calafate beer—a beer of Patagonia—and we drank together. He could speak English well and was on business looking for places to set up hot computer servers in the cold climate.

It was nearly 7:00 p.m. when Devin and I decided to leave the airport. Jackson's flight was early the next morning. We told him we would be only a kilometer away. My Achilles wouldn't let me walk any farther. We said good-bye and left. An air force base was next to the airport, and inside the fence were three dogs chasing a big rabbit. The rabbit was trapped, and the dogs were gaining on it. The fastest dog caught it and quickly snapped the *conejo's* neck. He did not share with his friends. Devin and I wished the dog had killed it on our side of the fence so we could have chased them off and eaten it.

We lay down in our bivouacs using the airport's entrance sign as protection, less than one hundred yards from the air force base.

"We could never get away with this back home." Devin said thrilled.

"Arrested on the spot!"

I was just beginning to doze off when Devin nudged my shoulder.

"Do you hear that? I think that's Jackson"

In the distance, Jackson was shouting, and he showed up a few minutes later.

"I needed one more night outside in Patagonia." Jackson said epically.

He left early the next morning. A half an hour later, Devin and I got up, and we had just started leaving the campsite when three military men appeared and asked what we were doing.

"Oh, so this is a *perro Argentino*; that's very *mal*," the officer said, while petting Cumbrecita. The Beagle conflict is the reason why there are so many officers in Patagonia. It is also why there are land mines here. The Beagle conflict was a series of repeated posturing by the two counties regarding territory in Patagonia. Though neither country experienced direct casualties, Chile permitted English pilots to land and refuel years later during the Falklands War, which was another act of Argentine aggression, and something Chile was quite used to. Many Argentine leaders, especially the members of military juntas, have been rumored to love making decisions while absolutely wasted, and the Chileans love these rumors.

Argentina was indeed more advanced than both Canada and Australia, and was receiving many more immigrants, up until 1930. These were all from Europe, as Argentina was historically known as the last great land for the white man. Argentina has since that time experienced a relatively unparalleled reversal of fortunes. This is being studied by economists the world over and is known as the Argentine paradox. I had obviously stumbled on one piece of the puzzle.

The bored Chilean officers said they would drive us the three hours to Puerto Natales, and seemed to be desperately looking for something to do. Hours later, fighter jets performed low-altitude passes right above our heads, and we narcissistically assumed they were for us.

I was able to walk only six kilometers that day, my Achilles still burning. There was a ditch off the left side of the road and a small pond further down. There was a lot of trash, and we made a wall with old tires.

The next day, we walked over to a big iron building that had a car pulling in. It was raining in sheets, and pelting us with force from the wind. A long-haired guy greeted me and filled up our Nalgenes. We felt weird asking for water during a downpour, but it was easier than pumping.

We got a lot more attention now that we were just two guys and a puppy. Three people seemed to intimidate motorists. Now cars were frequently stopping to offer us rides. Devin and I were getting along better too. It was easier to agree on things like rest breaks, places to sleep, and what food to eat. We didn't fight at all, and two seemed to be a better number than three for this form of travel.

We rarely carried Cumbrecita anymore. We pulled her. We yanked her collar each time she veered into the road. If she walked too excitedly, yank, and if she didn't walk fast enough, kick, and if she didn't walk at all, dammit, we dragged her. She was barely 3 months old, but needed to grow up now, and she soon learned the rules of leash walking that were necessary not to encounter abuse. Cumbrecita became a show dog in one hundred miles.

Later on in the day I came across a nine-hundred-gram bag of Nestlé instant powdered milk. It had a couple holes in it, but I could tell they had formed from falling out of the back of a truck. It had just rained the day before, and the powder showed no signs of moisture. I raised up my discovery.

"Milk!" I shouted like a caveman.

Devin ran up, and we started dancing. This was nearly a day's worth of calories for both of us. Warm powdered milk had become one of our favorite things to drink.

The road took us back along the ocean's Magellan Strait. There was water everywhere—puddles in potholes, little ponds were on the land, but that required a long walk and pumping. This meant that we would do the water dance tonight instead.

To our right, along the coast, we found a large incomplete structure. It appeared it was going to be a fairly nice summerhouse at some point in the future. Around back, we were able to crawl in through the only window not nailed shut. The place hadn't been worked on in a while. A newspaper in the kitchen was dated January 20, 2011. It was eleven months old, and we assumed the workers hadn't returned since the previous summer.

The place had a lot of potential, and many storage buildings surrounded it. The windows facing the ocean were huge, and we could see them from both floors. There was still enough light to see the ocean, and the crashing waves. We went up to the second story, up the spiral staircase, and unpacked. The second story was open and floated above the first floor. Through the huge windows, the curvature of the earth was apparent in the sea. The world felt small—not because I had a satellite phone, and not because of any technology, but because a person could walk across it. Then I hurried back to Ruta 9 and tried to do the water dance as it was just getting dark.

The first car stopped, and the driver gave me half a Coke and apologized profusely for not having more. Two cars later, a van pulled over, and the driver gave me a liter of orange juice, a Coke, and crackers. Then he got out and searched through his car for anything else he might have. I went back to the building. Devin was trying to cook on the wood-burning stove.

"What are you doing, man?"

The place was filled with smoke, but it wasn't worth fighting over. Devin finished cooking, and we ate instant mashed potatoes. It had become dark outside, and I went up the stairs to grab a headlamp. When I did, through the window I saw light moving around in a small building out back. It was someone else with a headlamp—someone who probably didn't want us there. I shouted softly at Devin from above.

"Devin, we've got to go. Deviiiin, let's go. We gotta go."

He hurried up the spiral staircase.

"What's up, man? What happened?"

I was already frantically packing. "Someone's outside. We have to get out of here."

We hurried out the back window and ran up the driveway to the main road, not encountering anyone along the way. We stopped, not knowing what to do. Where would we sleep? It was too dark for anyone to see us, as the night clouds blocked all light, but we were too scared to use our headlamps. Across the main road was a small public bus stop. It was small, but at least it was protected from the wind.

Devin opened the flimsy wooden door, and it bumped a man sleeping on the ground. We bolted back in the direction of the unfinished house, wondering what was happening. We slept behind a pile of rocks.

The next day, we got started early. All the road's potholes were still filled with water, so it was no problem for Cumbrecita to drink, but Devin and I still had to ration. We hated carrying water, but we also hated pumping it. This meant we never carried much, and when we had it, we tried not to drink it. A trucker stopped and offered us Powerade.

The road forked, and there was a small convenience store with a Tehuelche name and a bunch of dogs. The restaurant was closed, and the kiosco had only candies. We asked for hot water and made warm milk. It began to rain, and I went inside the kiosco to offer the tall, heavily wrinkled old man some of the milk.

"No, gracias." He paused for a moment, as the strange and friendly gesture had caught him off guard. When I smiled and turned to walk out, he said, "But if you want to, wait out the rain in my barn."

When we got inside, we laid out the sleeping mats and began to take a nap. The many dogs kept wanting to show Cumbrecita their dominance, and we kept shooing them away. The entire barn was filled with wood, and behind the barn was a mountain of logs—a reminder of what it takes to survive a winter in southern Patagonia. The man had four small rooms that truckers often slept in, and he offered one to us when he came in the barn and saw us sleeping. We slept more in the room, the structure rattling with the wind, and taking blows from the rain.

A few hours later, the sky was blue, and we left. We walked for a long distance, meandering up and around little hills. We found a spot to sleep above the road. The ground was wet and squishy, but the wind had already blown most of the dead limbs on the bushes dry. We gathered half a dozen old discarded fence posts and had a good fire.

Instant mashed potatoes and peanuts were our dinner; this was almost standard now.

It rained more through the night, and in the morning my bivouac was filled with humidity. When the road stopped curving, we looked out on an incredible wide and flat valley filled with innumerable sheep, and we immediately started talking about killing them. They were everywhere. This area was very remote, and it glowed with spring rainbows. "That ass hole Jackson, I'll kill a sheep right now, I would have killed that fox damnit, I'd be wearing fucking fox skin if it wasn't for him!" We missed Jackson, and kept him around as long as we could.

We hopped the fence and found a place that was out of sight. A few hours later, Cumbrecita started barking and we woke up. Standing above us were three imposing horses. I was curled up on the ground, completely vulnerable to a hoof. Their size was intimidating. They had come to check out what a bivouac was. When I sat up, they backed away, scared. It was hard to go back to sleep thinking about a horse stepping on my head.

The next day, my Achilles was back to normal. I felt capable, finally, of the task before me. We came to a small pond with a family of ducks. Devin and I immediately scrambled for the rock attack, but we never connected. I wanted the meat, but more so, I hoped to make Devin swim in the cold pond, retrieve and gut the bird. The rocks splashed, and the babies submerged themselves, but we never saw them come back up. I don't know if they ever did, and the parents searched for them, calling out for them. Perhaps these were the first frivolous deaths of the trip.

In the distance was a small town, and we walked that way in silence. The name was Villa Tehuelche. The town was named after the Tehuelche natives, whose big feet are thought to have given this land its name—Patagonia, or Land of the Bigfeet. Magellan's voyage brought back tales of giants.

There was a small restaurant on the main road. Tourist busses stopped there, and it looked cool, so we did too. We tied Cumbrecita up to the walkway, but inside the waiter was rude, and the air was stuffy, so we hurried out. The owners didn't want our dirtiness taking a table from the quickly passing, peso-filled pockets of Santiago tourists. These same tourists who were taking pictures with us and Cumbrecita as we left.

We walked a few blocks to the end of town, and Devin waited with the dog. I went to find a place to exchange my last remaining Argentine pesos. There was a small kiosco named Cacique Mulato or "the dark-skinned Tehuelche chief." A small round woman welcomed me in and started talking. Her husband had glasses and a gray wool sweater. He was just shorter than me and seemed completely normal—except he was really happy.

He said my Argentine pesos had no value, but was eager to pour me coffee and chat. They talked about their family and their daughter studying in Santiago. I went to find Devin, and we stayed there many hours. While we were there, we made a very thick powdered milk. I offered the Cacique the first pull. The milk was in the 1.5-liter Snow Peak titanium pot that we used for everything but we never cleaned. The parts of the pot that weren't blackened from ash or grease had turned various shades of purple as a result of the many fires. Pieces of older foods always floated. The Indian chief grabbed the milk from me and in big gulps proudly drank the whole thing. He slammed it back on the table in satisfaction, then wiped his face with the sleeve of his sweater.

His wife looked at him, embarrassed. "He didn't mean *todo*."

The Cacique ignored his old squaw and went on to tell us all his youthful adventures, and how he needed one more. The couple left us with small *regalos*, and I gave them a picture of the Grand Canyon. Pictures are the best gifts for a traveler. They show another part of the world, it is easy to carry a bunch, and they are great to look at when lonely.

After Tehuelches, we walked a little farther. Cumbrecita was being annoying, and it rained for half an hour. When we finished, the sky was again filled with rainbows. The area is populated only by sheep. There are herds of thousands. Small patches of trees about ten feet in height dot the flat green landscape.

We entered one of these wooded sections and incidentally scared off some corderos in the process. After a couple hours, a few of them began to return. They were close and coming closer. It was dusk, and this was the best opportunity we had ever gotten to kill a sheep with our bare hands. We waited there in silence. The sheep were passing through, and we were hidden in the taller grass near the trees. They grunted and moved forward, hopping over logs and inching closer. They were constantly nervous because they were sheep—not because they remembered us. The slightest noises we made resulted in sudden hesitation.

"They are moving over there. We gotta move up closer," I hissed.

They were moving into the highest ground in the open pasture. We started to creep up behind them. Cumbrecita could sense something was going on, and she wanted to be a part of it. We tried to stay low. The sheep were on constant alert for foxes, and we crept out of the trees where we were able to see the entire herd. It was beautiful the way they worked together to stay alive. Sentries were standing lookout at the farthest points in all directions. The circle of the sheep became denser with each layer of mothers. The youngest, hundreds of newborns, were packed so densely behind the backsides of their mommas and crowded together in the center. We never stood a chance at killing one, but we watched the herd for an hour, admiring the smart animals always compared to the dumb humans.

The next day, we were having trouble finding the energy to walk. We would go a few kilometers, rest, and go a few more. There was a small fox in front of the entrance to an estancia.

"If we could kill that, I bet they would take us in and give us lamb."

The monotony was making us restless. The food was too plain and the landscape too mundane. Everything was so big, humans were so far apart. The land was flat, except for the Morro Chico—a brown rock formation the natives used to paint the walls of. Few tourists seem to stop there, probably owing to the uninspiring signage and lack of funding. Argentina was only a few miles to the north. In times like these, anger was the only thing that pushed me forward. I was angry at myself for deciding to trek across South America, and at how I would be a failure when I couldn't do it. For now, that anger drove me.

We reached a large river where a couple people were fishing, and a guy in a silver Peugeot pulled up, washed his face, and then filled up his bottle straight from the river. He drank it, filled it up again, and drove off. I felt weak using a filter, but I kept on pumping anyway.

Not too far past Rio Pendiente is the Estancia Maria Antonieta, and when we arrived, we both agreed to hitch to Puerto Natales.

Armando y Soledad picked us up. They were in a rental car on their way back to Puerto Natales. Soledad was fit, and Armando liked to drive fast. They were from the capital, Santiago, and were on vacation. They smoked Marlboro cigs, and for this ride, Devin and I did too. Armando hit the accelerator, and at times we topped one hundred miles per hour. After walking, it felt even faster. I was trying to study the road and not think about how fast it was moving below me. I was terrified, and Armando delightedly took his eyes off the road to ask us questions.

8   Puerto Natales

If I saw you hitchhiking, I'd smile and return your thumb's up, just for
you doing such a great job of being a positive roadside influence.
—Jarod Kintz

As we arrived to Puerto Natales, the mountains returned, with giant rock ledges falling just short of the sea. Their valleys descended rapidly to the waves. The ocean was filled with rocky outcroppings—the snow-covered heads of massive subterranean monsters, ready to catch a ship and take it under. Immortally epic is Natales—a town where tourists stay before and after visiting Torres del Paine. The foreign tourists are mostly European, but there are also plenty of Israelis. Patagonia's many hostels have signs in Hebrew. About a month after Devin and I left Natales, one Israeli was said to have accidentally set the national park on fire. It burnt over thirty-one thousand acres in the center of the park. The winds had picked up a campfire and spread it. It was the third time foreign tourists had accidentally scorched the park. I was always careful, this would never happen to me. The Israeli must have been careless.

We got food and pisco and decided to look for a place to crash. We found a spot on the far side of town, on a steep hill and across a narrow creek. It was an abandoned shack. There was no roof, only cement walls, and it was covered with Spanish obscenities like *"la puta madre"* (the whore mother). It was perfect.

I asked a lady in one of the houses below if we could sleep there.

She did not mind. The only risk was getting our stuff stolen when we went to town, it appeared. To avoid this, we stuffed our belongings into nearby bushes, and covered everything with trash.

We walked back to the center of town and then along the road next to the ocean. At the main entrance to town is a statue of the mylodon—an extinct enormous ground sloth native to the caves that weighed 440 pounds and were ten feet in height when standing. It was shaped like a bear but had a thicker hide. Specimens were discovered just before the start of the twentieth century, and a British expedition was sent to find a living mylodon. Testing later showed the thick frozen skin to be ten thousand years old. Thomas Jefferson had hopes, though highly reserved, of Lewis and Clarke discovering a live mylodon.

We returned to camp, and the trash had not been disturbed. Our bags were still there. We had a fire and, for the first time in a week, ate some meat. The meat allowed us to drink the pisco heavily. We were in town, and even though we were the dirty homeless ones, it was great to be near people. To hear the sounds of human life was needed. It was nice having the walls of a house and the Milky Way painted on the ceiling. We slept the longest we had in weeks.

The next day, we found a coffee shop to pass the time. The girl behind the counter was a short gordita named Barbara who owned the place with her mom. She was just about to turn thirty and grinned behind her glasses with shoulder-length unadulterated brown hair. Every song that came on her playlist was good. There were big pictures of the naked natives on all the tables and walls. We spent a few hours there hanging out with Barbara, and listening to her music. Cumbrecita was tied up outside and getting free food from everyone.

We left to drink a six-pack in the park. This was our homeless responsibility—the need to feel numb. We were in the most beautiful place in the world, and we didn't have the energy to do anything but turn bottles upside down. I could have spent a month, or a lifetime, in Natales, going on new adventures without end. Now all we could do was rest in inebriation. The freedom I had promised Devin, and had dreamt of myself, resembled more of a jail. We were confined to the road, our bodily pain, and our sinful minds.

The next day, we had more coffee and said good-bye to Barbara. We did not think we would return to Natales; the border crossing was just north of it. We walked down the main road to the beach and passed the mylodon statue. Here was the exit for Ruta 9, and we waited there with our thumbs out, but no one was stopping for us. Every driver passed with a finger pointing to declare, "I am just going over there."

"Dude, hitchhiking is like trying to pick up chicks," I said. "It is no, no, no no no, no … no, no, no, no, no, no, no, no, no, yes!"

I had been able to charge my phone in the coffee shop, and I turned on Grover Washington and played Funkfoot. I stood out in the middle of the road, attempting to block traffic, dancing with soul power, and shaking more than just my thumb.

"No, no, no, no, no, no."

"At least they are enjoying it," Devin said.

A truck pulled up. The driver was young, and so was the passenger. He pointed up the road looking uncertain.

"Yes! Yes! Siiiiiii!" I screamed.

We hopped in the back of the truck and were off. He could take us only twelve kilometers up the road, but it would be easier to get a ride from there. We got out near the road leading to Dorotea—another border crossing for another time. We immediately got a ride now that we were outside of town. This driver was on his way back to Punta Arenas. His rally team had a race in Tierra del Fuego coming up. He could speak English and was well dressed in clean jeans, a navy windbreaker, and Oakleys.

"We saw a dude racing his rally car between Porvenir and the border a couple weeks ago!" I said.

He laughed. "Really? They aren't supposed to do that before the race."

His team was out of Santiago. I thought he was lying because he drove fast but wasn't good at it, and appeared as frightened as me during the curves. His driving was perhaps the only area of his life where he lacked confidence.

"Do you work on the cars?" I asked him.

"No, I really don't know a thing about cars."

He said he moved his way up in the company by being good at what he did and making friends with the right people. He was the team's manager, and he spent a lot of time trying to get sponsors. "Prostitutes get you sponsors," he said. He had spent the weekend in Puerto Natales with a French girl he had just met, and I imagined he was good at his job. He talked the whole time and left us with four Red Bulls. "Have as many as you want," he told us. His trunk held boxes of them.

Hitchhiking had taken much of the day, and neither of us felt like walking. I suggested we go ahead and set up camp. It was only about half a mile from where we started. We were surrounded by trees and near a small pond. I reached into my backpack and showed Devin the hidden bottle of pisco. It was only a few hours till dark, and we made a large fire under an old tree on the edge of the woods.

I don't remember going to sleep, but I remember waking up. The wind had blown a coal through my bivouac and Feathered Friends sleeping bag. Duct tape is vital for adventure. My Nalgene bottle had been covered with it, and now I pulled the last pieces off. I was extremely thirsty from all the pisco, but the water hadn't been pumped. It was from the pond, and I waited for it to boil. A big piece of charcoal fell in the water. It tasted bad, and I drifted back to sleep.

The next morning, I told Devin we needed to chill. He was ready to go but didn't press the issue. I drank more charcoal water, and he walked the kilometer-plus distance to the pond to pump. I started throwing up before he got back. I couldn't keep anything down, and was not just hungover. Once the water became warm enough to digest, my body purged it. I couldn't quench my thirst. Devin began to get sick too. The hours crept on. I felt like I was going to die lying beside a tree stump a few hundred meters from Ruta 9.

"We have to walk back to the estancia."

It felt impossible to hop the wobbly fence and make it back to the road. Devin dropped his flashlight, and neither of us cared. A big travel bus stopped and gave us water right when we reached the road. Everyone on the bus was looking at the two zombies unable to walk straight, but the water tasted so pure, and provided an instant rush of health. My eyes saw colors again. Devin threw up in the middle of the road while the bus was driving off. We made it to a little white ranch house at the Estancia Mirta Antonieta, km 170½, Ruta 9. I had been planning what I was going to say. We knocked on the door.

"Disculpame, Lo siento. Estamos muy enfermos. Estamos…"

I was trying hard not to cry. My voice was cracking, and my eyes were tearing up.

"We are really sick; we are good people. I am sorry."

The main farmhand was inside. He was named Dante; he was built like a brick and was over six feet tall. His hair was short and light brown, and his last name was Kusanovic. Devin and I were led to a separate house on the property. Inside, a television ran on a car battery—the same battery that ran the old Land Rover. I crawled into bed in the back room. The mattresses were bare, and I got in the sleeping bag. When I told him about the water, he laughed, "We don't even let the animals drink that," and if I understood correctly, gas and a few other contaminants leaked into it.

Dante came in later that evening to have dinner. He was with another farmhand—Digo. This made it easy to remember. Dante had studied animal husbandry in college, and he showed me the handwritten records he kept. The pages were filled with date on every cow and sheep bought and sold, their weights, price per kilo, health, etc. It was meticulous and humbling. His true passion was wool, and he wanted the find and breed the best. They were cooking lamb on the stove. The pan had a quarter inch of grease from corderos long past. Devin felt better and made sure to tell me how good it tasted.

The next day, my stomach was okay, but I still felt weak. We fed a baby cow milk out of a bottle. The mother had died, and they were hand raising it. Dante and Digo unplugged the car battery from the TV and went off deep into the property in the white Land Rover that had been driven with reckless abandonment for three decades. A few hours later, they came back looking busy and excited. A truck was coming in, and they were herding the cows. Extra workers had arrived, and they squeezed the cows into the back of the truck. The smallest among the workers took pleasure in beating the *vacas*; he spit on them. His eyes glared with hatred for the lives of the animals that fed him in more ways than one. The dogs were barking and nipping at the cow's feet. More than half of the dogs had mangled, unusable limbs that flopped around lifelessly. They had a miserable existence and loved every minute of it—much different from the short man who loathed his miserable existence.

"I don't really like that little guy," I told Dante.

"*No tenemos muchas opciones.*" He replied. Dante never hit the animals. He understood them, and he had a future.

We took a warm shower in the main house. There was a library on how to farm sheep, containing books on the hundreds of different types of wools produced, what they were good for, how fast it grew, etc. Dante was here learning. His family owned thousands of acres and many thousands of sheep near Porvenir.

I was able to eat some of the cordero that day, my body's insides having purged whatever had caused the sickness. The meat was cooked for hours in the grease—not the best after being ill. I topped it with mashed potatoes. We modeled all the different gaucho hats they had, but I was informed that a Chilean cowboy was not a gaucho, but a *huaso*. Similarities with Argentina were never permitted.

The next morning, Devin and I felt good enough to leave, and we reached a restaurant/hotel. They served cold beers, exchanged money, and had world maps with pins so customers could mark their hometowns. Out back, people were fly fishing, and the place appeared quite successful, being the only place with refreshments and structured entertainment for many miles.

Farther along we passed a couple streams and a giant wooden preaching Jesus. The road climbed and opened to a large crystal-blue lake. The water constantly pulsated from the multitudes of fish kissing the surface, the insects just above, the birds dipping in. Beside it a car pulled over, and a cute young girl offered us a ride.

We kindly refused.

"Do you have any water?" We asked.

She only had chocolate, but she gave it to us. We went over to the lake and rested. There were signs saying "private property," so we didn't attempt a rock hunt. It was pristine and wild. The sounds of life were out playing the wind.

It was now getting late, and we decided to hop the fence and camp in the trees near the lake. It seemed like a great spot, but by nightfall the mosquitos were incessant. They would attack the bivouacs, searching for the opening. We made the fire bigger and threw on horse manure, which only made it smell bad. It was an impossible night.

The next day, we had twenty-six kilometers to go till the border crossing. The highway from Arenas to Natales is called Ruta 9. Offshoots of the road are everywhere—failed attempts at misguided construction. These stretches of accidental road would go off in various directions, leading nowhere, and stop. They went up the mountains at too steep an angle, or around them unnecessarily.

In the middle of the afternoon, an SUV pulled over.

"We saw you almost two weeks ago. The dog was smaller."

The dad asked if we would take a picture with his daughter. She got embarrassed but was clearly happy her father had stopped. The mother was wearing a New Mexico–style shirt with a big eagle head on it. Her eyes spoke of incredible vistas I would never see but that I admired in her. They told us about their travels to Isla de Pascua.

Easter Island is so far from the mainland that just getting there is an adventure. Chileans who have had the opportunity to visit always mention it with pride. The family gave us coconut chocolates and left.

We still had a few hours of walking. Devin's intestines were wrenching. He was holding his left hand just under his belly button and walking bow-legged. He had to take a squat, and there was no hiding place for miles. By the grace of God, there was a fair amount of traffic today, and just as Devin took the oath, a pack of cars came racing into view. It was a clear, beautiful day and there was no missing Devin's performance. He was only thirty feet from the road and using a telephone pole for support. His butt, the only skin on his body not dark from the wind and sun, was glowing. The first car neared, and my moment arrived. With all my enthusiasm I began to jump up and down to get their attention. I was screaming, and with dramatic gestures, pointing at Devin. He was grinning in my direction with hate, and I fell over laughing.

We crossed a creek that was filled with lupine flowers. The water was clear and cold. We put our aching feet into it. We were on a high note. I had just found three duck eggs filled with enormous orange yolks. Unlike the seagull eggs, these had not begun to form.

We got to the Chilean border and gave the officer our paperwork. We didn't realize Cumbrecita had only a thirty-five-day pass.

"She has to go get more shots," he flatly told us.

Devin and I were both livid at the prospect of having to return to Natales. We walked back to the ruta and stuck our thumbs out. The chauffeur was a gay hairstylist. He was coming back from Argentina, where he had crossed over and bought three cartons of cigarettes. The price to smoke is shockingly low in Argentina. We were back in Natales twenty-five minutes later.

We found a hotel we could sneak the dog into, and we used the Internet most of the day. It was the weekend, so most places were closed. We were going to try to make a small fire in the shower to cook the steaks. It was a ridiculous idea, but we thought it would be feasible if we took a few precautions. I walked outside alone to look for twigs, and a brunette, roughly my age, approached. We will call her Loca, but for now, I was so glad to finally have female attention without a male companion.

"I like your shoes," she said, pointing to my FiveFingers.

Loca was wearing flip-flops with rainbow-colored toe socks.

"I like your socks," I responded enthusiastically.

We started walking together, and she asked what I was doing. I told her I was looking for wood to build a fire.

"Oh, I know the perfect place," she said.

We walked, and she talked. She lived in Natales but assured me she was from Santiago.

"I am from the city, not this little town."

After only a few moments into the conversation, the crass and crude language of Loca dissuaded any initial hopes of fornication. She was hungry. Her English was fluent, and she talked constantly about sex and how she had guys in town that followed her. I didn't have any cash, since I had only been looking for streetside firewood. Buying chips and beer only to leave during a bathroom visit wasn't an option. I soon wished Devin was with me, feeling now tied to the whimsical wonderings and increasingly depressing musings of this strange girl.

"I need to get back to my buddy; he is probably worrying about me."

Loca acted as if she couldn't hear me and continued on about how she would get in fights with other girls. She told me about her daughter. Loca had a C-section scar, and she lifted her shirt above her bra to show me.

"But I am still perfect, you see?"

She would often stop me, stand in front of me, look into my eyes, and then continue pulling me forward. After an hour of meandering down side streets, she told me some guy owed her money. I waited for her on the corner, wondering if I should just run. She came back upset and empty-handed. She never stopped talking, though, and wanted to go on the trip with me. She said, "I will do whatever you want every night," but now I had no wants she could fulfill. I convinced her to come back to my hotel to get Devin. We passed three Europeans on the main street. She started talking to them, and I could tell she knew them.

The two guys and girl were slowly backing away from Loca. The European girl was made visibly unhappy by the chance encounter. The shorter curly haired guy looked at me, and I turned my back to the others to face him.

"So you know this chick?" I whispered.

"Yeah, man, we met her the other day. She followed us for hours. She kept talking about anal sex."

"I know dude, she's fucking crazy."

"We asked around, and people said she is bipolar... good luck, man."

Loca and I walked off in the direction of my hotel, while my eyes looked up into my mind for an escape plan. We arrived.

"Oh, this is your hotel; my dad is friends with the owner," she said this while trying to follow me inside.

"No," I responded, putting my hands in front of me indicating she should stop. "I gotta go in by myself. He might be naked or something."

She could see I was trying to make my getaway. Distressed, she grabbed my hand and looked deep into my eyes.

"Is it right for a dad to hit his daughter? Because that's what mine did. Is it okay that I hit my son? Because I do, and I can't help it ..."

I tried to say sorry, but things had just become too real.

"Relax, okay? I will be back outside in just a minute. I promise," I said, attempting to sound positive.

Inside the hotel, I let the lady at the front desk know the girl outside was crazy and to not let her upstairs. When I made it back to the room, Devin was on the bed reading Benjamin Graham's book on investing.

"What's up, man?"

"Really crazy night, dude. Look out the window."

The girl wasn't outside, though, and when Devin looked, the phone rang.

"Devin, you fucking answer it; I can't!"

He picked up the phone, and his lips curled upward to a smile as he listened to Loca.

"No, I don't know a Caspian; sorry." He hung up the phone and began laughing hysterically.

We never had a shower fire that night, and we set the meat on the windowsill to stay cool.

The next morning, we went downstairs for *desayuno incluido*. It was cheese, ham, bread, butter, and jam—the same as it was everywhere in Argentina and Chile. The lady from the night before was still there. She came over to our table.

"You didn't lie; that girl was crazy. She waited for an hour," the friendly receptionist said.

After breakfast we sneaked the dog out of the hotel and went to the vet. It was a somber walk, and when we got there, I bent down and gave Cumbrecita a big hug. She was looking for my fingers to bite, when she grabbed them her ears flapped, as her head twisted and shook. She was always good now, but she required so much. The trials at the hotels, the problems with hitching, carrying extra food, and just being a puppy. Outside the door to the vet's office was a tree and small square grass patch near the road. I tied her leash to it. Next to her I placed a big bag of dog food, a bowl with water, her shot records, and a note that read, "Hola! Mi nombre es Cumbrecita. I walked here from Rio Grande, Argentina. My friends can no longer take care of me. I need help. I know my name, and I am very good on a leash. Please help me!"

She barked at us as we left. Cumbrecita knew something was wrong, and I felt bad for ever having accepted her. My heart ached with each step. Her cries echoed, the cries of a lonely wolf, and though no people were looking at us, the spirits were. We walked to the supermercado to buy a six-pack of beer and food for the trip. Devin shopped for a long time, looking at all the products. He loved browsing the supermarkets, and I left to go sit on the bench outside.

A couple stray dogs came over to me, and I thought about Cumbrecita. I hoped that if she were going to be an unloved mutt, maybe someone would feed her. A few minutes after I had given the strays sandwich meat, I heard barking. It was Cumbrecita's puppy bark. A kid on a bike was standing outside the supermercado, holding her leash. Cumbrecita was barking at another dog trying to sniff her. She stood there puppy strong.

I started to worry that if the boy went home, his parents would not allow him to keep her. Cumbrecita never looked at me, and I tried not to attract her attention but to just observe the moment. A few minutes later, a woman and two girls walked out carrying dog food and toys. The mother grabbed the leash, and Cumbrecita walked off with her head high. She walked perfectly—not so far ahead as to pull, but not so close as to get in the way of the feet. She never got distracted. She didn't stop to sniff anything. Her walk had earned her Eukanuba for life. I was so proud. She had been with us for over four hundred kilometers and would never crawl into my bivouac again. I am sure she became a great dog.

Devin came out, and I told him what had just happened.

"Are you sure it was her?" he asked, and I wasn't sure if it was sarcasm.

"Fuck you, dude!"

9 Leaving Chile and New Dogs

Stealing, of course, is a crime, and a very impolite thing to do. But like most impolite things, it is excusable under certain circumstances.
—Lemony Snicket

We found an old, poorly maintained backpacker's hostel, and it was only five dollars a night. The manager was a young guy who lived the party lifestyle. He, like everyone else, loved it.

"A huge group was just here. There were so many girls. This one … Oh, Dios, I think I need to go to Punta Arenas and spend one more night with her."

"Don't worry about us; I'll make sure the door is locked," I responded trustworthily.

The manager left us with the entire hostel to ourselves. I went to have a sandwich and beer in town alone. The bad person inside me wanted to run into Loca again. I'd had too long to think about all the deviant things she had said to me, things I had never done. My mind festered.

Inside the restaurant, I had a sandwich and two local beers brewed a few blocks away. Afterward, I went to the store and got a pair of Salomon trail runners. The FiveFingers had holes. My feet were never going to get tough enough to walk a marathon in them daily. The image I had of myself globe-trekking in FiveFingers was over—another pipe dream smashed. The comfort from the new soles quickly erased the worry.

I walked back to the hotel, and I watched Devin play zombie-killing video games. We passed out on the couch, and the next morning, we went back to the mylodon statue to hitch a ride. When we returned to the border, the *carabinero* laughed when he didn't see the dog.

"She has a home now," I said with a slight degree of scorn.

It is seven kilometers from there to the Argentine border post. A white dog began to follow us. She lived at the border with the Argentine *gendarmeria*. The white dog would stay in front about fifty feet, and frequently take long sprints out into the fields. When I called her, she came back, tail wagging. While we were resting inside a shack, she came up to me for love, burying her snout in my crotch, and sniffing. Here a sin was committed that would later cost my spirit a fortune: I gave her cheese.

A few kilometers into Argentina, we passed some *callejeros*, and like road workers everywhere, one man was working while the others watched. They were drinking yerba mate. Devin and I stopped to drink with them, and they gave us clear plastic glasses to keep the dust out of our eyes. The road was entirely under construction till it reached Ruta 40, and we took a shortcut to get there. Ruta 40 would be our home now. It is the most famous road in Argentina, running the entire length of the country.

From there it was twenty-six kilometers to 28 de Noviembre—just a little town in the bottom corner of Argentina tucked around mountains. It exists mostly from of the discovery of coal a century ago. We went to a supermercado and stayed there a long time. We wanted to escape the white dog, but she was waiting for us the instant we came out thirty minutes later.

We saw a shack that look abandoned from the distance, and we walked through high grass to get there. Inside it was in disarray and looked as if a person were living there. We decided to leave before we ran into the person who did.

On the southeast edge of town, just as the steep hill began, there were a couple of houses. Outside a well-kept yard, a man was unloading his truck.

"Conoces donde podemos acampar?"

I tried to repeat it slower because of my Spanish. He looked inquisitively at us and the dog and then said we could camp right in front there, but the *policia* might bother us. Up the steep hill would be a better place. The clouds and rain were coming in fast, so we hurried up. We had made it only a hundred yards when the storm began, and the skies released everything at once. The man below was calling and waving for us to come back. Devin and I ran down the hill, and he took us to the big shed behind his house.

Inside, the shed was clean and organized. Normally the ones we had been to were for storing firewood. This had wood for building—not burning. It was a workshop. The man had constructed his kids' swing set, merry-go-round, and teeter-totter. I imagined he'd built many more things inside the house, and probably the house itself. The family came out to meet us. The man had three young kids and a happy wife. From inside they brought us wood for a fire and fed us. They wouldn't let us refuse. They were impressed we liked yerba mate and that we knew when to say thank-you.

The next morning, the white dog was standing above me, looking at me, ready to go.

"Get out! Get out. You have got to go home, dog," I screamed at her, frightened at now being responsible for another dog. I had been trying to get her to leave since the moment we reached Ruta 40. We had kicked at her and screamed at her, and she hadn't eaten since the piece of cheese, but she wanted adventure, and quickly ran up the hill outside waiting for it to begin.

The family came to say good-bye The kids had to go to school, and they complained about it. The mother gave me a real mate gourd to drink from. Everyone wanted a hug and kiss.

We left, and the dog led us down the street and into town. I think the adventure caused her to release pheromones. She strutted with her head and tail held high. She was leading the way, only looking back to make sure we were still coming. It wasn't long till a dumb happy lab wanted a piece of the action and adventure. He followed her, smelling her butt with perky enthusiasm. He wanted to play, but to hump was definitely his prime motivation. As we got farther into town, two other male dogs took to the chase. They wouldn't leave, and we stunk too much to hide from them. They could smell us for miles, and it didn't matter how mean we were; they all wanted the adventure. Even to animals, an adventure at first feels like freedom—though not for long. Adventure often causes the greatest loss of freedom. Adventure can mean death.

Just two days after I had gotten rid of Cumbrecita, our pack had grown to six. None of them were good dogs like Cumbrecita, though. They all loved to chase cars. That morning, before work hours, there was a good amount of traffic between Rio Turbio and 28 de Noviembre. The dogs were zigzagging between them. Horns were honking. Many cars were slowing down to avoid them—but some were not. The happy golden-brown lab had found roadkill and was carrying it in his mouth. He was trying to show it off to the female. He was so proud and was smiling like only a lab can. He was someone's pet.

"Look what I found you," he said to her, shaking the roadkill while flinging his last happy drops of slobber from his long tongue.

Car brakes screeched, but it was too late. The lab was sucked up into the space between the tire and body of the car, and "bumpff," the sound of death went deeply. The lab's fur exploded in every direction, and he hit the ground. The second tire hit him again and bounced over his chest. "Arrue," came the painful surprise. It sounded like powerful blows from a playful pillow fight, and the game was now over. The car drove off, and here the lab lay dying. He was trying to bite at his back, where the tire had struck. His eyes were full of fear as they fell into the void of his mind. The dog's dying body was instinctively trying to twitch and turn back on. Nothing worked anymore. He was pleading for mercy and for death. He was pleading for life, and the happiest dog on earth felt no peace in his final moments.

"I knew this was going to happen, man; I fucking knew it. We have to get rid of these dogs!" I was crying. "We fucking did this, man!"

"No, no, man no!" Devin said not accepting what he saw.

I wanted to run across the road and smash its head with a rock like I had done to the kelp goose, but there was too much traffic. It would have been too barbaric. We didn't look back. Devin was gritting his teeth. His neck muscles remained clenched as he tried not to turn his head. His eyes were full of tears. The lab didn't scream for long, and his suffering ended. Ours had just begun. The other dogs didn't care.

"We have got to do something; another dog is going to die!" I said.

We put our thumbs out and kept walking; a guy in a truck picked us up.

"Those dogs yours?" The mustached man asked.

"No, but they won't stop following us; you've got to help," I pleaded.

The truck drove off, and the dogs ran along till we couldn't see them anymore.

Rio Turbio is a blue-collar, coal-mining town on a hill. We first went to get on the Internet and give the dogs time to disappear. We exchanged money, went to the panaderia, got bread, and put our thumbs out. We talked only about the lab and how we had killed someone's pet.

The memory of the impact was in still in high-definition and on replay. Another pickup truck brought us back. There were no dogs in sight.

The road followed a small river with cattle sometimes near it, and was another place with land mines—this time on Argentine territory. No one else was here, and no cars passed for long stretches of time and distance. It was easy to get water, and we were able to cover a lot of ground. Far off to the west, our left, we could see Torres del Paine. It was the closest I got to the most famous rocks in Patagonia. Even from one hundred miles away, they are glorious—three needles of granite so spectacularly beautiful and sharp they are said to be nature's equivalent to three Egyptian obelisks, one of which was re-erected in Central Park, commonly named Cleopatra's Needles.

We stopped in a wooded area to camp for the night. There were sheep everywhere. The wind on the mainland was still constant, but it was nothing compared to Tierra del Fuego. We were about to exit the latitudes of the furious fifties and enter the comparative peace of the roaring forties.

The next morning, we woke up to car tires screeching. Looking out from the woods, we saw a guy driving in reverse as fast as he could go. A male passenger jumped out of the moving vehicle, hopped the fence, and took off after a group of the sheep. The hunt was on, and I watched, laughing. It felt good knowing others were bad too. There was a woman in the backseat shaking her head in embarrassment. They never saw us, and they drove away unsuccessful.

Weeks before Devin and I had seen a man kill a sheep from his truck. He had done it with a shotgun, and he was quickly gutting it on the side of the road when we passed. He nervously yelled, "There is a banana in my truck if you want it," attempting to buy our silence, though we had no one to tell.

Today we headed down the road, and finally ended the hilly section. The Andes to our left were becoming more real and apparent. We passed a little-used and often closed entrance to Torres del Paine. This entrance would have made the mountains more accessible to tourists.

The Argentine government had, it appeared, decided not to spend money on a road that provided tourism dollars to their rival.

Ruta 40 opened up and went straight for hours. There was a large cordero in front of us, and it couldn't get back to the other side of the fence. It ran every time we got close, trapped between the barbed wires. We used calls we had learned from Dante at Estancia Maria Antoinette to keep the sheep moving.

"HEY! HO! Ho-Oh, heyHO, HO-HO-HO!"

It took the sheep three hours to decide it was time to turn around. Throughout the encounter, we were hoping it would run into a car so we could scavenge.

We came upon a hotel that had been out of business for many years. Up ahead we made camp and had a fire with old fence posts. We were behind a huge boulder that gave no clues to its origin and seemed oddly out of place.

I had spent two days feeling strong, and I woke up feeling even better. We could now just walk, with no dependent dogs following. Devin was still wearing his FiveFingers, and the skin on his feet was in a dreadful condition, but he didn't say anything to me about it. Early that day, we passed some bikers coming from Alaska. They were Americans, and it made us proud. They were the first we had met on our trip, and they were adventurers—just like us, we wanted to believe. The bikers were nearing the end of their adventure. They had thick faces, muscularly perfect legs, sculpted necks, and coarse split hair. They were dripping with the sweat that causes the Holy Spirit to lust.

"You have about ten kilometers till you get to the turnoff," one of the bikers said. "You guys need any water?"

"No. You need any food?" Devin gave them some lentils without letting them say no. "Go to the Panaderia La Union in Tolhuin. Congrats!"

We always told people the cool places to go to, and they did the same for us.

We were heading toward Ruta 40 *viejo*, the old ruta before pavement arrived. It is a seventy-kilometer stretch, and it gave us our first glimpse of the dry Patagonia of Santa Cruz province—the least populated place in South America. This was the land of cowboys and Tehuelche natives. The new Ruta 40 is quickly changing this. Progress always does.

We were thirsty. The *tierra* was morphing. The grass was nearly all brown, with fewer blades surviving with each step north. We were entering the Patagonian desert. On the right side of the road was the pueblo of Tapi Aike. The only place in the town of twenty was a gas station covered top to bottom with colorful stickers from passing travelers. On the left was the turnoff for Ruta 40 viejo. A military checkpoint was there, but no one was outside in the wind. The flag was slapping against the pole, the beautiful blue flag of Argentina with the shining *sol* in the white middle. I wanted to steal it.

We went to the sticker-covered gas station, but it was locked. A sign on the door said the owner would be back. We waited about twenty minutes and used the surprisingly clean bathroom outside. The man arrived. His house was around back, and his skin was leather, with whiskers on a square jaw. Inside wasn't much—just crackers and chocolates, tables and chairs. He also had *cafe*, so we sat there for an hour and drank three liters of it. He leaned forward against the counter, watching us and trying to hear what words he could understand. After his mind got tired, the old owner said it was time for siesta. We were wired from the coffee and ready to venture onto the famous old road.

It was nice walking on the dirt road of old Ruta 40. It was soft, and we were completely alone. Only a handful drive it, either for the adventure or to bypass the town of La Esperanza. That's what we were doing, and it was saving us nearly four days of walking. The government has changed the route of the new Ruta 40 to make it connect to all the pueblos, which are few and far between in Patagonia.

We were pushing each other like we never had before. We wanted to, but we also needed to. This was a remote and dry area; we had to cover as much ground as possible. In one hour we walked over seven kilometers. The map showed two rivers on the route. We planned to arrive at the first river and camp there. We'd need water before then, and we had seen only two cars in five hours on this road.

We heard the next car coming long before we saw it. We were on the shaded side of a rock face and out of sight. I laid on the ground with my shirt off, and was using the shirt to shield my face. Devin waved the car down when it rounded the corner. We made our situation look desperate because we didn't want it to become that way. The car stopped, and the woman in the passenger seat looked concerned. They asked if we needed a ride and left us with a liter of water.

After nearly eight hours of walking, we found ourselves surrounded by corderos in a U-shaped valley. The green hills around us were steep and closed in tight. We could see cars coming from either direction for nearly a kilometer in both ways. Corderos were everywhere, thousands, all ages. Here was my chance, but my legs were shot. We had already walked over a marathon that day. Still, I had to try, there were so many weak targets, so many babies with the soft wool of new life, babies that I could kill, a bare-handed baa baa baby kill to become a legend.

Off to the right, about six feet below the road and maybe ten feet from me, was a large group of prey, probably twenty, of all ages. The ground was sandy, with sharp grass and small bushes. I was just above and out of their line of sight, and I squatted to get closer. One more step and they would know. One more step and the hunt was on. I jumped down with a mad burst of energy. The group spread in every direction, and I searched out the youngest, the littlest lamb. My wide eyes and slobbering mouth were filled with a rabid ferocity.

The most innocent of the babies—with big, scared eyes—spun around and took off, trying to get every bit of spring from her three-month-old legs, the first time the baby's leg had ever ran from death. Devin was screaming in excitement.

"YES, Kill'er C! KILL HER!!! Yeeeessss!"

Now it was just me and the baa baa baby running through the field. I was gaining on it, but I felt my legs start to cramp. Still, I was within reach. We would eat baby heart tonight. I had thought this moment would never come, and I extended my arm back to launch the rock right as I dove. Gently, I released the stone, and it connected with the baby's butt who let out a cry and bolted off to her family. I was glad not to have hurt her, but I was much happier knowing I could have.

The road curved left, and we were able to walk down the embankment on the right side. It was steep enough that cars couldn't see below. We again had instant mashed potatoes, peanuts, and extra crackers from Tapi Aike. Both my legs and stomach growled at me, but I felt good.

The next morning, we got started early because we had another marathon to walk. We were determined to make it to the river early and get water. It had to be close. After we walked for a couple hours, our morale was really low. The wind was picking up in ferocity. We had pushed it so hard the day before, and now we couldn't find water.

Finally we reached the river, and alongside it was a police station. We went up to it, hoping to seek refuge inside. We knocked, but no one answered, so we walked around to inspect the place. By looking in the windows I could see it was used more like a house than a police station. Today was Saturday, and we assumed the occupants had gone to town. We walked around back to lean against the wall of the station and escape the wind.

We chilled there a long time. I was hoping the family would return. I wanted to sleep in a bed. We made a big fire in a metal drum there for that purpose. Devin went and pumped from the river. We drank as much liquid as possible, and for an hour we both dozed off.

When we left the police station, I was again eyeing an Argentine flag flying from a policeman's pole. It only made sense. I needed a flag to cover my backpack with. Stealing the flag was also good for our morale—even more so because we were stealing from the police. This was our patriotic duty.

We crossed the river and crested the plateau. The road leveled and straightened. Glacier-covered mountains on our left were too far away to be distinct. Sand and shrubs surrounded us. After a couple hours, we began to question the map.

"That must have been the second river. We have got to be right here." I pointed.

We were much farther than we had thought, but this also meant there was no more water. The main ruta was five hours away. After four, we still hadn't seen a car. We were conserving water and still had almost three liters a piece. The mountains were off in the distance, and I knew from the map that El Calafate sat somewhere among them.

Finally we saw a car, and Devin started shaking our only empty Nalgene while I waved at them. The Chevy hatchback drove a little ways and stopped at the last moment. I ran up to the driver's window. He was in his early thirties and wearing shades. His girlfriend was in the passenger seat. I tried not to look at her revealing shirt while I asked her boyfriend for water. We had plenty, but Devin and I wanted to cook extra tonight. The driver told me he didn't have any water. He looked at me for a second, and then he reached behind the seat and pulled out a tallboy Quilmes. He turned back with a big smile on his face.

"Tomas cerveza?" he asked, already knowing the answer.

"Si! Si! Siiiii, mucho mejor!"

We went over to a ditch and tried to get out of the wind. We wanted to drink the *cerveza* while it was still cold, and we did so quickly. Just half the can gave my head a desert numbness. The inhospitable landscape seemed to vibrate.

Now we were less than ten kilometers—just under two hours—from the ruta, and we got there just as the stars were coming out. We decided it would be better to camp again instead of trying to hitch to Calafate.

"We don't need to go to town and pay for another night," Devin said. He was right, even though the beer had made me want comfort and the woman in the passenger seat had made me want girls.

10 The Land of Glaciers

Every job is good if you do your best and work hard. A man who works hard stinks only to the ones that have nothing to do but smell.
—Laura Ingalls Wilder

We stood back out on Ruta 40 *nueva*, the paved road, early the next morning. A driver stopped and said he had room for only one. I told Devin to go, and I stayed waiting for another ride. A few cars passed, but nobody was stopping. Cars were driving too fast. The road was straight and deserted.

I brought out the Argentine flag, tied one end to my backpack, and held on to the other with my arm raised in the air. The wind was blowing strong. Patriotism was flying. A Volkswagen truck pulled up, and I hopped in the backseat.

It was a dad and his daughter, and they were taking furniture to their grandmother in Calafate. They were from Rio Gallegos, and the girl spoke English well; she was probably sixteen and seemed quite pleased her dad had picked up a hitchhiker. She spoke with a British accent. This embarrassed her, and she said she wanted to speak "real English, like an American." Her dad was a local politician in Rio Grande, and he approved of the stolen flag. They were taking furniture to their grandmother in Calafate.

When the truck neared town, the dad said to me, while pointing in the distance, "Is that your friend there?"

Devin was on the side of the road, walking with his thumb out.

The politician stopped, but with all the furniture, Devin had to get into the bed of the truck. Six kilometers outside Calafate, there was a checkpoint, and this forced Devin to exit the ride. It was illegal to travel in the back of a truck. I told Devin to check his e-mail for my location. Then I waved at him with the utter delight of chance, laughing like a gambler as we left.

The road wound down to El Calafate—a small but rapidly growing town. The largest freshwater lake in Argentina sat next to it. Everything was very nice, new, and expensive. There was construction on every corner of the town packed with old people and money.

The name Calafate is derived from the dark, purple Patagonian fruit that is about half the size of a blueberry. The fruit is mostly seeds but is extremely sweet and full of antioxidants. A Tehuelche legend says that if you eat the calafate berry, you will return to Patagonia. This legend is always true, and sometimes comically so.

El Calafate is the hub for people wanting to visit the Perito Moreno glacier and the entire glacier national park. Here exist some of the world's largest frozen waters. In the summer, Perito calves in dramatic fashion, with giant pieces of ice falling from the glacier, and creating big waves in Lago Argentino. There is a beautiful viewing area that we saw in the pamphlets. Now was summer, but it cost too much for us to see the calving. My only interests were beer and sleep. I found a room at the cheapest hostel in town. It was clean and new.

Devin was walking the street looking for me, and we soon made our way back to the hostel. It was a square two-story wood house with ten rooms. There were eight beds in our room, all of them bunks. We were the only people currently staying in the room, and we spread out. After relieving ourselves of clothes, I was the first to take a shower. Afterward, while I was brushing my teeth, I heard Devin apologizing: "*Lo siento, lo siento.* I'm sorry." An unhappy American accent was also on the other side of the door. I opened it, loosely holding the towel.

"What's the problem, ladies?" I said to the forty-year-old woman from the front desk and a blonde girl who I would later find out was from Cleveland. At this moment Cleveland was covering her nose and shouting.

"*Huele Mal*. No. I can't sleep here. No, Huele *muy* mal. No. *No!*" The situation ended abruptly. We put our shoes outside the window. Owing to this level of soap-defeating reek, we were afforded a private room for the price of a shared one.

Later on we saw Cleveland in the kitchen, and I tried to be friendly, inquiring about her cooking. She had spent the entire day on the Internet and was now peevishly attempting to bake a lonely dinner.

"This kitchen is the worst; they can't even keep it stocked with normal pots and pans. What a joke. The Internet said a fully stocked kitchen!"

Cleveland was the reason American tourists had a bad reputation, and after this behavior I decided to be an asshole. While she was waiting on her food to finish, Devin and I talked loudly about people always complaining.

"How can someone be in the middle of Patagonia on vacation and hate their life?" I asked Devin and the empty room.

"What a fucking loser you would have to be!"

We drank a bunch of Quilmes in Calafate with the much friendlier European travelers. We never made it to the glacier, or even to hike around the lake. Hikes were free but were nearly impossible both physically and mentally. An Irish guy talked about the different blues he saw in the glacier.

"I have never seen ice that color before. It is constantly making noise."

We let them have their moment. Humility is almost impossible during adventures, but now I was used to the adventure, and I could hold my tongue. I was settled into the trip. It wasn't about spending a week at Torres del Paine or spending nights on the ice. This trip was about putting one foot in front of the other. All that towns were, was a new drinking spot at the end of long week of work. How foolish it would all have been had it not been destiny. How foolish destiny required me to be.

We got a taxi to the edge of town and then stood a good distance past the police checkpoint to have better success at hitching. It took nearly an hour, but eventually Devin hauled down a ride. I had been attempting to make a sign out of cardboard trash.

The driver had a new Chevy hatchback and lived in Rio Gallegos, almost four hundred kilometers away. He had been visiting his son in Calafate, and consequently his ex. He drove with frustration. The trip had not ended enjoyably for either party, though I couldn't understand everything he told me. We began to climb the steep mesa out of the valley. The man was driving in fourth gear and sped up to maintain it. His anger at his wife was morphing into a desire to kill us all.

We were flying when we crested the ridge and leveled out. I kept looking at the speedometer, never seeing it go below 190 kilometers per hour. At one point it hit 225. I thought death was imminent. The driver didn't care that my face was screaming at him with terror. Devin was thrilled by it, making me feel powerless. We took blind corners in the wrong lane. I couldn't speak and was white-knuckling the door and seat. The Chevy's engine was torqueing, and the wind would randomly push the car into the opposite lane. The tires were barely holding on to the uneven, potholed road. In the distance was the old farmhouse near the intersection with the old ruta.

"ESTAMOS ACA! ESTAMOS ACA!" I started screaming as if I had won a game show, pounding on the dash board.

We had a long week ahead and so were carrying lots of food. Our packs were full, bulging with cheese and sausages. Devin was even holding a plastic grocery store sack in his hands.

"I am sure you can shove that in your pack, man; it is going to suck holding it all day."

"I don't want to squish my bread man, and now I can eat candy whenever."

We were well rested and making good time. The road was at a slight incline, and it was thirty kilometers back to the lookout over the valley. Right before we got there, a trucker pulled over and gave us water. It was in a tank below the cab on the passenger side.

"This water is from Mendoza," he said proudly as it flowed out. Mendoza was the destination I now considered the bare minimum I could walk, and consequently home to unmet old family acquaintances. Walking to Mendoza, or anywhere else, was horrible to imagine, to think a million steps in the future, and then to take one.

There is a small lookout over the valley of Rio Santa Cruz. It is enormous and difficult for the senses to grasp. The visible landmarks seem all at once close and impossibly distant. Off ahead, the Rio Santa Cruz formed at the east of Lago Argentino. Here is a desert river formed from glaciers. That day we also saw two rare Andean condors flying above—the big, beautiful black bird of the cordillera, with fingers at the ends of its wings. The air thunders when they fly.

We were looking for a place to rest when we saw a large red-roofed estancia. It was huge, and just below us to the right. The road leading to it was rock and well maintained. Devin found the only litter, an old cig on the ground, and smoked it. No one was there. We knocked on doors and walked around barns, and finally a gaucho invited us inside. He wore a black gaucho hat similar to a beret. He was clean shaven and much larger than us.

We all drank mate, and he gave us *torta frita* (fry bread). The place was very bare. There was a long wooden table with a bench, and an old TV with the news turned on. A couple of outdated calendars were on the wall, but the place was mostly empty and clean.

After an hour's rest there, we left and decided to take a shortcut through the property. After almost two hours of hiking through desert sand and sharp plants, we made it back to the road. Right when we did, a big white Tacoma was there waiting for us.

"It's the guys that were praying earlier," I said as I started to run toward them.

During a rest, two older gentlemen had pulled over to ask if they could pray for us. I asked if they had any water. They didn't, but now they had returned, looking for us, with four sandwiches and three liters of water.

We kept walking and passed a small creek, where we rested for a while. It was nice and was shaded with the only trees for miles. A few buildings were near, and there were a dozen workers. We were too tired to be friendly and had already been noticed so we decided to keep looking for a better place, though we knew there was not one.

We found a big drainpipe under the road. A truck stopped and gave us many liters of water. We didn't need it, but we were in the desert, and we drank yerba mate all night.

The next morning, we made it to Lago Argentino. It was hard, but my morale was still high. It was almost Christmas, and we discussed where to spend it. Devin was not giving much input, just agreeing halfheartedly. At the end of the day, we were low on water again. We found a spot to sleep a few hundred yards from the road, and I returned to do the rain dance, the empty Nalgene in hand.

In twenty minutes, only three cars had passed. Each driver looked at me apologetically. I was just about to give up when an old truck rattled to the side of the road. The shirtless driver was sweating and went to the bed of his pickup. I hadn't noticed before, but now, I saw the many bottles of water he had in the back. He started handing me liter after liter. After four liters, I told him thanks, but he just kept saying, "Yo tengo, I have, yo tengo." I returned back to camp with nine liters—everything he had. We drank and cooked with nearly all of it that night, and I didn't mind getting up to pee in the dark.

The next morning, Devin and I decided to walk the river instead of the road. It always seemed like the better idea. The road was monotony; the river could be anything. We hopped the fence, and headed in the direction of the flowing water. There were some tire tracks at first, but soon we were following animal trails. Purples, blues, reds, oranges, whites, and yellows—the colors were everywhere. Each plant had a different flower. From a distance, the desert was bland; but up close, it was vibrant. The river was farther than we thought, but it felt good being away from the people with much faster modes of transportation.

Devin's FiveFingers were filling with sand and making his blisters bleed. Everything soon became significantly more difficult, and after an hour we began looking for a place to climb out. We got back to the road, and Devin was lagging behind fifty meters. He was in a bad mood, and the blisters were now entirely covering his feet. Between each of this toes, the skin was raw. The calluses his feet had built up were now gone, replaced by raw flesh, as if they had been rubbed away by sandpaper. He was walking with a bit of a limp. I saw a small sign on the fence that said, *"Observatorio."*

"This is the place! I have seen pictures of this on Google Earth!"

I jumped over the gate and rushed inside. Devin followed me, not wanting to walk another step. The observatory telescope was huge, made of stainless steel, and hadn't been used in decades. It's round base looked to have a twenty-foot diameter, and the earth reflected off the shiny walls. The clean, dry air of the desert is the best for looking at stars. There was a house right below the old observatory, but no one was there. Devin and I laid out the mats and planned to sleep with the old stargazer.

Just when it was starting to get dark, I heard a truck pulling up. We were in the open, and it was only a matter of time before they noticed us. I decided to walk down and introduce myself before that happened. There were two workers near my age and a very old man with a full head of entirely white hair. His name was Ramon. I told the trio that Devin and I wished to sleep next to the telescope. The shorter worker with dark skin and hair sat down his box of wine, and he looked at me with wild eyes. "Plata!" he said, rubbing his thumb and fingers together, then pointing to his open empty hand. He seemed angry, and I didn't know what to do. Both the workers had holes in their clothes.

"Lo siento; we can leave," I said somberly, and causing both the workers to laugh.

The old man smiled and stepped forward.

"Come inside, *tomamos mate.*"

I ran up to get Devin, and we went inside the old gaucho's house. It was filled with knickknacks from a long gaucho life. Ramon was a collector/hoarder, and unlike most places we had seen before, this house was filled with personality. It had never been cleaned, but there was a duster made of ñandú feathers hanging from the ceiling in want. The ñandú is a native bird similar to the ostrich and is wild in Patagonia. On his walls were prints of old Molina Campos calendars. This is Argentina's most famous painter, known for his paintings of gaucho life. There were armadillo skins, Mapuche signs carved into wood on all the walls, strange antlers, animal skins, a radio, and a collection of old books. He took the time to show us his dictionary of the Mapuche language. Here was a man who had lived in Patagonia his whole life, and all of his fathers' fathers had too. His house was so refreshingly unique and culturally interesting that I forgot entirely to ask about the telescope. Ramon invited us to sleep inside, but we told him we wanted to sleep under the stars. There was no need for a roof, as the Milky Way glowed.

The next morning was spent on the sagging wooden front porch. The two workers were drinking from another box of wine, and they talked about having an asado—the argentine barbecue. The truck had come back the night before filled with old produce, and now the workers were feeding the chickens and goats. They knew the personality of each animal and would smack the tail of the meanest goat. When the goat lowered his head to charge, the alcoholic would grab the horns and hold on tight. It was time for us to move on.

Before we left, I asked Ramon if there was a quicker way back to the road. Immediately his cataract-covered eyes sparked with life, and a return of energy ran through his slow-moving spine. He was excited about showing off his knowledge. This land was always and would forever be his home, and now he walked with purpose, erasing years in a few steps. This was a man who had a vision. He took us over to a lookout and guided me through. *"No hay nada más derecho,"* he whispered. Ramon's old eyes forward, looking out over the vista, not seeing the river or the plateau or the condors, but seeing the adventures of his distant life. Every memory was a spirit dancing in the vista below him. Ramon's spirit was the reason the wind blew relentlessly, because the wind was born to make spirits strong so they can live forever, even when they are forgotten. This was a Patagonian pure-blooded gaucho, and no one in Argentina wanted that life anymore. Being a gaucho was too hard and lonely, but I was full of excitement.

"Dude, Devin, I understood everything he said: 'There is nothing straighter!'"

In under an hour we were back on the road, and a half kilometer ahead, we were approaching Lago Viedma, another glacial lake. With each step, we were getting better views of Mount Fitz Roy. We looked at nothing else for hours. The rock faces were so impossibly steep. The clouds raced past it, showing the narrow icy peak for only an instant before it again disappeared in storms. Beneath the mountain was El Chalten. The small town, existing solely from the mountain's greatness, was ninety kilometers west down Ruta 23. We passed the intersection, tired. I had resigned myself to not getting a better view of the Patagonian mountain whose outline sits behind the brand name of a world-famous clothing company—the thing most people think of when they hear the word "Patagonia." Monte Fitz Roy is the most anonymously famous mountain in the world

The following morning, we were twenty kilometers outside of Tres Lagos, and it took us four hours to arrive, rarely looking back at the great mountain behind us. Tres Lagos is a small town with a few thousand people that covers a dozen or so square blocks. On the edge of town was a place for camping, but we wanted a break from the bivouacs. We soon arrived at a kiosco that sold beer, and we each bought Quilmes Negra. There was an unfinished house across the street and under perpetual construction. We sat inside the roofless building and drank, each of us having a liter of the dark beer, and it hit me hard. My tired body went numb, and my mind shut off.

Two hours later, we woke up and started walking farther into town. We found a small hosepdaje with WiFi, so we got a room and took showers. Later I heard a noise in the hallway, and when I popped my head out the door, I noticed the owner had lit multiple sticks of incense. Our smell was not good for business. I fell back asleep.

The next morning, we sat around drinking as much yerba mate as we could in the small kitchen in front. Devin was hungover. He had been unable to sleep the night before. He had instead consumed Fernet. Neither of us had heard of it before, but it was cheap Italian liquor.

Devin was drinking from the bottle that night, and this morning his mind was still somewhere else. At 11:00 a.m., we had to leave or pay for another night. I wanted to get started and put Fitz Roy behind me. It felt wrong and right at the same time. Devin talked me into putting my thumb out. He really wanted to go.

"We are ahead of schedule; we can rest a few more days," he said to me.

He was right. We were ahead of schedule, and I had never felt so strong and capable. My legs were rocks, and their muscles were finally ready for the challenge. Each toe was ready, and the balls of my feet were flat and thicker than before. My back never ached, and I walked leaning forward, like a caveman. My neck and face were chapped, my dark brown hair had been made lighter by the sun's rays, my lips bled, and my mind was dulled by the stillness of the walk. Nothing bothered me except the wind.

"You're right; we've been killing it, man. Let's go."

Though I was unaware of it, Devin's desire for human companionship and his hangover would change my life forever.

There was no traffic. An hour passed with only a few locals driving by. A van entered town from the north and circled around, making a couple quick stops. With the battery charged in my phone, I turned on James Brown's "Mind Power." We gave it all we had, and the driver stopped. He had curly shoulder-length hair. He liked adventure as much as we did; it was his job.

"You guys are really lucky; most people going to Chalten don't come through this town."

He spoke English and ran tours from Bariloche—a town much farther north that is the Aspen, Colorado, of Patagonia. The tour guide had just finished taking a couple on a honeymoon excursion. They had visited the most remote locations. Now he was alone and looking for gas. Tres Lagos didn't have any, and he was hoping Chalten did. If not, he would have no way to make it back north.

He talked about how slow business was. A volcano had erupted in Chile, sending mountains of ash across the border and into Argentina.

Ash filled the sky almost every day. Near the border, in towns like Villa La Angostura, the ash was over six feet deep. The airport had shut down, and the vital stream of rich Brazilians entering Argentina had vanished immediately. The story was told to me repeatedly. Brazilians were looking elsewhere for snow.

As we approached in the twelve-person tour bus, the massive blue green Lago Viedma was on our left, and the mountains in front. A giant sky-blue glacier with parallel streaks of earth, like beaten paths, entered the water on the west. It was huge, even from a distance. The van cut deeper into the side of the steepening Andes. We passed a condor lookout next to large walls of granite. These ledges provided unlimited areas for the giant birds to perch. We passed a few streams running toward the lake, free of man and cattle. The moment we entered El Chalten, we were placed under her spell.

11 El Chalten and the Girl

On how vast a scale, and of what duration must have been
the action of those waters which smoothed the shingle
stones now buried in the deserts of Patagonia.
—Captain Robert FitzRoy

The mountain overlooking Chalten, Monte Fitz Roy, is one of the world's most beautiful peaks—and one of the most difficult to climb. It wasn't first summited until 1952. Less than half the height of the Himalayas, Fitz Roy is still the ultimate mountain. Enormous granite faces and rapidly changing weather patterns leave climbers dangerously exposed. It claims many. The successes are few, as are the attempts.

The driver let us off at the entrance to town. There was a pretty entrance sign with flowers surrounding it. The town was colored with backpackers and new shops catering to them. The mountains were again blanketed in clouds. El Chalten means "the smoky mountain" in Mapuche because there is always a trail of clouds at the summit.

We found a hostel, and inside were three Israelis—one guy and two girls. The girls couldn't stop asking us questions, and our enthusiasm was rising with the encouragement. The guy wouldn't even look up.

"We are going to look for a brewery if y'all want to come." I said encouragingly.

Israelis frequently travel to Patagonia in big groups. It is one of the premier destinations after the military service. Many signs across Patagonia are in Hebrew, especially along the Carretera Austral. I had concluded that though they came for adventure, more than a couple secretly hoped to find a hidden Nazi compound and practice their training. We liked to imagine some were spies.

Devin and I left—just the two of us. The guy at reception said a place around the corner "had all the good beers."

In less than a block, we arrived at La Vineria. A handmade wooden sign was hanging in front. Inside they tried to carry every wine and beer made in Patagonia. We didn't look much at the wine, but there were multiple fridges filled with beers that I had never seen.

It was the coolest place we had been to, but from the time we entered, I couldn't keep my eyes off the girl working. I wanted her to see me looking, and when she did, I smiled and looked down, hoping to find my courage. Her hair was long and walnut brown. Her oval face held big round eyes, and they were opened completely when she spoke to me.

"Kay teepo day cervayzuh es teww favureatoh?" I asked, and somehow she understood me. Her favorite beer was the Araucana red bock. Devin and I sat outside at the picnic table in front of the store. Drinking commenced.

"That girl is really cute, man," Devin said between gulps.

"Yeah, and she likes good beer."

A car pulled up and waved us over to ask us for directions. I pointed them in the way of an ATM, and before they had driven off, two Swiss guys on BMW motorcycles pulled up. Devin and I had met one of them a few days ago. They had the blondest hair and bluest eyes possible. Two days earlier, one had been stuck on the side of the road, out of gas. At the time, he gave us water, joking that he had decided to drink his vodka and would not be pouring it in the tank. Now a third biker pulled up. We knew him too, and I puffed out my proud chest, hoping the girl behind the counter was watching. Sofia was her name, and I wanted her to think we were celebrities.

After two big bottles of beer, Devin and I were feeling the effects. My face was fire drunk, and inside I was feeling a rush of energy. I could feel the town humming, and I wanted to beat on the table. I wanted to rip my shirt off and scream. My eyes were wide, as though they could see for the first time.

"I don't want to pay for that damn hostel!"

"Me neither; let's go." Devin responded.

We went back to the hostel with our drunk mission to retrieve our backpacks. The Israelis were still there on the Internet. They saw us grabbing our packs.

"You are leaving?"

"Yeah, we're out. Beer's too fucking good over there; we spent the money. We're going to sleep in an abandoned house. Chau." It was so awesome, being able to say that, it was the greatest thing I had ever said.

We then took our bags to La Vineria and left them with Sofia. Devin and I explored the mountain town with the vague notion of finding a place we could sleep. It wasn't long till we were back. We would find a place to sleep later; I just wanted to be around her. She was the only one working, so she was unable to escape my pestering whenever I felt bold. Throughout the trip my Spanish had been improving, but now I couldn't form even the most basic of sentences. I said words like *"linda"* while pointing at her and blushing. I felt like a fourteen-year-old, except I was hammered.

It became dark. Devin and I were both *borracho*, and we decided that in all our macho bravado, we had been wrong. We did, in fact, want to sleep in a bed. We couldn't go back to the first place, however; that would have been humiliating.

Instead, we went across town. In the middle was a large open area, and a designated spot for camping. There was a big group set up, and a fire was burning. All the good people were enjoying their night under the Chalten stars. Here was a party of peace signing kumbaya to the gentle strumming of the guitar, and I wanted to yell obscenities at them, so I did.

"Euro-trash, using your fucking tents in the middle of a town. The mountain is that way!" I yelled, pointed, and jumped.

The fact that almost all the tourists we had seen were from Europe or Israel was pissing us off. This was the Americas. Where were all the cool Americans?

The guitar playing stopped, and Devin stood in front of me to scream, "Euro-trash! You are trash!" We then ran to the next hostel. We were certainly not prepared for any potential retaliation.

At the hostel, the guy behind the counter showed us to the room, but before he did, I tried to pay him. He calmly assured me, "Che, no, *en la mañana.*" I insisted on paying, but he wanted me to wait until morning. That night I crawled into bed with the money curled in my hand. The next day, we got up and drank mate. There was a young Danish couple in their early twenties, both our size and blonde. They were going to Antarctica to celebrate New Year's. Their adventure had just begun.

It was an hour after checkout, eleven, and no one had shown up at the front desk. I rang the bell on the counter. No one came. I went behind and called out. No one came. We made the beds and left. The money still in my hand.

The four of us went to the Vineria and started drinking and play-ing cards. She was back, and she told me to call her Sofi, not Sofia. I watched her all day while the other three focused on winning the card game. My senses were elevated. I listened to the sounds of her voice, noticing the inflection points in her words. She was confident with who she was and where she was. I noticed the way her hips pivoted when she walked. She was tall and slim, and her coworkers called her Flaca (skinny), but her hips were wide. She was mountain fit, and I tried not to gaze too long into her big brown eyes. She touched my right shoulder and laughed. The electricity traveled from her fingertips to my toes, and it shocked me.

Devin and the Danes wanted to go to a brewery a few blocks away.

"No, don't go there; that place is *feo,*" Sofi said. I thought how cute it was to call a brewery ugly. After just one beer, we returned to Sofi and the Vineria.

"*Si es mejor aca,*" I said with a smile, my Spanish returning only because it had been prepared.

Like Sofi, the Araucana strong red bock was my favorite beer in Patagonia. In the bottom of the bottle is a layer of sediment. It is nine percent alcohol, malty but clean, with Patagonian-grown bitter hops. That afternoon I felt myself crossing the line to debauchery. I have never been able to hold my alcohol, and I did not want to lose whatever level of cool credibility I had built. I went across the street to a house under construction to nap. Devin stayed playing cards.

I woke up a few hours later and sat there leaning against the brick wall, alone. I was in the same clothes I had used for months. In front of me I could see a family eating dinner. They looked happy together. I didn't want to go home, but I did miss it. I thought about staying in Chalten and giving up one dream to pursue another.

I went back to the Vineria. They were still playing cards. Sofi was making empanadas. They had quinoa in them, and I told her how good they were by using exaggerated movements and saying, *"Muy rico!"*

Devin and I went to the small supermarket and bought all the food we would need for a week. Then we went to have dinner with the Danes. Later that night, we returned to the Vineria. I had a box of chocolates with me.

"You gotta get her something, man." Devin had told me.

I felt dorky buying chocolates for a girl I didn't know and could barely talk to—one that would pass as such a brief encounter. Still, I went inside the Vineria nervous and with candies in my hand. Sofi's boss was there with her, and I said only "Para ti" while placing it on the counter next to her. Then I left quickly, before things became more awkward. I felt like a kid running away from his crush after just giving her a letter, it was a short letter, a question really, and it asked her to answer by circling yes or no. Devin and I were continuing to drink in front of the store. Sofi came outside and put something in my lap. I went to open it.

"No, not yet," she said, and then I realized what it was.

I waited a moment and then went inside to say good-bye to her. The boss was still there.

"Estoy triste," I said, looking at him, but really at her.

"Why are you sad?" he asked me. He had seen his share of people claiming to be adventurers. He was one.

"Because I am never going to see Sofia again."

"There are plenty of girls on the road," he said, not realizing I wanted the right one.

"Yeah ... but nobody has the *buena onda*, like her," I said.

Sofi looked into my eyes, knowing she would never see me again, and I left like a gringo, uncomfortable, unsure, and without a hug or kiss. She would always have a place in my heart. I felt as if our spirits had been together before, though we could barely communicate. I could only watch her, but somehow I knew her, and it was over.

Devin and I ran to the abandoned house where we had decided to sleep. We climbed up to the second story. There was a big window looking out and a small room in the back. I went there to unwrap the present. It was 11:00 p.m., and the stars shone in through the large, windowless frame. We made a flame, and the smoke entered our lungs. I held it there as long as I could, and it rumbled inside me. The plants returned to our bloodstream after considerable absence. At first I didn't feel anything, and we passed the tightly rolled torch back and forth in the dark, giggling with anticipation. Soon my world changed.

This being the first time a philosophical fire had been burned in months, the normally subtle effects were now surprising me. I was next-level. Devin's face was no longer in pain. A look of relaxation had come over him. The most pleasant, mild, devious grin appeared under his resting cheeks and barely opened eyes.

"Man ..." Devin exhaled, "I need to take a shit," and he was much happier to be doing it with the assistance of induced relaxation.

I looked out the window, resting my forearms against the frame, and I began to cry, and to ask God for forgiveness. I was selfish for leaving my family. My sister was pregnant, and I was going to miss the birth of my niece. The walk felt more pointless with every step. It didn't mean anything. No one cared. No one would ever care. I couldn't even answer the question so often asked of me: why?

Devin came back up the ladder.

"I just had the *best* shit in my life. Under the stars, not giving a fuck, dude, it was … Are you okay, man?"

I turned my sobs into laughs and played it off.

"Yeah, man. You know what would be hilarious …"

We spent the rest of the night laughing and imagined picking fights with all the Europeans. A police car kept circling town with its lights on. We were paranoid and thought they were looking for us since we had left the hostel earlier that day without paying. Mostly we did what people do when plants are burning—we did nothing. It was the greatest night in Patagonia.

The next morning, we got up and burned the last of our prayer-inducing substance. We bought some empanadas and walked out of town. I almost cried again when we passed La Vineria. Inside was all the gold of El Dorado, but Patagonia was between us, and if I went on a new path too early, I would certainly get lost. There would be no bushwhacking my way to paradise.

We sat on the outskirts of town, waiting for a ride. A group of travelers walked by us. They had nice mountain clothes and glasses. When they passed, I heard one say, "Looks like they have been at it for a while." It was the best thing ever said about me behind my back, and this lessened the sadness I felt for leaving.

An older Swiss couple picked us up. They had a big van and were going all over the continent. The happy gray-haired couple told us about a guy that was running across Argentina. A South African was jogging thirty kilometers a day with his girlfriend driving a van behind him. Devin and I looked at each other, feeling awesome. We were averaging thirty-five kilometers a day with packs, no cute girlfriend, and no van to sleep in!

Outside of Tres Lagos, we returned to the walk. Both of us were sad. The adventure wasn't fun anymore. Fun was Chalten. We had left the fun. We were alone in the middle of the desert.

12 Alone

Ordinary men hate solitude. But the master makes use of it, embracing his aloneness, realizing he is one with the whole universe.
—Lao Tzu

Ruta 40 was under construction here like everywhere else. The mountains were blocked by hills that were closer and brown. The part of the road under construction was flat and nearly paved. This made it smooth, unlike the old road, which was uneven, rutted, and filled with potholes. Cars were not supposed to drive on the new part, but evidence spoke to the contrary. The new sections of road suddenly ended in places with no warning, and there were huge gaps where drainpipes would one day go. Black tire streaks showed close encounters.

Devin was far behind. The blisters on his feet were not getting any better. They hadn't had time to heal in Chalten. We were walking slowly, and after five hours, Devin was ready to stop. I looked at the map and talked about us spending Christmas at Gobernador Gregores. He agreed, but his eyes and mind were elsewhere. We crawled to the side of the road, behind dirt moved by construction equipment, and sat in silence. The plants had made us nostalgic about that good life we had wanted to escape.

We woke up with the sun and started walking. Devin's limp was worse. The road was dirt, and his feet were bleeding again. After four hours, Devin started yelling at me, and I waited for him. He looked like a guy who was trying to complete a marathon after surgery. His body was giving out.

"I think this is it for me, man."

"Yeah? You think so …"

I didn't know what to say. We had been through so much. I loved him. I hated him. I wanted him here, and I wanted him gone. Many things in my past, present, and future were and would be a result of Devin. Every day I wanted to outwork him. We had gotten strong together. We were brothers.

"I am sorry to do it here man. I know this isn't the best place to say good-bye."

"This is where we spend every day, man. It is a perfect place."

We paused, not knowing how to take steps in different directions.

"Let's drink some mate first" I suggested.

We shared a few cups but didn't say much. Then we embraced firmly and parted ways. Devin was going to hitch back to Tres Lagos and then try to hitch all the way to Buenos Aires. Today was December 23.

Only an hour later, I came upon some road workers. They lived in a shipping container with six bunk beds and a sink. One of them was wearing a hat that said "Callejeros." I thought it was because they worked on the road, but later I found out that Callejeros was an Argentine *rock nacional* band. During one of their concerts, a fire broke out, and many young people died. It became known as the Tragedia de Cromañón. The band fell into depression after the incident, and the drummer supposedly set his wife on fire in a fight.

I started drinking mate, but only one other worker drank with me. The five others sat around, each one laughing at his own jokes.

"You are lucky," one of them said. "We are supposed to leave at any moment."

They were waiting for the bus to take them back to Rio Gallegos so they could spend Christmas with their families. Two liters of mate later, I was feeling more confident about walking alone. At the bottom of my backpack were a dozen or so bags of caramel-coated peanuts. They were Christmas packs and had been on sale for twenty-five cents each. It was the best price-to-calorie ratio of anything in the supermarket. I couldn't eat them though, they cracked my teeth.

"*Regalos para todos! Feliz Navidad!*" I said, assuming the candies could at least provide me the benefit of looking generous.

I had just left, but one of the workers started running after me. I stopped, and he had two cans of lentils, a kilo of sugar, and five hundred grams of peas. I wanted to refuse all the weight but was unable to politely do so. My bag was now four pounds heavier, and I immediately dumped out the sugar near a hill of ants. The road was approaching Lago Cardiel, but I still could only see it on the map.

A few hours passed, and I saw a man in the distance. His dog was next to him and barking at me. The man bent down to try to calm the perro, but the dog was too excited and ran to me The animal first welcomed me with hugs, and then the man followed with much the same enthusiasm. His name was Ronaldo, and he was a little shorter than me, with big, unblinking eyes. No one else lived on the estancia with him. The owner lived a few hours away. This place "is essentially mine," Ronaldo told me. His face was hard, intimidating, but he was very outgoing. I liked him from the start, though he was clearly a little insane.

The block house was big and clean, and had thick vines manicured over the white walls and tin roof. The living area and kitchen were furnished with only a wood burning stove, a table and a bench. There were five rooms upstairs, with all of them empty and dusted. In Ronaldo's room, things were different. He had hundreds of books, pictures, and flags. There was art, writings, an old globe, and *National Geographic* magazines. Everything was organized, and he was knowledgeable of the location of everything.

"Oh, let me show you this," he repeated often, going directly to the object of his thought.

He showed me one book in which he hid all of his money. He had a lot.

"*Todo para mi bosillo*" (It all goes in my pocket), he told me.

He lived a solitary life and said he preferred it that way. He liked to listen to the radio and roll his own cigs. His crazy eyes never blinked when he spoke, and they never looked away.

"The Bolivians, they won't look you in the eye," he said to me.

The Bolivians, he told me, came to work the *campo* and were taking jobs from gauchos.

"They work for less, work longer, and they don't even drink mate! They are changing our culture."

They would, as he said, "Work *por un mango*."

Here was my first experience with the Argentine prejudices against the Bolivians, the new immigration into Argentina. Originally the immigrants had been from Spain and Italy, and many of Ronaldo's old gaucho friends had gone to the city, replaced by lower-paid Bolivians.

I had my small American flag in my pack, and I thought Ronaldo deserved it. Our countries faced similar issues. Ronaldo was not a bad man, but an old man experiencing change, and whether or not these changes indicated progress, Ronaldo's opinions were stone.

"The government and the people are different," he said, proud to have the flag, though like many Latin Americans, Ronaldo knew everything the U.S. government had done south of the border. I had always felt it was the traveler's duty to perform personal diplomacy—this being especially true for a US traveler, whose generous government has often given guns, money, and training to bad people.

Ronaldo, while holding the stars and stripes, said he was saving up money to buy a couple of sheep. The estancia hadn't produced anything for a long time, and this clearly hurt his pride. He was dreaming of production and growth, and he kept asking me if I wanted the skin of a *gato*.

"No, gracias. I am okay, really."

I didn't really want a skinned cat to carry around, but after the third time he asked, I conceded and walked over to the barn with him. Hanging from a rafter, over scattered hay on the floor, was the skin of a wildcat. He called it a *gato de campo*. He told me to stuff my hands inside the body to stay warm at night.

Before I left, Ronaldo offered me money. He was disappointed I wasn't staying, but this was still my first day alone, and I now wanted to be alone. He gave me a big pouch of La Mariposa tobacco and rolling papers for the road. I gave him my last picture of an ex-girlfriend. She was quite voluptuous, and Ronaldo was quite happy with it. I walked seven more kilometers while thinking of Sofi and ended up sleeping next to some red religious icons. Rolling and smoking cigs now gave me something to do.

The next morning, I walked over to the red religious box I had slept next to. It bore the name "Gauchito Gil." There were candles and unsmoked cigarettes inside. I thought a little gaucho had died, and later when I told this to Argentinos, they thought it hilarious. Gil was no baby, but I didn't know that yet.

The road was under construction in the hills surrounding the emerald-colored Lago Cardiel. The lake seemed enormous sitting there, the lonely body of water in the middle of the brown desert. Wide tan patches of spiky grass stood near the shore. Only a handful of people lived anywhere near it. I was provided with many expansive views, and at times I shouted to no one. I was alone.

"Pataaagonia!"

My map showed a small river ahead, and that was my goal. The road was straight for as far as I could see. It was the afternoon of Christmas Eve, causing there to be even less traffic than usual on the road never frequented. One car gave me two liters, and I drank them fast. The road had never come within a manageable distance of the lake, and I was thirsty. Four hours later, I had only one liter of water left. Another car approached while I was sitting down, resting. I held up a bottle from my crouched position unenthusiastically, my head down. Again I tried to look miserable enough to ensure assistance. The car stopped. The driver was a man in his fifties with his wife and extended family.

"Is it okay if we film this?" The woman asked.

The camera was already rolling. My normal nature returned, and I responded enthusiastically, "Si, si, si. *Tienes* agua?"

The driving grandpa looked down disappointed, having just failed on home video. He began to apologize to me.

"No, no *tenemos* agua ..." Grandpa said defeated, and now he was staring into the future, and he was watching the home video, and he was watching his son rewind the video, and watching his grandchildren laugh. Here was the grandpa who drove his family across the desert without water. They would still be laughing at him even after he died. This would be all anyone remembered about him.

Suddenly Grandpa's eyes lit up. He knew he had hit the jackpot.

"Tomas cerveza?"

"*Yes!*" I exclaimed in English.

Happily, he got out and handed me a Quilmes *bajo calorias* tallboy from the trunk. It was so cold, and enjoyed more than any low calorie beer has ever been.

Then gramps drove off a legend. His family in tow, his right hand on the wheel at twelve o'clock, and he left the windows down. Here was the famous grandpa who drove his family across Patagonia with only beer, and there was proof. This would be all anyone remembered about him, and he loved it.

The creek on the map was dry. Down a steep hill where it should have been were spots with little pools of water in hoof-prints. There were feces all around. It was nearly night, and the next river was over thirty kilometers away. I had five hundred milliliters of water.

An old 4Runner was throwing up dust in the distance, and I was finally feeling what might be described as desperation. Tomorrow would be Christmas, and traffic would be nil. This was my only chance. When the car drew closer, I began to jump wildly and wave my arms. I was standing in the middle of the road, trying to force it to stop. I had empty plastic bottles upside down in both hands. Inside the Toyota were three young *machos* with their shirts off. I noticed climbing ropes in the back, but I couldn't think of the word for "climb." I pointed at the rope and mimicked the action.

"Yeah! We are going back to Chalten after Christmas; you can come."

I thought about seeing Sofi again, but knew the way was north. The only liquid they had was backwash at the bottom of a couple bottles amounting to 250 ml. They drove off, and I slept by the dry creek. I attempted extracting potable water from the dirty puddles, but it was too gross. Never before had I gone to sleep so thirsty. In the night, I dreamed about finding water and woke up feeling crazy and scared.

Without a thought, I drank the climber's backwash and went back to sleep.

It was vital that I started early. If I didn't make it to the river before noon, the dry sun could make things dangerous. At five in the morning, I opened the two cans of lentils the callejeros had given me. Lifting the can above my mouth and turning it upside down, I pressed the lid up into the can, squishing the lentils and letting the water drip into my mouth. I turned it back over, pressing down now more firmly to retrieve every drop of liquid. There was a small scorpion under my sleeping mat, and seeing the creature here made me feel vulnerable. With chance, so many things in life happen; and with chance, so many things end.

I walked quickly, keeping my focus on the river. It was a great distance to my right and down steep ledges. I thought about going straight for it. After five hours, I still had not passed a single car, but I was close. The road dropped in elevation, the humidity changed, and I couldn't see far, but I sat down to finally have my first sip of water. Performance in need often comes much easier than expected.

I leaned up against the rock wall and started rolling a cig. I could relax, and smoking had quickly taken the place of Devin and Jackson, whom I now thought nothing of. With every step, I was thinking of Sofia, and I didn't want our previous farewell to be the last time I saw her.

As I had just lit the cig, the first car of the day drove up, and I hurried to put out the tobacco. The occupants were another three-generation family. They were traveling to one of the estancias to spend a Christmas riding horses. They told me the river was about three kilometers away and gave me a five-hundred-milliliter bottle of water. I took a small sip and put it in my bag. Another grandfather, this one in the passenger's seat, seeing my action, handed me another bottle.

"Toma! Toma!" he said encouragingly.

I drank the entire half liter in big gulps before him, showing off my yellow unbrushed teeth.

"Quieres oh-ray-oh?" he asked now.

I had no idea what he had said and looked at him oddly.

"Que?"

"Ohrayo. Oh ... ray ... oh."

He finally held up a blue package, and I felt like an idiot for not understanding him. They drove off, and I sat back down in the shade, eating the entire twelve-pack of Oreos he had just given me. I instantly felt the sugar and walked light-footed the rest of the way to the river.

It was just before noon when I arrived and set up my Christmas spot. I put the stolen Argentine flag across a tree and hung my clothes and equipment up there with it. It was a backpacker's Christmas tree. I smoked cigs and drank mate all day. The river was cold, and I swam naked in it. Never before had I done this, and it was liberating.

In leisure my mind kept returning to Sofia. I had her e-mail address, and I wanted to do something corny. I tore out a page from my journal and wrote her name on it. Then, with duct tape, I attached it to the metal sign in front of the bridge. The river had once been called Rio Chico, but it was now Rio Sofia. I snapped a photo of the sign and thought about how long it would be till I had an Internet connection. I spent hours dictating the e-mail in my mind.

"I'll bet no one else named a river after you for Christmas!" I said out loud and to the wind, wondering if she had already forgotten me. Did she feel what I felt? I had every step to think of her. I was alone, and for the most part I was without music or any form of companionship. I had only my thoughts, and I imagined a million lives. All of them were real, and each life gave me pleasure in my current state. There are parallel universes in Patagonia.

A few hours later, a tour bus stopped and the passengers got out to look around. I was lying by the river in my boxers, using the Argentine flag for shade. A few people took pictures of my Christmas from the bridge.

The next morning, I returned to the pavement, a forty kilometer stretch without variation in direction or elevation. A large black-and-tan plateau stood to the right, while Rio Sofia was running west to east five miles to the south, visible only through the break in the brown landscape. The Andes stood in front of me, covered with snow—my only visual motivation. I was constantly looking for things to do to keep me entertained now that I was alone. I often made up songs, normally singing about God or sex—one to make me feel good, and the other because I liked a little bad. I was the cab driver from Rio Grande. The scenery changed so slowly. Life was monotonous.

Currently my most entertaining game involved cigs and the tour busses. To be successful, I needed to have the cigs pre-rolled and on standby. The tour buses could be seen for miles, and anytime one was in the distance, I would quickly pull one of these pre-rolled *puchos* out of my pocket. Lighting the cig was the hardest part. To do so, I would put my face inside my blue button-up shirt, crouch, and get behind my backpack. The wind still battled everything I did. When the bus passed, I would be posed, attempting to look like James Dean with a lit cig in his mouth, taking the biggest drags possible. I started smoking at every break. There was nothing else to do.

I arrived at a police outpost thirty-two kilometers into the day. It was called Tamel Aike. A nice family lived there, and they invited me inside. The two kids, a boy and girl, were excited to have company. The mother was thin, with dark walnut skin. The man liked to joke. He talked about *futbol* and Boca Juniors, the most popular team. He was skinny and quick. The two of them had started dating when they were fourteen.

I stayed and drank mate. It was the holidays, so they had sugary bread with fruit in it. They call it *pan dulce*, and it is really popular in Argentina. It is also known as panettone. The family offered me a bed to sleep in. There were a few extra, but my mind, now used to the solitude, was done trying to communicate. They sold me a loaf of non-sugary bread for a dollar.

The last kilometers went fast. I found a spot under the road to sleep. There were always some feces, animal or human, in these spots, and they required initial maintenance.

Early the next day, I came across an estancia. It was near the road, so I ventured to it. Most of the estancias were far from the road, so normally I never bothered. Two men with dark features came out. They looked to be in their mid-thirties and were from Bolivia. They didn't seem to understand me, and they wouldn't look me in the eyes—not once. Nor did they say much at all. I decided to ask if they had yerba mate. One of the guys went inside to get it. They didn't drink the mate with me, and they said it belonged to the owner.

Their dirty black dog had come over, and they looked at me strangely when I bent down to pet him. It felt good seeing the mutt's tail wag, a dog's happiness being the only reason for having the animal. I didn't stay long, and their dog started following me when I left. I went back to tell the Bolivianos, but they didn't care.

The dog continued following me. I could not control him, and he would take off into the fields, running as far as he could. Then he would turn around and start scanning the horizon for me. I tried to hide, but he could always pick up my scent. I was low on food, and I wasn't going to let another dog die. It was time to hitch a ride into town. The problem was that no cars would stop because of the black dog.

The road turned to gravel again. A car came by going south and kicking up dust. The dog went after it, and I took off the other way. His adventure had taken another road, and he didn't come back. A few minutes later, a van pulled up behind me, and I had my thumb out.

The driver's name was Roberto, and he was from Bariloche. He knew the land well, and could tell me all the good fishing locations, as well as the names of mountains, birds, and animals. He had a big gray beard and was skinny but with long, old man muscles. He still gave trekking tours, but not many anymore; this was not because of his age—Roberto was the best—but because of the volcanic ash from Chile. He was on his way back home, which was eighteen hours north.

"You can ride all the way there if you want." People frequently said these horribly nice things to me. Everyone wanted to let me out of my unlocked cell, and I wanted out too, but I needed to keep walking. I needed the pain. I hadn't covered a distance that was meaningful—not to me.

His English was better than my Spanish, and we got along quite well. We stopped at the historic hotel/bar El Olnie, named after the river next to it. I had seen pictures of this place on Google when planning for the trip.

"Why's it closed?" I asked, surprised and disappointed. I had imagined drinking in the famous establishment.

He told me the gaucho running the place had died, and no one had been there to take his place. The trees remained and provided good shade to drink mate and eat the candies he shared with me.

We passed Bajo Caracoles and the less-used southern entrance, *cueva de las manos*. Fewer than fifty people lived there, and I decided the more populous Perito Moreno would be a better place to relax for a couple days and to get food.

An hour and a half later, we arrived, and I found a hotel on the outside of town. It was overpriced, but I wanted a room to myself and needed a private bathroom. There was a TV in the room, and I fell asleep with it on.

Perito Moreno isn't much. It's a small, square twenty-block town, but slowly it is becoming a tourist hub for people looking to see the caves. It is named after Francisco Moreno, a scientist responsible for many of the early expeditions into deep Patagonia. Legends say he was captured and escaped from the Tehuelche natives, though some say the stories were only told so he would sound legendary. Francisco was given the title of Perito (expert) for proving Argentine territorial claims against Chile.

I spent two days with the workers at the hotel. A guy, barely twenty, had come to Moreno looking for work. His name was Ariel. He was tall, skinny, and had black hair. He said he had been working there only a couple of months, and I could tell he was bored. He lived with his aunt and had made few friends. He was slightly awkward, and not yet prepared to take his eventual step out of the closet. Juanita cleaned the place and helped wait tables at the restaurant. She was in her early twenties and was from Salta, a city in northern Argentina. Juanita had a young kid and had also come to Patagonia looking for work. Paula was the other worker. She was thirty-three and proud of her figure. Ariel told me she had sex with everyone. Paula had lived in Perito Moreno her whole life and had four kids. Her oldest was sixteen, and I was shown a picture of this daughter posing provocatively.

I sent Sofi an e-mail with the photos I took of Rio Sofia. When I finished typing the e-mail into Google Translate, I signed it in English, "your American boyfriend." I was so excited to get a response. I couldn't wait for one. I kept clicking the mouse to make the page refresh, but it was soon time to leave. I gave Juanita a few of my things to hold on to. I didn't want to carry anything extra, and I would soon be back after walking south over the distance I had hitched with Roberto. The owner of the hotel had refused responsibility for my luggage.

My plan was to arrive in Bajo Caracoles on New Year's, and for weeks I had been imagining celebration scenarios. I dreamed about meeting a van of longhairs who were going to spend New Year's hallucinating in the caves of floating hands.

The landscape was changing from brown and sandy to different shades of red, and there were large areas with only sculpted blood-colored rock. The road went up, over, and around a few hills. There was a large valley with a little bit of water still in the creek, and I spied there the last patches of grass. I went down a steep embankment and laid my sleeping bag right next to the bridge. I pumped water and made a fire. It was nice under the stars with the cars passing above my head. Not a single person on earth knew I was there smoking cigs. I had started sleeping under bridges and in drainpipes nearly every night. I no longer thought about killing animals, but I still thought about the goose. Now I was a vegetarian nine days out of ten, eating instant mashed potatoes, bread, and peanuts for every meal.

The next morning, I went to take a pee, walking just upstream from where I had pumped water the night before to admire the morning view. I looked to my left, and in the grass, submerged in four inches of water, was an almost entirely decomposed sheep; the only things remaining were the wool and bones. I emptied all my water bottles. The pump had probably worked, but psychologically it had to be done.

Then began a long, steep hill, and I could see the former Ruta 40 off to my left. There were one-lane bridges and snaking curves up this same hill, with hardly any variation between the road and the surrounding red ground. Only the indentions of old tire tracks remained, slowly fading in the face of the new road. Ruta 40 veijo was historical and unimaginably rough. Now it is gone. The five-thousand-kilometer cattle trail has been almost entirely paved. I often thought about George Meegan, the Brit who walked from Ushuaia to the tip of Alaska—one of my inspirations for the trip. I would never feel what he felt.

This part of Patagonia was the most arid I had encountered, and the land was an incredible mixture of rolling orange, red, and brown rock hills. Here was where the natives got the materials to paint the caves. The sky was free of clouds, and the sun gave fire to the earth. Everything burned.

Six hours into the day, I crossed a trickle of a creek and made lunch. I rested there for an hour with my shoes off in the shade. When I came out from under the bridge, I saw a lone biker about one hundred yards ahead of me. He was stopped on the side of the road, drinking water.

"*Hola!*" I yelled as loudly as I could.

He waved and waited for me ahead.

His name was Matt, and he was from Alberta. Just nineteen months before, he started riding his bike from Alaska. His forearms were huge. He had dirty blonde hair and blue eyes that glowed with excitement. We met here, fifty kilometers north of Bajo Caracoles, in the middle of the Patagonia desert.

"I am really not pressed for time, if you want someone to walk with."

He pushed his bike along. Matt was twenty-three and full of information and crazy stories about what lay ahead for me. Matt began with his obvious favorite.

"So, we needed to get across the Darian Gap between Panama and Colombia eh. A boat took us on for free in exchange for work ..." We continued walking, and he got more excited. "Throughout the day, the captain of the boat had been watching me, and the first night on the boat, I was taking a piss off the side eh ..." Matt stopped pushing the

bike and grabbed my shoulder for effect. "He came up behind me …
He tried to grab my dick, man. And I ran down to tell my buddy, but
of course my buddy thought it was hilarious," but Matt had more. "So
seven days later, we arrived in Colombia and we got free lodging in a
church eh. In the middle of the night, the preacher got in bed with my
buddy, and grabbed his dick, and whispered that it was okay," and still
Matt continued. "I just heard from a kid on Facebook that the preacher
got murdered with a machete while taking a shower, and you know
the moral is that you just shouldn't go on an adventure and not expect
your dick to be grabbed eh." I could only hope.

After ten kilometers, Matt and I came up to an estancia and asked
if we could camp there. The man wanted to charge us twenty-five pesos. Matt refused, saying he never paid for lodging. In cities he slept at
fire stations, called here *"bomberos."* We kept walking to an abandoned
building in the distance. I wanted to sleep outside under the bridge.
Matt wanted to try to get in the locked building. We found a small
window to the kitchen that was unlocked.

"I think your skinny ass can squeeze in there," he said to me, leaving me no choice but to try.

When I got inside, I opened the door, and we boiled some water on
his stove. I was jealous of how much a bike could carry. He was eating
polenta and told me it was the cheapest and easiest thing one could get.

"Damn, dude, you make me feel weak," I told him. He had arrived
here on a bike from Alaska and never paid for lodging, while I still appreciated the peace and comfort of a private hotel room.

"You are a long-distance walker, man; I have only seen two others,
and they were legitimately crazy." That made me feel good and strange
at the same time.

The next day, I got started about an hour before him. He came up
riding behind me soon after. We were planning on meeting in Bajo
Caracoles for New Year's Eve. The forty kilometers would be a short
day for him but a marathon for me. I wouldn't be able to party tonight
if I walked the eight hours today.

After I passed the north entrance to the caves, the new entrance, I saw a truck, and I put my thumb out. The driver stopped immediately, and I hopped in. Forty minutes later, I was at the pueblo, and I walked around looking for Matt. He wasn't at the lone gas station built of rock, but I figured it would be a good place to wait. He'd come by eventually.

In the *estacion de servicio* was an older Danish couple, and the man bought me beers. After a couple hours, I walked around the tiny town of tiny homes looking for Matt. I talked to the first guy I saw. He had not seen the biker but let me take a nap in his warehouse. I slept for a few hours and woke up at 6:00 p.m. The same guy saw me and gave me twenty pesos.

"Comprame una caja de vino."

I thought it kind of strange he wanted me to buy him box wine since he had the truck and the town was so small, but I did as he told me. I figured Matt had just kept riding, and decided it would be best if I continued as well.

I felt depressed. Of all the ideas I had imagined for New Year's, this wasn't one of them. After walking a couple kilometers, I pulled out the business card for La Vineria. I wondered if Sofi was still working, if she had read my e-mail, and if she had responded. I decided to find the nearest bridge and to call her from the satellite phone, feeling a desperation from the loneliness of adventure holidays. Before I started dialing, the guy I bought wine for pulled up in his truck behind me. Matt was with him, and I got inside. Matt had been at the small hospital. He told me they always provided help or lodging, and that nurses were easy. It was the only building I hadn't gone to. I hated hospitals.

I followed him there. The two workers smoked cigarettes in the small kitchen, and we watched TV together, drinking mate. A male and female nurse were there, filling in for the holiday. I leaned over to Matt.

"You were right, man; this girl is really *caliente*."

"I told you she was horny," he whispered.

She touched us, got close, stuck her chest out, and loved doing it all. The night was uneventful, though, and after the midnight countdown, Matt and I headed to the earlier-used shack sober.

The next morning, I was able to take a shower in the hospital and get cleaner. I had to get started earlier than Matt, but we planned to meet twenty kilometers ahead at the abandoned hotel/bar Olnie. I walked the twenty kilometers, resting only twice. When I got to the Olnie creek, I used duct tape and wrote "Matt 2" on a street sign with an arrow pointing forward. I arrived at the old hotel bar thirty minutes later. Behind it there was a fire pit and a nice flat area for sleeping. A few cherry trees were above me, and the cherries were all ripe. I ate as many as I could. The container on the roof still held water, and it looked and tasted clean. That night I slept under the cherry tree, assuming Matt slept under another.

The next day I walked forty kilometers. The ground was no longer red, but brown and filled with dry struggling grasses and small struggling bushes. I kept thinking Matt would pass me, but I never saw him. It was 6:00 p.m., and I went down into the ditch so no cars could see me. There was a string of horses loose. The male was wearing a bell around his neck. Occasionally I would hear a flurry of hoofs and the bell ringing, not sure if I was about to get trampled, and this eliminated a night with restful sleep.

Early next morning, a truck pulled up beside me. The man rolled down the window; he was a callejero.

"There are two people on bikes that stayed with us last night. One is from Japan; the other is from Canada."

I walked over and found both of them eating tons of free food: cheeses, crackers, jam, and bread. The extra kilometer they had traveled the previous night had done them well. They had passed me without ever knowing it. It was good to see Matt again, and I kept feeling as if life would be better on a bike.

"So you definitely had sex with that woman," I said, but he was a gentleman and left me unsure of the outcome.

We left about an hour later. He and the Japanese guy rode off, leaving me behind. Matt had told me that during his whole trip, he had been alone for only one month. It is easy for bikers to find partners. Bikes meant options. Bikes meant freedom.

One of the callejeros walked beside me. He walked fast, and I could tell he wanted to feel what I felt, if only for ten minutes. In this moment, it meant a lot to me—walking in silence with another person. I could see the mesa off to the left, and I knew today I would arrive back at my hitching point. I wanted to walk northward again; it felt strange doing otherwise.

It took six hours to finish, and I spent the last hour looking for the spot so I wouldn't "cheat" by not covering a few yards. All the surroundings were familiar. The mesa was on my left, ahead was Rio Sofia. To my right were the snow-covered peaks of the Andes. I kept walking to be sure.

After considerable certainty, I took a seat and waited for a car. I was low on water and held out the bottle. People were much more willing to stop and give water than give a ride. It took an hour for the first car to arrive. The car was full, but they had agua. As they were handing me the bottle, another car pulled up. It was a younger couple, and they were happy to take me back to Bajo Caracoles. I witnessed this phenomenon on a daily basis. Traffic travels in bunches.

The young couple was talkative. They were from Cordoba, and the guy driving told me I spoke good Spanish. Sofi had told me that, but I assumed she was just flirting back with me, and here were the long Latina legs in the passengers' legs, and they were the only thing I could look at, and they looked like Sofi's long legs, and oh my God these Latina legs were in yoga pants too. They dropped me off at the gas station, and I bought cigs, having rolled all of the gifted tobacco, but I had no intention on spending a second longer in this little town.

I walked for a few more kilometers and then lay down by a pile of gravel. I was in plain sight of the road. I didn't want to hide; it was a challenge. I wanted to be alone and was so lonely I wished someone would come fight me, if only so I could challenge another person and stop challenging myself.

To the southwest, I watched the sun set behind the beautiful San Lorenzo—one of the tallest mountains in in the Patagonian Andes. It is less than thirteen thousand feet, but because of its prominence, it looks much larger. There are three glaciers continually carving away at the sides. San Lorenzo is normally climbed from the Chilean side, starting in the town of Cochrane.

It was a starry night, and I thought about the Cueva de las Manos only fifty kilometers away, a place I would not see. The caves were named after images of hands that are painted on the walls. The paint was made from the dark red rocks I had passed earlier. When the ingredients were mixed, the artist would press a hand to the rock, bring the mixing device— similar to a straw— to his or her mouth, and blow the paint on the wall. This formed a negative of the hand. Most of the negatives are left hands, and thousands of hands cover the entire walls of many caves and bring this desiccate land to life.

I woke up the next day and made my way north. There was a lot of construction, and there were many different levels of road to walk on. The sun was hot, and the flies were relentless.

The road curved up the side of the plateau. The guardrails had all been crashed into, and there were crosses of remembrance. A truck was approaching, and I was standing on the side of the cliff. The driver never slowed down and passed only a few inches from my feet. I threw my hands up in the air and yelled, *"la puta madre!"*—the most famous of all Argentine insults, and as translated earlier, but again because of it's frequent use, and not only because I love it; the whore mother.

When I finished the hill, I felt rejuvenated from the climb and wanted to keep walking. I had begun to despise breaks and now would take them only if the spot was perfect, having good water, good shade, protection from the wind, or a good view. Finding shade was rare, and the views were of the same browns and bushes I was used to. I kept walking. A few hours later I found an enormous drain under the road and crawled in for a nap. The dreams came quick and were vivid in these moments.

I woke up from my nap frightened by nightmares. My dream state had returned me to the US early, and my subconscious mind was mortified. This gave my conscious mind strength, afraid the dream could be reality. It was a couple more hours before I found the hitching spot next to a small plot with sheep.

I kept walking with my thumb out. A small SUV pulled up, and I started limping so they would feel sorry for me. Inside the SUV was an older man in his late sixties. His son was driving, and was a *bombero* (fireman). They lived in Perito Moreno, and I went back to town with them. They let me stay at the fire station. I thought about Matt and how he would have slept here on the couch.

I wasn't going to stay at the Hotel El Viejo where my buddies worked. I wasn't going to give the owner any more business, but I wanted to say hey to my friends. Close by were camping grounds that also had cabins and shared baths. It was ten bucks for a cabin and five to camp. Quite a few people where there, and I crawled in a cabin to rest.

13 Into Chubut Province

Poets say science takes away from the beauty of the stars – mere globs of gas atoms. I, too, can see the stars on a desert night, and feel them. But do I see less or more?
—Richard P Feynman

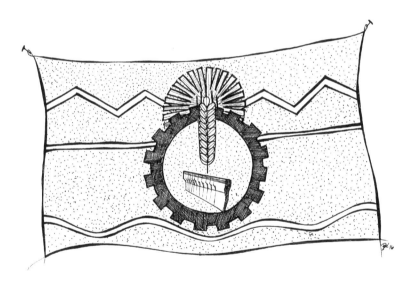

That afternoon in Perito Moreno, there was a group of local guys in their late teens playing guitar and drinking Quilmes. Going from desert solitude, begging for water, to a place with people and beer is spiritual. Anytime I arrived in a town, my charisma would rival a young Bill Clinton's.

"De donde sos?"

"Are-kan-saw, R-Kansas … you know *el estado de* Bill Clinton." Everyone knew Bill.

"Walmart, the first Walmart ever, is thirty miles from my house." Everyone knew Walmart too. This didn't necessarily excite them, but it gave them an idea, and often led to good conversations.

The locals were acting outrageously, all of us sitting around tents and cabins on a picnic table, saying things that only young men say. They wanted to party. There were five in total. The one that worked at the cabins had long hair and played the guitar, and he wanted me drunk, and so everyone else did too. They couldn't believe I didn't have an iPad for walking. Males aged sixteen to twenty-four always inquired about my music. I had noticed this, and it made me want to introduce funk music to the youth of Patagonia. Grover Washington's "Funkfoot" was the song I repeatedly wrote down because it did not have lyrics, and James Brown "Mindpower" because it did.

"*Vamos a fumar mucho porro esta noche,*" The guy with the guitar said after listening to Grover.

My eyes perked up at the word "porro."

"Yes, me encanta porro!"

We were getting low on beer, so I walked to the supermercado and grabbed three bottles of wine. Three cute traveling *Argentinas* were there when I returned, and this filled all us boys with testosterone. It was starting to get dark, and drinks were being handed to me at an elevated frequency. With big, laughing smiles, they proceeded to inebriate me heavily, just as I had done to Jackson earlier.

After becoming drunk, I became restless. Sitting around all night was too boring. I stumbled over to see my friends at the El Viejo. I had the last bottle of Malbec in my hand and was continuing to drink it through the street as I stumbled. The hotel's restaurant was packed, and my friends were all working hard. I was belligerent, and they gave me fries. Ariel came outside with me to smoke cigs. During the smoke break, he complained about the same problems every waiter on earth has ever had. All I could do was black out.

The next morning I woke up in bed, though my night had ended standing in front of the restaurant. I was in the right cabin, and I quickly made sure all my things were accounted for. There was another guy in the room.

"Did I smoke *porro* last night? *No recuerdo nada. Estaba. um. Estaba bien,* I was okay?"

He laughed, informing me that plants had not been burned. That was good. If they had, I wanted to remember.

"*Estabas tranquilo.* You were chill," he told me.

I walked out of the cabin at the moment the three girls from the previous night were driving off. I waved to them. They smiled and said *"Chau"* out the windows, their sunglasses covering eyes whose judgement I could only imagine. My mind was working hard to remember the stupid things it had done the night before.

I shook off the hangover by drinking mate all morning, still aggravated at the eraser that had made last night disappear. I went running errands and got caught up with the world. Thanks to Matt, I bought two kilos of instant polenta. Sofi had responded, and I copied and pasted the text into Google Translate. She loved her newly named river, and she signed "Your girlfriends." I smiled inside and out, not knowing if she had done it on accident, and not caring, and did she know that she was the only one?

I had sent her hundreds of messages without the use of electronics. I will never know how many reached her, but her email mentioned some already had. For over a month now, cars of people had been showing up at La Vineria, looking for a girl named Sofia. These were the cars that had stopped to offer me water or rides. There was a crazy guy walking the Patagonian desert telling everyone about the Patagonian princess, and they had promised to look for her.

"You have got to tell her I said hey," I pleaded with them all.

That night, when the hotel workers got off, we walked to Juanita's house. She still had all my supplies. It was nearly midnight, and we went only a few feet inside. Her son came up, and I gave him a toy motorcycle I had bought earlier that day. Juanita was a good lady, beautiful, and like many in Argentina, was raising her kids alone. Many children born in Argentina are born to single women. Getting divorced is incredibly difficult in the Catholic country, and now a whole new generation has decided instead to just not get married.

I got started the next morning out of Perito Moreno, going north. Sixty kilometers down the road to the west was Los Antigous. There were the big alerce trees and a beautiful lake I would never see. There were also forests of cherry trees. It was January 5, 2012, and the Festival de las Cerezas started the next day. People were coming from all over the province for the cherries. Cars were passing constantly.

I was walking against the direction of traffic, going deeper into the desert, away from the party, the trees, and the ripe cherries. Nearly twelve kilometers into the day, I was feeling strong. I waved like a crazy person at nearly every car, giving them a big smile and thumbs up. I figured that if they saw me on the way back from the festival, they might give me water. My phone was charged, and I had James Brown playing. I was dance-walking.

Some kids pulled up to me, and the driver rolled down the window. There were five of them. I said hey, and a kid in the backseat started yelling. People often yelled at me. They did this to help me understand.

"*Teeee … nnnisss*. Marihuana? *Mary*-juan-a. *Ten-m-os plata*. PLATA!" he screamed, holding up his wallet.

They gave me two sandwiches and drove off while insulting their friend with names like *pelotudo* and *boludo*. After four hours, I came to the turnoff, Ruta 40 went to the left, and continued north. I saw another big red monument like the one I had slept next to on Lago Cardiel. Earlier I had asked Ariel about these strange red monuments. "Is it some famous baby gaucho who died?" I knew words ending in *-ito* usually meant "small," and this brought laughter to everyone in earshot.

Guachito Gil is Argentina's Robin Hood, and Gil's skill was as a farmhand. He was from northern Argentina's Corrientes Province, and Gil had a heart to fill. He was a romantic, and Gil loved a widow, a rich one. Poor Gil whom the rich widow's brother had decided to kill, and so Gil fled for the hills. He enlisted in the army, fighting first against the Paraguayans and then fighting in Argentina's civil war. After these wars, Gil deserted the army and fled into the pampas, where he led a Robin Hood campaign. Gil would never again fight wars for ones in power, but would now steal whatever he could from the landed elite and give it to the needy. Only two years after he began his career as a Robin Hood, the police tracked him down.

Famously before the execution, Gil said to the officer, "Your daughter is very ill; release me and she will heal." This only further infuriated the policeman. Gil was tortured, and his body ripped to pieces. The police chief returned home to find his daughter near death. Legend says that when the man started praying to Gil, his daughter recovered without pill. Gil's remains were then gathered, and he was given a proper burial. In Latin America, the one percent of the population owns all the land, and this distribution has resulted in not only war but also inescapable economic stagnation of continental proportions.

For years Argentina has pestered the Catholic Church to make Gil a saint. These markers throughout the country are a testament to the faith the *Argentinos* have in Gil. They are everywhere. When I arrived at Gil's monument, there were three unsmoked cigs in it. I silently went to one knee staying still and gave thanks to the Gil for these cigs I would steal. Gil is pronounced "heel".

From here, Ruta 40 is rarely traveled. Most people going to the cherry festival were from the east in Rivadavia. Water was getting low because I hadn't asked any of the many cars for help, and it was now starting to get dark. A few truckers passed me as I was doing the water dance, but they kept driving. It really pissed me off when truckers didn't stop. There was supposed to be a code! I knew they had water, but I slept thirsty.

Tonight another mythical story from Argentina's history came to mind as I was dry-mouthed and under attack by pesky flies. The story was being repeated to me constantly. It was of another person considered a saint by many Argentinos, and her name is Difunta Correa, and her monuments were the best. They had water.

Difunta Correa was a woman who walked through the desert in

northern Argentina with a baby in her arms. Her husband was dying, and she had to reach him, but Correa ran out of supplies. She would not make it to town. All hope was lost for her entire family, and Correa with the dry tears of dehydration, laid down to die. She was holding her child, the child that only knew to suckle. Correa's body was discovered days later by gauchos, and there, miraculously, curled under Correas's stiff lifeless arms, face down against a bare chest, a baby nursed a mother, a mother whose heart would no longer beat, but whose soul power would not leave. The baby had survived. The saint was still producing milk. A mother never dies.

I lay next to the road in a drain. The flies were bad, and I closed my eyes, trying to ignore them. A couple of dragonflies came swooping in. I could hear them zipping right above me, and I opened my eyes, preparing to strike. Right as I was about to swing, a dragonfly jetted in front of me and snatched a fly out of the air. Instantly the fly fell to the ground. The amount of precision required to kill a fly midflight was incredible. I never knew dragonflies did this, and in thirty minutes the area was nearly free of flies.

In the morning, I had a steep hill to walk up, and very little water left. A couple of trucks drove past me, but none stopped on the hill. I had never run out of water entirely, but now I was wondering if it would soon happen. It was another hot summer day, and I was far from signs of life. The adventure left me entirely dependent on random and infrequent strangers.

When I made it to the top of the hill, there was a mining company off to the left. I headed that way. No one was at the entrance, and I walked up to the first man I saw. He looked as though he worked hard, and he only nodded affirmatively at my question about water. Then he grunted and kept walking.

There was a converted shipping container next to some large steel equipment, and I went inside. Four men were there, and I asked for water. They were playing truco, a Spanish card game that is very popular in Argentina. It is similar to spades, but far more entertaining when played well. The four men were waiting on water delivery too. I took two of their six liters and said thanks. The walk was going to be harder.

From here there was no water—not a drop. There were no creeks, no stagnant water—nothing. I was lucky, though. Argentinos are famous for littering. Anytime there was a plastic bottle on the side of the road, I went to check the contents. Oftentimes I found Sprite and Coke backwash to drink, but many of them contained pee, which made testing contents risky. I found a piece of cardboard and wrote "agua" on it. A few hours later, a van stopped. A tall, athletic French dad in extra-short shorts hopped out. His wife did too.

"Where do you need to go?" He asked.

"Hey! I just need water." We conversed in Spanish.

They had three young boys in the back. They were traveling for two years through South America. I told them they were awesome parents, and they gave me two pears. Fruit is nearly all water and low in calories. This meant I never carried it, and that these were the best pears I had ever eaten. I found a place to sleep under the road shortly after.

The next day, I made it across the remote and under-construction border between the Santa Cruz and Chubut provinces. I had just walked across the most incredible province in Argentina, and I was able to get water at the border from the gendarmeria, but here was void of human life, dusty, and inhospitable. I wasn't feeling up to walking twenty more kilometers to Rio Mayo and celebrating.

The land was flat in all directions until hills blocked the view to both the east and west. In front of me was haze. The road was sand and had no pipes beneath it, so finding a place to sleep was difficult. I kept looking for a big calafate bush to huddle up behind. The bushes were everywhere, but only a few were big enough to completely shield me. In the distance was a huge one, and I made my way toward it. The calafate bush had berries, but they were still green. The bush was also covered in long, painful barbs. There are small but abundant orange flowers that precede the berries, and some still remained.

Normally the east side of the bush, the side shielded from the wind, is free of grasses and brambles. This side, however, is never free of feces. Behind the bush was a semicircle of sheep droppings decades deep. The sheep used the bushes for the same reason I was now—to escape the wind.

That night I dug a hole a half foot down in the sand and gathered twigs to make a fire. It wasn't hard to make fire in the desert. The hard part was keeping the fire under control. The winds make hikers responsible for wildfires in Patagonia every year, and I was always careful.

Tonight and every night, a game I played was to light the fire with one match. I always carried a Bic with me, but starting a fire with *fosforo* felt pure and right. The grass in Patagonia is very spiky, and for every patch of living grass, there are three dead ones. These are easy to grab from the base and pull entirely from the ground. Shaking them a few times removes all the sand. It is a perfect fire-starting material. All of the bushes and larger plant life are half dead too. Small, very dry, twigs are everywhere. After it rains, the dead twigs at the tops of the bushes are dry in an hour. The wind keeps them that way. The wind is in charge of Patagonia.

I put some dead grass under the twigs and lit the match. The grass began to crackle as it took the flame. The flames reached a few inches above the hole, but the fire stayed small because air wasn't able to feed it. I filled the 1.5-liter titanium pot and balanced it on a few sticks above the fire. Next I dropped a chicken-flavored cube in the pot and stirred.

Anytime the wind blew really hard, it would lift sand and its contents into the air. I did my best to keep the pot covered with the metal top, but both were so dented and warped that the exclusion of flying particles of sheep shit from the food was impossible.

When the chicken-flavored cube had dissolved, I added the polenta. This is instant corn mash. On its own it is bland, but with the flavor cube, instant mashed potatoes, and peanuts, it was a power meal. I hadn't put out the miniature fire yet, and suddenly the wind arrived stronger than it had for weeks, and she had something to say, and she screamed into my little fire, and out shot two small small coals. Each coal wedged into a separate patch of dying and dead grass, and it was now that Patagonia burst into flames. My bare feet were stomping a spreading fire, and I was losing, and I was throwing sand and shit over burning fire, removing flammables that were close, and still the fire spread, and now was quite large. Then the thin flakes of barely-burning carbon started to fall straight back to the ground, the wind had paused, and I got everything covered in sand. The food was ruined, and my body was dirty and burned. The wind blew again, and I was the Israeli, and *Yo, Judío*. I burned down Patagonia, if only the she had chosen me to.

I lay down and read Proverbs. During the trip, I read the New Testament start to finish, but the words of Solomon were still my favorite. I thought about how it was better to live in a desert than with a quarrelsome and ill-tempered wife. Then I thought of all the lonely gauchos of Patagonia and wondered if the man with seven hundred wives was right, and maybe I was just blowing in the wind.

The stars were coming out individually in the dry, clear air. The Milky Way makes a line so alive with light. The Southern Cross is the most recognizable constellation in the sky and was the place my eyes rested each night. The constellations here are unseen in the Northern Hemisphere no matter how dark the night. Billion-year-old photons were captured for the first time by my lens. My meditative stare shifted focus only when a passing satellite went through the sky.

"A shooting star," I kept whispering aloud, only to realize it was moving much too slowly.

14 A Side Effect of the Plant

I woke up with the sun. Since the wind blew from the west, I always slept facing the sunrise. I was looking forward to arriving at Rio Mayo. At kilometer six, I took my first break behind a bush about twenty feet from the road. Up ahead one hundred meters, a van stopped. Since I hadn't moved, the driver hadn't noticed me. I got up and started walking toward the vehicle. As I got closer, I noticed the entire van was painted in an African safari motif. It had a cheetah, rhino, and elephant on it, but no one was in the driver's seat, and I didn't knock.

Thirty minutes later, there was a guy jogging toward me. I said hey, and we almost parted ways. Then I grabbed his shoulder, as my brain had finally put the pieces together. This was the guy the Swiss people from Chalten had told me about.

"You're the South African running the entire Ruta 40!"

His running clothes were clean, and he looked like a professional.

We chatted for a few minutes. He was going to run to the van and then meet me in town for coffee. He told me about a shortcut I could take to get there. It would save me a couple kilometers. We planned on meeting at the YPF gas station, and I started walking faster, excited to have coffee with such a cool dude. The road split, and I went to the right. After half a kilometer I realized my road stayed along the bluff line and was never going down to the town. It was a few hundred feet below. Another shortcut had gone wrong. I slid down the steep hill, filling my pockets, underwear, and socks with sand. When I got into town there was a policeman.

"*Conoces donde esta* the *Sud* African with the crazy van?"

"*Dos cuadras y por alla.* They are waiting for you," he told me, smiling.

The van was parked outside the gas station. I walked in and sat down. His girlfriend was petite with a short bob hairstyle, and she wore a long hippie dress. She drove and he ran. They had started the trip a month before me. When they first arrived in Buenos Aires, he saw a guy doing graffiti and offered him $300 dollars to paint the van.

"It was the best investment I have ever made," he said. He was not a professional, but was running to raise money for the national parks in South Africa. He had picked up the pace recently.

"Almost a marathon a day for the last few weeks," he said mildly but with adventure pride.

They needed to arrive in Rio Gallegos in a few months. His family was meeting him in Antarctica to run another marathon. After that race, they would have run 26.2 miles on every continent. We looked over the map, and he told me to be really careful with water in a couple of locations.

"I am going to run across Canada in a couple years in honor of Terry Fox. Now that I met you, I can't do it with a van; I would feel so weak."

"Dude, if I had a cute girl with me, I'd be sleeping in a van too."

He left, and I stayed drinking café. Later two teenagers walked in the door. The kid had a black jean jacket and greasy black hair, and he was carrying a guitar case. His girlfriend had purple hair and a cute smile. All their clothes were black. They were from Coyhaique, Chile, and had been to the cherry festival in Los Antiguos. Their mode of transportation was hitchhiking.

"Fumas?" Black asked almost immediately. He brought two fingers two his lips and inhaled to make sure I understood. He had a few rings and piercings. So did his girlfriend, Purple.

"Si, si," I said, nodding my head affirmatively.

We walked outside with his girlfriend giggling. Around the gas station, he pulled a *rama* (stick) out of his jacket.

"You think it is okay here?" I asked him, feeling vulnerable.

"I am fine," Black said confidently.

He was seventeen years old, and part of me felt he was too young to burn plants with, but I didn't hesitate once the fire was lit, and instantly the colors became more vibrant. The wind was no longer an issue, except that it caused the stick to burn rapidly.

"You want to smoke another?" Black asked as the first one ended.

We walked over and sat down on the sidewalk in front of a random building. I was a little shocked that he decided to light one up so publicly. People could have easily walked by. I reached in my pocket and lit a cig.

"Una diversion" I told him, but Black didn't share my paranoia.

This was the first time I had burned fire with a South American, and when the roach got small, I told Black that I was good, but in his pocket he had a Copihue brand matchbox named for the red national flower of Chile, a flower which grows only in Patagonia, and the inside case and all the matches had been removed, thus leaving only the outer shell of which a hole had been cut in the middle and on the top side of matchbox. In that hole Black put the roach. His pointer finger went over the back, and at the other end Black inhaled.

"Que intelegencia!" I said, impressed by the famous roach hitter of Chile.

Learning smoking tricks from a seventeen-year-old Chilean was fun. We returned to the gas station to find his girlfriend. They had a tent, and we decided to camp together by the river. The plants seemed to make me fluent in Spanish—or at least I thought so. I spoke with no hesitation and without pause.

An anarchy symbol was spray-painted on the sidewalk. Black gestured at Purple so she would see it. We found a good place to camp by the river, and I went to the store to buy wine and food for all of us. When I got back, they had their tent set up.

"It isn't much, but it works," Black said, slightly embarrassed.

I showed them the bivouac.

"Que economico," Purple said.

They both saw the tuna I had bought, and Purple clutched it with love.

"Atun!" she said cheerfully.

Black started talking about politics. He was very passionate and very angry. He talked a lot about the World Bank, and sounded exactly like I had when I was seventeen. Angrily, he went to make a fire for cooking, but it wouldn't stay lit. I went over and got it started.

"Que profesional," Purple said.

We cooked and ate rice mixed with atun. It was now dark, and we went inside their tent.

"What do you call it when you smoke somewhere small where the smoke can't escape?" I asked Black.

He thought about my question for a second, making sure he understood perfectly. Then he responded happily, "Submarino!"

"Ha ha! That is the best! We call it 'hotbox' in English."

After we submarino another stick, he started playing his guitar, but he soon put it down.

"What's your religion?" Black asked me.

I was caught a little off guard.

"Well, for many years I never had one … but I have always been able to feel something. I know the spirit is real. I mean … I know you can feel something. Yes bad things happen, but there is a god, certainly … It's just I can't see what he can. I can't know what he knows." Black didn't say anything, upset that the pithy philosophy might be right, he did feel something, *but damnit why did God seem so unjust?*

Purple stepped in and said she used to be Catholic but didn't know anymore.

"What's yours?" I asked.

"My religion is anarchy," Black said, looking down, fiddling with his knife.

He went into a long tirade filled with adolescent absolutisms.

"Well, I believe in anarchy too a little, but not because I want chaos, but because I think people are good. I think we can take care of each other without the government. I would never have been able to walk this far if people weren't good."

"People are not good," Black said.

Now he was flicking his knife open and closed, harder and faster. Black wasn't happy, and I was not sure he liked me anymore. Would he kill me in my sleep? The paranoia began to build, this being a side effect of the plant.

"Yeah, hey guys, I am sorry—*la verdad*. The truth is I need to walk a few more kilometers today. *Yo tengo mucho energia* from the plants. I am really sorry."

I left quickly. It had been dark a couple hours already. After five kilometers, I stopped under a tree on the hill leading out of town. I had no desire to walk to level ground. I felt in my pockets and realized that I had left my camera in Black's tent—this being the second side effect of the plant.

I tried to sleep for a few hours but couldn't stop thinking about losing my photos. At five in the morning, I walked back into town. I wanted to get to the anarchists before they packed up and left. When

I arrived at the camp, Black unzipped the door of the tent. The camera was waiting for me, and I felt like a jerk. These kids had been so nice to me, and I didn't trust them. Black thought people were bad, but he had been good. I had said people were good, yet had worried Black was bad. Having a high opinion of myself, this event bothered me, and I no longer wanted to walk that day and instead slept in a hotel.

The follow morning, in the restaurant of the small western-themed hotel, a middle aged lady asked if her family could have breakfast with me. I sat by two young boys, both happy and rambunctious, an unhappy teenage girl in a revealing shirt, a mom in a flower dress, and a father in navy pants and a tan leather jacket. They gave me cheese and yogurt, and I asked the man what he did for work.

"I work for the policia."

"Do you work in the office, or are you out on patrol?" I asked him, not able to think of a better question.

He looked at his wife humorously.

"Wait … You are the boss, aren't you?" I said, knowing a flattering guess is always acceptable.

He grinned. Here was the head of the PDI in the second-largest city of Chile, Concepcion. His position was similar to being the head of the FBI in Los Angeles, and my mind returned to the other night, burning plants with the anarchists, seventeen year-olds former Chilean leader Pinochet would have killed.

"What are *las problemas más grande* in Chile?" I asked the Chilean head of investigations.

"Drogas," he said.

It was always drugs, and he told me marijuana and *paco* were the biggest problems. Paco is essentially crack. He gave me his card and told me to call him if I ever needed anything. He wrote his personal cell phone number on it, and his wife showed me pictures of nice houses with pools.

I started walking again after the big breakfast. There was an old dirt road nearby. It would save me twenty kilometers by taking it. People in town had told me not to. "It is really dangerous," they all had said.

Someone, sometime in the past, had been killed by somebody somewhere on that road. People always said walking was dangerous. It was fifteen kilometers outside of Rio Mayo, and I took the dangerous road to Facundo.

15 Facundo to Esquel

Water is life, and clean water means health.
—Audrey Hepburn

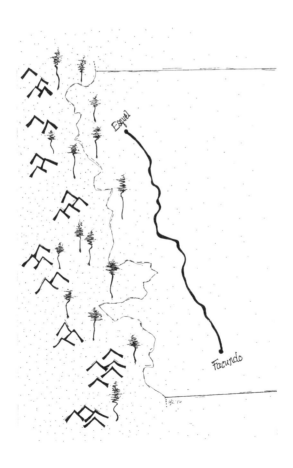

The road was empty and gray. There were a few small creeks to get water from where the only shades of green could be found. A few old trees shaded the only house for miles. Only two cars rattled past in the four hours. Both were very old and surprised me that they still ran. In the distance, a motorcycle was approaching. It came up to me and stopped. The man asked what I was doing, where I was going, whether I was okay, and if I needed a lift into town.

"No, I am walking, but I should be there in a couple hours," I told him.

"If you need a place, you can stay with me tonight." He didn't mention how or where to find him, but when he turned around and drove back into town, I read the back of his jacket, and it said "Chubut Policia" in big, bold letters. Word had already made it to the police that there was a lone walker on the dangerous back road, and he had come to check it out.

Almost all the pueblos in Patagonia are near rivers and are usually down in a valley. Facundo is like many of the others, only more beautiful. The desert plateau breaks apart, and the land falls into a lush sanctuary. The river meanders slowly, surrounded by hundreds of large, narrow trees one hundred feet tall. The entire town—only a few square blocks—can be seen entirely from the plateau above. Facundo is a true oasis, and only a few hundred people know about it.

I walked into town and headed to the police station. Next door was a kiosco, and I decided to drink a couple tallboys first. In front of the small concrete police station, a huge rottweiler was chained up. He was very unhappy and would not let me approach the front door. I walked around back and knocked. No one answered.

I went into town and asked a few people if they knew where to find the policeman. Everyone told me that now was *siesta* time, so I found a house that had bread to sell and left.

Right outside of town on Rio Senguer was a place to camp. When I walked up to the reception, no one was there. No one was camping either, but the place had running water, which allowed me to fully hydrate. I made a quick fire on the concrete grill, ate, and lay down to sleep. It was still light outside, and after a couple hours I opened my eyes because I heard footsteps. It was the owner of the campground. He was from Salta, and after seeing my condition, he let me go back to sleep. He never asked for money.

I woke up the next morning and walked up the road out of the valley. The sun was low, and I was able to stay in the shade until the top. Now I was out of the oasis and looked forward at the limitless vistas of greys, browns, bushes, and flies. A truck pulled over to the side. Inside was an older man and his wife, probably in their early fifties. He seemed really excited to talk to me.

"Te gustan cerezas?" he asked before the window had been fully rolled down.

I jumped at the thought of getting to start the day off with a beer.

He got out and went to the back of the truck and pulled out a big bag of cherries.

"Hay dos kilos aca."

"Ah, *cereza*, not *cerveza!*" I said, smiling. "I love these too."

I walked over to the side of the road and sat down to eat four and a half pounds of cherries.

Each day was getting hotter. The farther north I walked, the deeper into summer I went. It was a constant battle keeping my shorts pulled up tight. The backpack pushed them lower, and I was skinny. The unclean crack of my ass ran with sweat. This always caused chafing with precision at kilometer twenty.

The days where I didn't need to squat became my favorite days. The hour after excrement was the worst hour of the day. Too many times, a clean wipe was not achieved. The sore ankles, pain in my feet, and aching back never came close to the pain of chafing. I would soon resort to rolling up my boxers, wrapping them in duct-tape, and walking with a self-prescribed wedgie, but still the chafing continued.

I was low on water, and a couple of cross-continental motorcyclists stopped and gave me a liter. Beside the road were piles of rock left over from construction. I went around behind them to make the polenta mix and to sleep.

My water was still low the next morning, and the few cars that passed didn't stop. In the distance, there appeared to be something shimmering, and I wondered whether or not the desert was playing tricks on me. Before I arrived at the shiny object, a car pulled up behind me. The man gave me three liters of water and turned around. He had just passed me, driven to Facundo, bought water, and driven back to give it to me.

The shiny objects in the distance were a handful of 18-wheelers. They were next to an old convenience store / museum. It was the only building for many kilometers. I bummed a couple cigs from the truck drivers while I waited. The drivers were delivering cars from Santiago to Punta Arenas. They had to drive through Argentina because there is no clear path through Chilean Patagonia. The rainforest, mountains, and fjord make it impassable. The Carretera Austral, the road through the incredible Chilean Patagonia, is not conducive to commerce—only adventure.

The old farmhouse museum rest stop opened. I sat down and drank multiple cups of instant cafe. After my third, I looked at the waitress and told her I was ready for the tour. The guide was an eighty-year-old great grandmother. She had lived here forever, and she led me around the place showing me relics of her families' old life. There were winter shoes made of guanaco skin thrown in a corner. She had sun-bleached family farm pictures that looked similar to ones my great-grandmother had. There was a huge jug of wine that they call a *damajuana*. Fossils, lighters, and every mate gourd the family ever owned filled the counters and display cases. I drank another cup of coffee and signed the book they had for visitors. She told me they had seen only one other person walking, and it was a long time ago.

Today was the hottest day of the new year. Here the bushes were much shorter and fewer, and they didn't provide any shade. There were no drains under the dry road. The baking desert sun had softened the asphalt to rubber under my feet. The road had waves and ripples on its surface from where trucks surfed. I tried to rest under a cattle guard, but it provided little cover and was filled with thorny plants and flies. Way off in the distance, I could see some trees, and here in desert Patagonia, trees are the way to life.

I had been shaking my water bottle at cars for a good while when a guy finally stopped. He was solo and shirtless. His windows were rolled down, and the AC was not working. There was no water, but he gave me his nearly empty oven-baked sprite.

"Cuantos kilometros hasta los arboles?" I asked him.

He told me the trees were probably seven kilometers away. That meant an hour and a half until shade. I don't know why I asked, the shirtless man had the same view as me and was heading in the same direction, but I felt better hearing it from someone else, and now I knew that I could make it. Halfway there, I was blessed with a row of huge drainpipes. There was a dried-up river, and I cooked food and drank almost all my water.

After a short nap, I woke up with an hour of daylight remaining. I hurried toward the trees. It was cooler now that the sun was lower, but my body was scorched and drained. Every pore breathed in exhaustion from the day's workload. I arrived at the trees only to find a big abandoned gas station. There were more trees up ahead, and I kept my fingers crossed someone would be there. I had only 300 milliliters of water left and had been thirsty for hours.

The road went up a slight hill, and for a more direct route, I hopped the fence and walked directly to the trees. Now I could see a barn in the distance and was almost running. No one was around the barn, but it was in good condition, and a driveway led farther into the trees.

A fire was burning, and the gauchos were all sitting around it, their backs to me as I approached. The gaucho's dogs saw me coming, but the gauchos themselves made no move toward me. They hardly acknowledged my presence. There were twelve gauchos surrounding a lamb splayed on a cross leaning over coals. There was a wall of sheet metal to hold the heat in. The gauchos were a mix of ages; the younger ones were strong, and the older ones walked with limps.

"Lo siento, I don't want to bother you, *pero necesito agua por favor ..."*

No one said anything, but a gaucho pointed in the direction of another man near the house. I set my backpack down and pulled out my empty water bottles and went over.

"Tienes agua?" I asked.

He was the farm cook, and he showed me the hand pump to the well. The kitchen and dining hall had been built around it. The water came through nine meters of pure sand filter. The hand pump worked only when used with vigor, and the sight of cold, clean water coming out of the faucet while pumping was baptismal. Life had been below my feet the whole time. Here is the incomparable water, the naturally cold, infinitely old, hand-pumped Patagonian water from a lonely desert well, and there is nothing like it.

After filling my bottles, I went back to get my bag and start packing. I planned on finding a tree to hide under and sleep. This was the biggest and nicest estancia I had been to, but I didn't feel entirely welcome, the gauchos being rather indifferent to me.

The cook came over, stopped me from packing, and handed me a plate. I was still unsure. I didn't know how to perform the gaucho eating act. They don't use utensils—only their big all-purpose knife that is kept on their gaucho belt, a long piece of tied coarse fabric, worn behind them. One gaucho hobbled up to the lamb, motioned for me to come over, and sliced off two ribs and a huge section of leg.

I sat on a log stump, and now they did seem interested in me and watched me eat. The meat was dripping in fat, and I was not selective with where I took my bites.

"He's hungry," one of them said.

The roughest-looking gaucho walked over, shadowing me with broad shoulders, and took the half-finished meat from my plate, threw it to the dogs, and went to get me some more. They also had potato soup. Everyone shared the same six plates, three mugs, and four bowls.

No one spoke to me the whole time at dinner, and for that I was thankful. It was the longest, hottest day of my life. Nearly fifty kilometers of desert had passed under my feet, and I didn't feel like talking.

As each of the gauchos finished eating, he would say, *"provecho"* before leaving. This is common in Argentina and is very polite. The word means "enjoy."

I asked the cook if I could sleep under the trees in the grass. He smiled and showed me an extra room next to the kitchen. It was empty except for a bed frame. The frame had a few loose, uneven boards going horizontally, and I laid my sleeping pad on top.

There were plain crackers on the kitchen table the next morning, and soon I was drinking mate with the cook and one of the more charismatic gauchos. The other gauchos were out "working." There was a schedule on the wall that listed times for everything, and right now was work time. The two gauchos asked me how people were in America. This question was always being asked, and I found it impossible to answer.

"Oh, I don't know; we've got some good ones ... No, not everyone walks around with guns."

I went around and explored the place. It was named Estancia La Laurita, and it was full of hundred-year-old trees and houses. The owner might have been one hundred years old too and was white and hard. He was working, and I never saw him not working. His thin skin was now blistering in places where the wind had broken through. He drove only Ford trucks, and he had a few of them. They all had armadillo skins on the trailer hitches. The armadillo is a delicacy of the gaucho, but I never got to try one. All the buildings, barns, and houses had red roofs, white walls, and green window trim.

Some gauchos were drinking mate and had lamb cooking in the stove. They invited me in, and I sat around letting the time pass. Younger gauchos were listening to music and showed me their pirated DVD collection. I didn't see anyone working except the owner.

I went back to the kitchen, and the charismatic gaucho was still there. He was thick from lamb fat like all middle-aged gauchos. His eyes were copper, and his hair was too. He wanted to show me around, and we went over to the barn. It smelled like sheep, and hidden behind it were thousands of them in a corral. They also had a few pigs that were so big they looked like hippos. I asked the gaucho about the river. He said there hadn't been water in it for three years. This was hurting the estancia, and it would die with the old man if the water didn't return.

Lunch was the same—a lamb slow-cooked since sunrise over coals. There were more gauchos for lunch—about twenty of them. The young ones had huge shoulders, wide chests, and strong arms. Middle-aged men, the ones who worked less, developed large, drooping man boobs. This is a Patagonian phenomenon among nearly all managerial middle-aged gauchos. The few older men still working all walk with limps. Hospitals are rarely an option.

After lunch I decided to keep walking north. I felt bad for accepting so much hospitality. This time I actually wanted to stay, but seeing the owner work his dying ass off made me incapable of accepting his workers' generosity. The gauchos told me about a French couple who stayed for a week. I should have.

Instead I followed their driveway up to the road and began to head north. I had a backpack full of fry bread the cook had gifted me, and I ate it as I walked. The road was in horrible condition, with edges of it falling off. It had molded under heavy tires and a hot sun. Within three hours, the Achilles of my left foot stopped working. The tendon stayed contracted, and each step burned with injury.

I had to hitch a ride to the next town, which was now eighty kilometers away. A hatchback pulled over. It was a mom driving with her teenage son. He was seventeen and wearing all black. He had many nose, ear, and lip rings. He was quite large, and his name was Facundo.

"Hey, you know there is a town just south of here with your name!" I said. When hitchhiking, it is best to quickly let the driver know his or her decision was just. This makes the rest of the ride easier socially, but today the mom was a nervous driver, and the condition of the road made things worse. I grabbed my backpack, prepared to quickly get behind it upon her imminent mistake. Every time we passed a Gauchito Gil or any other religious monument, she would honk the horn repeatedly. Then she and Facundo would both cross themselves and say "Amen."

Two hours later, we arrived in Gobernador Costa and I got out. All the places to stay in town were overpriced, but I was not going to camp. One building was painted safari style and called Hotel Sudafrica. I went inside. It appeared to be cool.

A woman checked me in, and I got a private room and shower. There was a TV in the common area, and I watched a few movies. I kept my aching Achilles elevated. There were big pictures of Peron, Argentina's most debated leader—that is, until Cristina Fernandez.

Most people in the States, thanks to Madonna, know more about Peron's wife. Peron, however, was a nationalistic nepotist, a populist, and when Argentina was arguably better off economically than both Canada and Australia, just after the Second World War, Peron wanted Argentina to be completely independent of the Western powers. Everyone has an opinion on Peron.

"You and I believe exactly the opposite! Exactly the opposite!" a short man with glasses and a bald head was screaming. The four-hundred-pound third-generation South African owner was shaking his head. "We can do it all ourselves! We don't need the Americans or anyone else." He winked at me. "We are Argentina!" He pounded on the table. The fat owner had seen I was alone and had invited me to dinner. I didn't understand much, but things were getting charged. Dishes were rattling; the tablecloth would need to be washed. I thought the short guy was rude for arguing so forcefully over a free dinner and wine. He hated Peron.

The next day, I walked around town. I liked going to the YPF gas stations. They had free WiFi, and there was always someone new there. A couple guys were hitchhiking in the middle of town, and I told them they needed to start walking if they wanted a ride. I left the gas station three hours later. They were still waiting, not any closer to their destination or a ride. Effort, whether walking or dancing, is the way to hitchhike and arrive on time.

There was a small supermercado by the hotel, so I stocked up on supplies, and then went back to rest. The night before, I had noticed a more serious injury and needed to lie down. A lower vertebra was protruding from my back. I had dropped all the weight I possibly could, and my back had still buckled. The protrusion looked gross, a herniated disk, and I could barely touch my knees when bending over. However, I had not felt this prior, and had only noticed it in the mirror. There was no pain—just a lack of mobility, and stiffness.

The television options consisted of *Law & Order*, MTV, and movies from the nineties. I cursed myself for watching MTV in Patagonia. I was drinking beer, and occasionally people would come into the common room and waste away with me. The fat owner invited me to dinner again, his face exceptionally red from wine consumption, for he never went outside.

"No, I am okay; I am just going to eat this bread."

I didn't want to take advantage of his generosity, but he implored that I come. It was the same people at dinner: an eighteen-year-old white hip-hop dancer, the short argumentative guy with glasses who was the dancer's uncle, the female receptionist who essentially ran the hotel, and the fat owner who had his chin resting on his chest.

We were eating a huge lamb feast with rice and everything else a four-hundred-pound man would want. He drank his wine with soda water, and during the meal, another woman came in carrying a sewing machine. She was being really loud, and I couldn't understand much of what she said. The receptionist joined and was being loud too. It was like a Latin soap opera, with women yelling, and it appeared now like they were flirting with the fat boss.

"You just wouldn't believe it! Things are so expensive here!" They touched his shoulder.

After a minute or two of this strange game, the receptionist looked at me and said, "How much does a sewing machine cost in the United States?"

I had no idea, and I let the fat owner believe the small machine cost two thousand pesos. At the time, that was equivalent to $500. Maybe it did. Regardless, the short man with glasses let the fat owner know that he had just paid for an imported product.

"Probably the fifth time you have this week!" He smiled approvingly.

I spent four days like this—going to the gas station for a few hours, talking to random people, getting drunk on the common room couch, and being invited to dinner. I still had to retrace eighty kilometers south. The four days had been the longest rest of my walk, and I was committed to finishing the distance in two days.

I went to pay the bill and soon realized why the fat owner had wanted me to eat with him every night. He had been charging me for it. Since I had thought the food was free, I never asked for seconds and ate very little. I paid my bill and left, chapped already.

Leaving Gobernador Costa, there were a few trees near the remains of the river, which the town was sucking dry. For two days during my stay, the city water had been shut off. The entire town waited on delivery. No, the river will not be coming back to Estancia La Laurita, and she will die with her owner, and the last gauchos will limp to the city. After thirty-five kilometers, there was just an hour of daylight left. I tucked away in a pit left over from construction. The fire was easy to start, and I made polenta mix. This meal was my constant. I was low on water after using it to cook.

I needed to push it the next morning, and I did the first twenty kilometers without rest. Eventually I found a well-off red house built with solid, thick slabs of wood. There were many trees in the yard. I went up to it looking for water and hollered out a few holas that were never returned. There was a hose in the back, and I filled up my bottles—more Patagonian well water. I hoped someone from this crafted house would see me lying in their yard and give me food. Farther down the road, I passed the caretaker's house, and he was outside working. He returned my wave and went back to his job.

I felt strong, and walked another twenty kilometers without rest. There was no shade, and I laid down under a few small, thorny calafate bushes. It was still early in the day. When I reached the kilometer marker, I put my thumb out, turned around, and started walking back in the direction of Gobernador Costa. The eighty kilometers done.

A few cars later, an old, beaten-up Fiat pulled over. The driver was shirtless, his wife was in the front seat, and in the back were his four kids. The oldest kid was maybe twelve; they were all boys, and I got in behind the mother with my backpack squished against my chest. The oldest kid next to me had the youngest, a toddler, on his lap. The two other brothers, six and eight, sat side-by-side behind their shirtless dad.

In less than five minutes, the rusted fiat sputtered and died. I started wondering if I should tell them thanks and try my luck with another car. I hesitated, not wanting to look like an ass. We had been stranded for no more than thirty seconds when the shirtless driver stuck his left arm out the window, and waved the first truck in.

A rope, ten feet long, was attached to the old Fiat. A 1980s F-250 farm truck with a fast driver led the way. Everyone in the dead car was tense. The rope was too short to see in front of the truck, and the shirtless driver kept his head out the window trying to see, steer, and stay ready on the brake.

The narrow road had been melted and warped by the heat. Potholes and broken off pieces of the road were impossible to miss. When 18-wheelers passed, the mother crossed herself. She reached to the backseat, grabbing her baby and holding on tight. I tried to ease the situation by offering everyone peanuts. It was all that was left in my backpack. The kids took them and started eating. Five minutes later, the eight-year-old was sick. He started sweating, and his face was red.

"*El mani, el mani, el mani!*" he shouted, staring at me accusingly. "The peanuts!"

He curled over and vomited in a clear plastic bag that had been used previously to discard yerba mate. He continued puking during the rest of the pull home. There were seven actual vomits. There was constant dry heaving. All of us were crowded in the Fiat, tied to a truck, about to die. The eight-year-old tossed the vomit bag out the window as instructed by his mother.

Hotel Sud Africa was still the best option, so despite feeling slighted over the dinner bills, I returned. The receptionist checked me in casually, and I went straight for the common area. A couple hours and a few beers later, the fat owner walked in, "Che … the receptionist says you didn't pay for a day."

I was astonished, and I assured him that I did pay. Then I got upset for having had this said to me.

"Why would I come back if I didn't pay?" I looked him straight in the eye.

He said okay, told me he was sorry, and invited me to dinner. I left the next morning, though not before teaching him how to use Skype so he could call a cute lady who had left her number. The number was indeed fake, and the fat owner was far too sad for me to hate, but damn him for seeming so happy.

On the outside of town, I stopped at a small clothing store and bought socks. Socks lasted only a week before holes formed. Sometimes the holes formed in just a few days. My Achilles felt fine, but I was still mindful of the bulging disk. When I walked, I concentrated on pushing this spot forward. At night I would put a Nalgene on its side and roll it up and down my spine. This helped, drastically improving the curvature, and since it didn't hurt, I did not worry.

Up ahead was the best Difunta Correa memorial. There was a walkway lined with thousands of plastic bottles filled with water, all leading to the memorial. The walkway gets longer each day with new prayers. I thought it looked like a rather interesting display of trash, and I grabbed a bottle from the row. I didn't need to drink it, but I could cook with it.

The road curved around to the left, and there was a big river. A dirt road led below the bridge, and there were grills and places to camp. It wasn't long before I was sleeping under the cement bridge. I woke up from my nap and got started.

Four hours later, after cresting a small hill, I found a drainpipe. It was a horrible place. There was human excrement from the travelers who just couldn't hold it till they reached town. The bugs were outnumbered only by the amount of litter. I tried the shaded side of the road, but it was overgrown and was not an option. I cleaned the sunny side, and from here I was still visible to cars, but the pipe was too small and would have felt like a coffin.

The next day, I had walked seven hours when I spotted activity at a house about a half kilometer off to my left. The house was up along the ridge-line. Finally the land was more than just flat. The colors were still mostly browns and grays, but now there were cliffs, and huge boulders with little mountains. There was also tan grass, with one blade per thousand alive. I needed water, and by the time I made it up to the house, the dogs had already announced my presence. A man and his son came to greet me. I began with my normal line: "Hola, I don't want to bother you, but I need water."

Both of them had grins from ear to ear as they led me to the garage. The son, an impressionable fifteen-year-old, was square-jawed and handsome; and like a good country boy, he was motivated by adrenaline. A four-wheeler next to the house looked to have enjoyed a number of collisions. It was clearly his, and covered in stickers and dried mud.

The father began to pump the well inside their garage. "This is the best water in the world," he told me. "There is nothing fresher."

I drank a liter and half in front of them to show my approval. The man's wife and daughter came out and said hello. Everyone was happy. Their huge grins made me wish I could better understand the words coming out of them. Being alone every day wasn't helping me become fluent.

"*Quieres venir conmigo?*" I said to the son, who smiled bigger. His father laughed, and the mom said no, nervously imagining the idea, and the potential, of her boy saying *si*. Her boy—in three short years— he would say *si,* because her boy had the spark, and she loved that spark, and she knew that spark needed more wood, and that yes he would go, somewhere, anywhere, he had to go, but no God, please not now!

Near their house was a big dried-out riverbed. There were three tunnels about ten feet in height and forty feet in length. The wind was blowing too much in the first two, but the third tunnel was just right, and I was able to get a fire started. The next day, I walked, found another bridge to sleep under, and bummed a couple cigs off a truck driver.

Then I arrived in the next town north. Tecka is a small pueblo with a YPF gas station and six square blocks of old rock buildings. Tecka was originally a settlement for both the Tehuelche and Mapuche peoples. The last resisting indigenous ruler of these tribes, Cacique Inacayal, was reinterred here. The hundred-peso bill in Argentina historically commemorated the conquest of Cacique Inacayal and the Patagonian desert. Recently changed by President Cristina Kirchner, the bill now has the face of Eva Peron on the front and a symbol of peace on the back.

No places in Tecka appeared to be worth sleeping at. I sat outside in the shade, waiting for the small supermercado to reopen. It was siesta time. After an hour, the door was unlocked and lights turned on by a kid who was about seventeen. I bought a couple liters of juice, two Speed Unlimiteds, a liter of yogurt, cheese, and bread. Speed Unlimited is Argentina's Red Bull knockoff.

The kid asked me what music I listened to, so I wrote down the funk for him to download.

Outside of town, I came across a French biker. He didn't want to talk; he had pedaled ninety kilometers that day. Just two kilometers ahead of me was the river. There was a large place that was once for camping but was no longer operational. It was a really fine spot with large trees and shade. I had ample space, unlimited water, and plenty of food from the store. I was pleased that I had not resorted to paying for a hotel room and for a place with less worth.

The next morning, the road started out flat. The sun was roasting. About two hours ahead was a spot with trees and a place for parking. There I made a fire and drank some mate. After the water got hot enough, I put out the fire and lay against a tree drinking mate with undergrowth behind me and grass below me A car pulled up, and I stayed still. It was a Ford Fiesta hatchback, and the driver was my age. He laid the seat back, and the passenger, a hot *Argentina*, climbed on top. The car rocked for a few minutes, and then she got out to pee. It felt weird staying hidden, but it was impossible to do otherwise.

Further on was an old out-of-service gas station. It was old, grandiose, built with brick, and dead. There were some gauchos working nearby, and I asked the nearest for a good spot to rest. He said up the road about ten kilometers was the most beautiful place.

"Con todos los arboles."

This was not the response I had wanted, I wanted to rest now, and just ahead was a bridge. The river was dry beneath, and the grass was tall—four feet in height. This grass, in a low area and in the shade, was mostly living. There was a small fire pit with rocks and burnt wood. The air was nice and still. I cooked the polenta mix again. This was my every meal, every day, and I had just about finished the food when I heard some gauchos on horseback. I put dirt over the fire, and lay down, out of sight. They passed by without seeing me. The dogs had not seen me either. Everyone was focused on lunch, slowly moving through the routine of the Patagonian day. After they were gone, I left. It had become easier being alone than talking to people. When I started walking, I was anticipating the beautiful spot that lay up ahead. "With all the trees," the gaucho had said.

After ten kilometers, it was still dry desert. An imposingly steep tan rock ridge began just feet from the road here, west of Ruta 40. I wanted so badly to reach the gaucho's spot. The chafing grew worse with each step, but in a haze of increased humidity, the beautiful place appeared after ten more kilometers. I was exhausted, attempting to appreciate the thousands of trees along the river that had been planted and maintained by generations of gauchos. The understory was filled with climbing vines and flowering bushes. The grasses grew in huge, round tufts, thick and dark green. It was a small ecosystem of its own.

It sounded different. Tucked between two steep ridges, unseen water was rushing deep in the trees. Instead of owls and desert birds of prey, there were colorful songbirds, and here was significantly cooler than anywhere else for miles. Along the fence were Private Property signs, and the gates to the entrances were closed.

Everything was steep, and this maintained ecosystem was incredibly thick. There was nowhere to sleep. I dropped and curled up uncomfortably. I couldn't go a step farther. It was a mostly sleepless night, and I was never to know more about the place with all the trees.

The next morning, around the first corner was a flat open area perfect for sleeping. It was always that way. I chose where I slept, but I never had more than one option. There was a constant battle of knowing when to stop, of knowing what was too short and what was too far. A car pulled over, and a lady rushed to me. Her kids were staring through the window of her Fiat 600. She had a water bottle in her hand.

"Do you remember me?"

I stared at her blankly for a second. *"Si, si,"* I said, trying to look confident.

"No me recuerdas," she said, disappointed.

"No ... si te recuerdo," I said, even though I did not remember her at all.

"I am from the museum."

Still, I was lost, and I could not, in that moment, recall ever having visited a museum. She gave me the water and left. It wasn't till she drove off that I remembered the little museum rest stop in the middle of nowhere north of Facundo. For months I had been living in a world inside my head, and it was getting worse.

Sometimes I tried to count my steps, but I never could make it past a couple thousand. During the walk, I had created hundreds of companies all between my ears. I had married Sofia, and we had taken our kids around the world. I had met the president of Argentina. John Stewart even interviewed me. These were all dreams I had created, and lived inside my head during my steps across the Patagonian desert. I believed each story to be true. I had already lived it.

I never thought much about the past. My mind was in the future. I would get so excited I would grit my teeth from adrenaline. I would say yes to myself, agreeing with a thought, pumping my fists in the air, encouraging more thoughts, encouraging my mind to live more lives. I talked to myself. Was I my soul? Were we two things? Was my conscience my soul? What is trinity? Whatever I was, and wherever I was, there was no escaping me, and here in the Patagonian desert, I realized that I could be happy anywhere, and be sad everywhere.

The following afternoon, I had a valley to climb out of. There wasn't any traffic. The only company was a family of ñandú, South America's emu. It was the second time I had seen the prehistoric birds, and now there was a family of them walking the road with me. They are half legs and half neck, with round bodies in the middle. There were probably ten babies. The ones I had seen a month earlier were smaller. These had grown. Now the kids stood two feet tall, the softest down feathers beginning to form on their backs. The two parents ran, and the kids followed. Up the valley we went together, the ñandús running up the road every time I got close. This ended when we finally got out of the valley and the family of flightless birds decided to turn around.

I was back on the plateau and in the extreme desert. I pushed it a couple more days and made it down. When walking, I often yelled with enthusiasm upon reaching epic views. Today my cries were returned, and I shouted back and forth with someone I would never see. It made me happy to communicate with another crazy person.

Esquel was still forty kilometers away, a town of thirty thousand, down the valley below. This would be the biggest place I had been to since Punta Arenas. Ahead were power lines feeding the city with a hum of energy coming off them, and when I walked below the power my mind became energy and instantly was transported to Esquel, and my mind was already drinking, and the Patagonian party had already begun, and my body had to catch up.

The thumb went out as my mindless body passed the powerline, and a trucker came and carried my body to a small vineyard—one of the southernmost vineyards in the world.

The way into Esquel from the south was immediate and spontaneous. The mountains were here; the desert was there. It rained here, and it was dry there. Trees grew here, while shrubs grew there. Here was green, there was brown. A trip that was so exceptionally different from walking, a trip powered by the fuel of fossils, a trip powered by the soul. Death to life is instant.

16 Esquel and Bolson

Without a struggle, there can be no progress.
—Frederick Douglas

Esquel was a real town, a college town, and a place often overlooked in Patagonia. It was located at the end of the Old Patagonian railway, which took lumber and wool from Esquel and brought back civilization from Buenos Aires and Europe. Esquel is the gateway to Parque los Alerces and trees that are thousands of years old. This is the mythical region where Walt Disney is apocryphally said to have been inspired to write Bambi. Meteorites strike here.

I found a hostel for twelve bucks a night. In the room with me was a huge black man wearing a yellow Kobe Bryant jersey. He didn't speak English, only French and some Spanish. He was a terrifying teddy bear. I liked him, which made me feel embarrassed by my stink. I washed my clothes in the shower with me.

After resting on a hammock for most of the day, I decided to do the most important thing when entering a college town and head to the brewery. The brochure from the tourist office showed two, and I went for the nearest one. A few blocks away, I passed a tall, athletic Australian coming back from the laundromat. He was staying in the same hostel, so I asked if he wanted to help me find craft beer. His name was William, and he used to work for Bloomberg. Now he ran marathons, and had been traveling for a year in the Americas.

We started looking for the brewery but couldn't find it anywhere.

We walked circles around the block where the map indicated it was located. We began to ask people. One person would point in one direction, and the next person would point in another. After a number of circles, we declared it a failure.

We grabbed a cab and headed to the other side of town, seeking the location of the other brewery. The driver had no idea where it was or the street name, but he took our map, and off we went.

After a few more circles, we finally arrived at the Esquel Brewery, wondering why we were not yet dizzy. It was in a shed in the owner's backyard. Brewing capacity was tiny, and he was surprised at showing off his equipment. We had seen a microbrewer before. We were here for one thing only.

"Y las cervezas, how much?"

The Esquel Brewery did not sell beer to individuals. He didn't even have a cold one. Three blocks away was a restaurant that did sell their beer. We took some stickers from the shed and left. The search for good beer was proving difficult.

We entered an empty restaurant and consumed the three local brews on tap: a roja, a rubia, and a negra. I was glad to finally have a beer.

"I mean, it is definitely better than a Quilmes, but it's no Araucana," I said, trying to show off my knowledge of Patagonian beer to the much cooler William.

I spent the next few days hanging out with him and the enormous black man—Simmi. Simmi always wore his Kobe jersey, but he never drank with us.

"No, no, no. I make babies when I drink," he said with a meekness that exists only in the largest of men. The three-hundred-pound giant was hiding behind his one-ounce espresso.

Currently there were two Latinas carrying his children. One was with twins. His brother was a Senegalese diplomat, and this meant Simmi traveled around the world hawking fake Oakleys and making babies.

"How many do you have back home?" I asked, but only got an embarrassed grin.

After a few days of asado, hammock, and beer, it was time to go back to Ruta 40. I didn't want to wait for a thumb-generated ride, so I hailed a taxi in the center of town and flew out of the beautiful Esquel valley.

I headed back to the power lines and started walking back. Then I would branch off north, staying on Ruta 40. In five days I was meeting my buddy Manny in El Bolson, the hippie capital of Patagonia and all of Argentina. Only an hour into the day, the rain started to come down in sheets. It was pointless to walk, and I tucked in early for the night. I was under the road in a sewage pipe and I was thinking about Sofia. I sent her short little emails, but it was never back-and-forth like text messaging. I had weeks to plan between one-liners.

"Walk with me across the continent. Your American boyfriend."

The next morning, I was making my breakfast polenta mix when a big gust of wind blew off my baseball cap. It was gone, flying through the tunnel and a thousand yards away in seconds. It was my only shield from the sun.

After a few hours of walking, it started to rain again. I found another drain and spent most of the day there. Just before it got dark, I was able to walk a handful of kilometers farther. It rained all night and all the next day. I tried to walk through the rain, but it came down with unencumbered force, and I was soon forced into submission. I was drowning under the road.

Finally the sun came out and I was able to pass the intersection with Esquel. What should have only taken five hours had taken three days. I finished that day fifteen kilometers north of the intersection. There was a pine forest off to my right, and I decided to make camp there. I had spent nearly sixty hours in drainpipes.

The rains came again that night, and they never stopped. I regretted not having chosen to spend one more night in the drain, and the next morning, I was determined to walk. It was miserably cold, and I needed to get warm. After a few kilometers, I was done, and decided to go to Bolson early and wait for Manny. I put my thumb out, hoping for a truck, knowing a car would not let me inside. There was decent traffic, with a car or two every couple of minutes, and I pleaded to many. Another one was coming, and inside were a bunch of young dudes looking at me. When they passed, I threw up my arms, began to jump, and started pointing at their truck bed. The driver stopped one hundred meters down the road, and I took off running.

The rain was biblical, and the driver pressed the accelerator with complete faith. We were racing. After twenty minutes, the only thing that mattered was staying warm. My neck and throat were sore from my teeth rattling, and all my extremities went numb. Finally we arrived at Lago Puelo, the small town right outside El Bolson. It was still raining, with thick, low clouds. Visibility was a rock's throw, and I could not see the pristine Patagonian mountain lake below. I went to the gas station to drink coffee, attempting to gain warmth. An hour passed before a bus stopped and took me the twelve kilometers to Bolson. Compared to the desert, this felt like the jungle.

When I got into town, I found a hostel right in the middle of it. This was the famed Bolson. For months I had imagined the town where Bob Marley's music could be heard from miles away. I headed straight to the park in the center. There was a festival of hippies doing hippie things. They were making hemp jewelry, trying to do circus tricks, playing Hacky Sack, and not showering. They were also passing around burning sticks of plant matter. We immediately became friends, and my lack of personal hygiene was finally appreciated. A short older guy who resembled Lieutenant Dan from *Forrest Gump* looked at me with crazy eyes.

"Quieres faso?" he asked, seeing if I wanted the plant that has many names.

Then he left with my order and money. I was trying to *chamuyar* with every girl there. My fluency in Spanish returned as the neurons in my mind began to fire with high frequency. One girl seemed to smile at me more than the others, so I continued on with her. It wasn't long before the Lieutenant came back with the plants.

I immediately took the flammable material back to my room to hide it. I assumed he worked with the police and it was all a big game.

The Lieutenant would sell me plants while informing the police. The police would take a bribe from me and give Dan back the plants. The scheme ran perpetually through idiots like me. This time it did not happen.

I came back to the park and flirted more with the girl. She was wearing a hoodie and still hadn't taken it off. I carried a few pre-rolled ramas, and we walked to the other side of the park to burn them. She didn't talk much and sat slumped over, her eyes cloudy. Then we went to a bar for a local beer. Not only is cannabis grown successfully in Bolson, but another plant of the Cannabaceae family also is—lupulos, the hops that give Patagonian beer its unique flavor. Beer has a strong relationship with Patagonia. The mysterious yeast of the low-temperature-loving lager can be traced back to the southern beech trees found only in Patagonia.

The hooded hippie girl kept telling me she had no place to sleep. For a week she had been sleeping in a tent with people from the carnival. My mind had images of dirty, dreadlocked sex. Back at the park, Lieutenant Dan was beginning to hate me for not rolling more ramas to *convidar* with the large group. It was time I bolted.

Saturday morning came; my buddy Manny would be arriving that afternoon. Today there was a big farmers' market around the park with a handful of local breweries in tents. I drank on tap in the park. After three dark liters of microbrew, I went back to the hotel couch to sleep it off. When I woke up, Manny was outside, knocking on the window. I let him in, and his red cheeks were so happy they made his eyes squint.

"Dude, I have a car." It was the first thing he said to me.

"Wait, what? You have a car!" I said jumping up and down and now screaming, "Freedom!" as I ran outside to go see. Manny had rented a silver two-door Volkswagen Gol and driven it all the way from Valdivia to El Bolson, over twelve hours. We got in and drove to the top of the mountain overlooking the town. Ever since I started walking, I dreamed about having a car. This was a way to explore the places my feet could never take me. A true appreciation of the automobile arrives only after a primitive mode of travel has been fully experienced.

The next day, we left town and headed south. Manny had short brown hair and was already losing a little on the top. He was pleasantly thick because of heavy light beer consumption, and he became a redneck romantic when drunk, and like a good southern boy, Manny still loved his childhood sweetheart, and he couldn't stop. When he spoke, his southern accent put my mind at ease. It wasn't like speaking English with a foreigner; it was like speaking to a brother. When we spoke to the locals, we did it like Spanish-speaking hicks.

"May goosetuh Arjin-tean-uh. Vohs s-tahs lean-duh."

It wasn't funny to anyone else, but we went from one mountain lake to the next, renting canoes, drinking, and me puking. We explored every back road, and that night we camped on the side of the dirt road, far away from people. Staring into the fire with another set of eyes made life better.

The next day, we went to Cholila for the Festival de Asado. Cholila was a town reminiscent of the Wild West. I could see the sheriff on a horse, a duel was occurring in the street, and natives were raiding the liquor store. Butch Cassidy and the Sundance Kid were here, but not today. Today the residents of Cholila and all of Patagonia had come to honor a life carnivorous—the slow-cooking, coal-roasting, cross-grilling gaucho way of living. It was incredible—a football field lined with hundreds of roasting cows and lambs. We feasted and got well sauced, but just as we were heading out of town, Manny noticed a roadblock.

"I knew they'd be looking for drunk people," he said in terror.

We drove to the far end of town and sat there for an hour. The police were only stopping people leaving from the main road, so we found a deserted dirt road and drove thirty kilometers back to Ruta 40.

That night we returned to El Bolson and went directly to party mode. At the beginning of the evening, older women from Buenos Aires were buying us drinks, but toward the end, I looked over at Manny and said, "Dude, we have to leave; it is all sixteen-year-olds in here."

Earlier, In Esquel, I had bought a cheap pair of white thong sandals, and I was wearing them now. A *boliche*, or dance club, was near, and we walked in, but before we had time to buy a drink, the bouncer told me that I had to leave. My anger was amplified by alcohol consumption, and I marched back to the hotel and grabbed the rest of my money.

"No, man, you shouldn't do that. I mean, you can't really dance in flip-flops."

"Dude, were are in fucking Bolson, Patagonia, and they are going to have a fucking dress code?"

I went back to the bar holding all the Benjamin Franklins I had. They were spread out in one hand like a deck of cards.

"You're an asshole!" I yelled at the bouncer in English, and I took off running back to the hotel, loving that he had given me the opportunity to be one too.

The following day, we ventured back south to see Parque los Alerces. An hour into the drive, I had to ask Manny to pull over. The night before needed to come out, and it did so at both ends.

"Dude, you had a double blowout; that is awesome!" Manny said while laughing uncontrollably, almost throwing up himself because of it.

We made it to the entrance. The fee was fifty pesos, and we had fifty-three. The exchange rate got better for me every day as the peso steadily lost value. This is why I never exchanged my dollars until pesos ran out.

Los Alerces is filled with lakes and rivers and is complete nature. On the other side of the lake, accessible with only a boat and money, are the old-growth alerces trees. Many of these trees, which I would not see, have been living on earth longer than both Islam and Christianity. We found one of the free campsites and set up. Immediately Manny was turned on to the instant polenta, instant mashed potatoes, and peanuts. Manny called it mash boy, and just like that, the famous meal finally had a name.

The next day was spent exploring the park, hiking to rivers, and driving back roads while drinking. We stopped at one of the private hotels to take pictures; they wanted money, so we left. On the way out,

I squatted in the middle of their driveway to make room for more mash boy. We camped another night under the stairs. The sky was clear, and it felt good to have a traveling buddy again. The freedom of Patagonia is immense—freedom to be a complete idiot.

After Los Alerces, we drove the four-hour journey to the border passing of Rio Futaleufu. This is the premier river in all the world for rafting and kayaking. This is deep Patagonia, and we were in the middle, between the Valdivian rain forest—the *selva fria*, or cold rainforest, of Chile—and the windswept desert of Argentina. Here were the steep green mountains of dense fern-filled forests and fast-flowing waters. Here was the beating heart of the Southern Andes. We turned the car around.

We spent the last night in Esquel and watched the Super Bowl. After the game, we went to a cabaret. I had never been to one, and it was a lot easier to find than the brewery. Everyone knew exactly where three or four were located. The building was dark and on the street corner. Black metal bars were in front of the windows at the entrance. The guy behind them looked at us for a moment, took our money, and let us pass. The entrance fee included our first drink. Inside, everything was black and barely lit. Manny and I were the only ones, minus the bartender. At the end of the bar was a dark door leading to a dark room that was never lit but kept the lights on. We sat down on the black bar stools and faced the scantly stocked shelf. A Speed Unlimited and Coke had been included. It was then that two women approached us from behind. They were from the Dominican Republic. One sat next to me and responded to my nervous niceties like she was certain I would be one of the weird ones, and she mostly looked forward, the whole time allowing herself to be crudely inspected. She had a forehead like a basketball, and I tried not to look at everything falling out of her clothes. Her eyes spoke of resignation.

I turned to Manny, "You wanna get outta here, man?" I said, after only a few moments.

"Yeah, dude; let's go."

Never had I been that close to a prostitute. At least not one who was working, and there was nothing pretty about it. The place smelled like sweat, alcohol, sex, and slavery, and it made me sick. How two Dominicans ended up as Patagonian prostitutes was most likely the result of modern-day human trafficking, and I felt naive. I had also, by paying the entrance fee, directly contributed to the congestion.

The next day, Manny dropped me off at the spot where I had hitched from during the rainstorm. Manny, the redneck romantic, he was brilliant, and he was going to back to Valdivia to study tree rings, to search for the rainbow trouts, and to forget the love of his life. Me and Manny embraced epically, neither wanting the moment to end.

17 Alone Again

The eternal void is filled with infinite possibilities.
—Lao Tzu

Now I felt strong and confident. I walked along the train tracks of La Trochita. The railway is also known as the Old Patagonian Express. Many of the men who laid the tracks became early settlers. I walked and slept under the tracks for two days. Here black sheep roam near the unknown town of Leleque.

I got back to the road just south of where it forked. Going to the left would take me back to El Bolson and Bariloche, and add eighty-six kilometers to the walk. I could go right and trek through the sparsely populated area from El Maiten to Pilca. It would be the desert over trees.

At this moment there was nothing I hated more than traffic, and with every step north there was more of it. I slept here under the road and was invaded by mice. The first mouse I saw looked so cute, with his pinball eyes balancing on his little head. I threw it a crumb, and the night was ruined. I ended up trying to kill the many who came to touch me in my sleep.

The next day, I made it into El Maiten, and stayed the night, stocking up on food and using the opportunity to take a long shower. I also shared a Quilmes with the town drunk, who was sitting on the sidewalk because he couldn't stand. The next day, I would cross the border into Rio Negro. I had just walked the entire province of Chubut. I needed someone to celebrate with.

It is totally barren past Maiten. The road is dirt, and there are huge boulders scattered among the hills as if thrown by the legendary giants. It is a rock climber's paradise, with first ascents beckoning. Horses were roaming wild in packs—families of them. There was a house and stream every ten kilometers. Most of the streams didn't have water, but everyone had wells. All the gauchos in Patagonia took pride in their water. Their houses were most often disgusting and without electricity, yet each man smiled with spirit and told me, "You can't get water like this in the city." The gauchos are right; there is no comparison—especially not with the water of Buenos Aires.

Norquinco was a small town of a few hundred people. I didn't feel like paying for another dirty hotel, but I went to the small convenience store and bought bread and cheese.

"Why are you walking? Are you a professional?" the man behind the counter asked me, his wife next to him.

"No, I don't really know why."

"Like Forrest Gump!" they said together.

Everyone had been calling me Forrest Gump. I smiled, but deep down I couldn't help but think they were calling me an idiot—maybe because under the bravado I felt like one.

There was a place to sleep beside the river. Here the trees drip with a strange goo.

The next morning, a few hours outside of town, there was a bridge over a dried-up creek, and I took a nap there in the shade. The heat was oppressive. The road forked, and a sign littered with bullet holes stood in the distance. I didn't try too hard to read it but kept going straight. This looked like the road most traveled.

I noticed that the berries on the calafate bushes had finally ripened, and I stopped every twenty minutes to pick them. This delighted me. I had watched the small orange flowers bloom in the spring, and I had been waiting for the day the tiny green fruits would turn dark blue. The berries are similar to an elderberry and are mostly seeds, but the drop of juice inside is an intense and unique sweetness that tastes mildly alcoholic. The bushes were everywhere. I walked hard for three hours up and down the hills, continuously munching, and becoming part of the Tehuelche legend.

I wanted to talk to someone just to reassure myself about the direction. There was a house off in the distance. A man there saw me approaching and waited. When I got there, he gave me water from the bucket at the bottom of his well. I stood there while he pulled it up from the depths. His muscles sculpted for this essential task, and his little boy squeezed his leg, and his chickens were free, and his car hadn't been used in many years, and it sat on cinder blocks, and he didn't need to go anywhere.

I asked him how to get to Pilcaniyeu. He told me I could keep going down this road and take a left, but there was no sign. I thought that sounded like a disaster, so I walked back the fifteen kilometers to the bullet-riddled sign. I had wasted an entire day eating calafate berries and believing the legend that I would return, and I had returned, all in a single day. The spirits of the wind howled in laughter.

I made it back to the bridge and started out the next morning. The next two days were great in their solitude and peace. They were lonely, of course, but I felt each step north bringing me literally closer to home. There was an older man, with a few gray hairs, ahead on a horse. He had dogs with him and they led me inside his house. His grandmother was there, and the man left us to go kill a lamb a mile away.

I was alone with the world's oldest lady who surpassed a century by decades. Every possible wrinkle streaked down her face and hands. Her pants were stained with pee. The radio was powered by a car battery, and she and I listened to music. The house had gone into disrepair. Shelves were leaning under the weight of old dusty magazines, broken dishes, and toppled religious icons. They were using old tin cans with wires as cups. The world's oldest woman got up humming with the radio and started cutting potatoes, onions, and garlic. The way she handled the knife was exceptional. I watched in awe as she cut with speed, precision, and organization. Maybe this woman was only 70. Maybe Patagonia ages the outside but keeps the inside young.

When the man returned, he hung a dead sheep from the roof and ripped out the intestines. They were filled with grass and unknowables, and the man tossed them on the ground raw for the dogs. I stayed the night there. A side room was filled to the ceiling with two-pound bags of La Mulita mate. He gave me three of these bags when I left. The gauchos are dying.

Two days later, I reached the turnoff to Pilcaniyeu in the early evening. There was a guy my age on a BMW motorcycle stuck on the wrong side of a locked gate. He asked if I had any tools. I didn't, but after some maneuvering, we were able to break down the gate and get his motorcycle across. His name was Lucas, and he told me that he was a class-b professional futbol player from Junin de los Andes. We rode the two kilometers into town on the back of his motorcycle. There wasn't much room, and I felt awkward with my package smashed so tightly against his backside. I bought a liter of Quilmes for Lucas and me to split, but he declined, and I was left drinking the whole thing by myself. He had just killed a big hairy armadillo and was going to Bariloche to cook it. He wanted me to go with him.

I camped under the train tracks feeling inebriated from the liter of beer post-marathon, and had just ripped my backpack climbing over some barbed wire. I woke up in the middle of the night with a fox walking slowly on the tracks above me, each paw silently landing on each railroad tie. I felt exposed.

For three days I had been walking through the ash from the Puyehue volcano that was causing all the economic hardship in Patagonia. The volcano was done erupting, but the ash would get picked up by the wind anytime it blew. Chilean Patagonia has many active volcanoes, and the ash always blows into Argentina.

Further on I came across a large estancia comprising of a dozen or more houses. There was an old man searching for a bullet he had dropped somewhere in the grass. I helped him look, but we never found it. I kept on walking and took a nap under a bridge an hour down the road. I woke up from my nap when the same little old man passed by me under the bridge. He was going to take a leak and was limping twelve kilometers to his friend's house. The man must have been in his late seventies. I picked us calafate berries while we walked together.

When we got to his friend's gaucho house, I drank mate with them and kept walking. I wondered what they talked about when I was gone, if they ever talked, or if they were just together, needing someone to be alone with. I slept on the side of the road in the *ceniza*, unable to escape the inch of fine volcanic ash everywhere.

The next day, the wind was relentless, blowing the volcanic ash into my lungs. After a full day, I found a nice driveway lined with tall pine trees. I walked down and asked the man if I could sleep on the grass in his front yard. He showed me over to a dust-filled two-room worker residence. There was a couch and wood-burning stove, empty shelves, and dust. Later he brought me some eggs and instructed me on how to pump water from the well. Covered in dust like everything else, and the only item on the shelf, was the *Book of Mormon*—a large hardback with etchings. The Mormon's Patagonian presence is worth mentioning, and if there is a lord, how on earth did he not come to the Americas and see Patagonia? At least that would be my argument.

The next day, I trekked hard. Finally I was about to cross the Rio Negro. It was a long day, but before nightfall I could see the rio, and when I crossed the dam, I was full of accomplishment. This river separated Argentina from the unconquered natives of Patagonia, and it wasn't until 1884 that Patagonia was finally under control. The true Patagonia was behind me. I was now on land known as "civilization" for over a century. Today it clearly was. I had no doubt that the fairy tale had ended. Every inch of Patagonia had passed under my two feet, and I would have to make my own fairy tale now.

Some maps draw Patagonia as the land south of Rio Negro; others, farther north. It is better for Argentina's tourism to include as much as possible in Patagonia, but the true Patagonia and the solitude were gone. The spirits of the wind were behind me.

I was in Neuquén province, and the next morning, I was back on a busy road. It was flat nothingness. Many cars were speeding south in search of the white peaks of Bariloche. It began to get depressing with all the people passing me by on their way to the land I was leaving behind. Because walking against traffic is the only safe approach, this caused me repeatedly to step off the road and step back on—there was nothing new to see. Here was the same dust, with the same rocks, and same nothing. Here was the treeless expanse, and the inhospitable beauty. Here was the same land, but this was not the Land of Bigfoots. No, Patagonia is not a place. Patagonia is a wild dream, and all these motorists ready to see with rapid eye movement, had woken me up.

The road descended steeply until it crossed a large tributary that had become expansive because the dam caused it to fill up a valley. The bridge was hundreds of yards long, and then the road split, going east to Neuquén, an industrial city of two hundred thousand in Patagonia, or north to Junin de Los Andes. I headed north and put my thumb out. A family soon stopped. Ten days had passed since I had done anything but walk, and I had covered nearly four hundred kilometers.

The wife got in the backseat with their two boys, seven and ten. We were off to Junin de Los Andes. The drive was beautiful, and for once the driver didn't speed. I watched the countryside roll across my eyes as we strolled through. The geological lines along earth's exposed crust ran parallel to the road, randomly bumping, shifting, breaking apart, and coming together. The road followed a wide, straight river. The dam had slowed the water. The now fertile unused land was heavily wooded with pioneer species. Here was life in the desert. We listened to Ricky Martin in Spanish, and I liked it. We sang.

In Junin I checked in to a splendid and secluded hospedaje with a nice trail that led to a stream out back. Then I chugged a liter of yogurt. They sell it in bags in Argentina. It is liquid, and I had become accustomed to biting off the corner of the bag and squeezing the entire liter into my mouth.

Junin boasts of incredible fly fishing, but I had other plans. It was my twenty-fifth birthday, and I was taking a bus to Chile to get my passport stamped and extend my visa in Argentina. Luck had me sitting by a Turk named Ghengis. Ghengis had made big money as a civil engineer in Iraq and Afghanistan and was now traveling the world for as long as he wanted. He was older with a few gray hairs, a big nose, and bushy eyebrows. He was thinking about climbing a volcano.

"I'll climb a volcano," I said.

On the border between Argentina and Chile is Volcan Lanin; it is an incredible mountain that takes two or three days to climb. It is a perfect cone volcano. The god Pillan, according to Mapuche legend, lives at the top, and he does not like people—especially hunters—climbing it. We did not risk it, and the volcano we climbed was Volcan Villarica. It is another nicely shaped cone mountain, easy to climb, that is often spewing sulfur. It took only four hours to climb and seventy dollars. Genghis brought Coronas, and we celebrated at the top. I smoked victory cigs, mostly to show off to the guides, to whom I wanted to feel superior. The views were obstructed because of sulfur gas, but I explored regardless. The stinking rocks were covered in mustard yellow.

The group had left when Ghengis and I got back. One guide was waiting for us, and we soon caught up with the group. On the way down the glacier, there were paths set up for glissading. We were sliding down the volcano's adult-playground using the icepick to brake and steer. Slides had been molded into the glacier which allowed riders to go bobsled fast.

Pucon is a beautiful town with lots of tourist attractions and lots of money. There are plenty of markets and restaurants here, and many former presidents have houses just a lake over, at Caburga. There is no town like Pucon. It has volcanoes, rivers, lakes, and old-growth forests of the famous monkey puzzle tree, Araucaria araucana—a dinosaur. Its leaves, like the scales of reptiles, are very sharp. Here is the national tree of Chile.

A few days later, I was back in Junin. I had decided to keep walking. I still felt as though I had accomplished little, but I dreaded going back to the road. The town had a marathon, and I cheered on the people finishing. It felt good giving people what I wanted so badly to receive. I wanted the finish line—an excuse. It was settled. I would only walk to Mendoza.

I got a bus to the intersection of Ruta 40 and began to hike south—back to where I had gotten the ride earlier. After fifteen kilometers, it started raining, so I hopped a fence with a Propriead Privada sign and crawled up under a tree near the river. I wondered why I hadn't chosen an adventure with more action.

The next day was nice, and I was about twenty-five kilometers into the walk when a Tacoma passed me going the opposite direction and the two men inside asked if I needed a ride or anything else. I told the men that I was fine. The driver was lean and clean shaven, and it looked as if he had a gun on his hip. He appeared to be military.

They drove off, and I kept walking. An hour later, the same truck came back, now heading in my direction. The driver was alone, and he waved me over. I hesitated, knowing that if I got into the truck with him, things were going to change, but my mind was weak, and I wanted change.

I got in the truck, and we drove a few minutes south. Then we turned left down his long driveway. He had a big walkie-talkie on his hip, not a gun. His name was Diego, and we walked into his small but very nicely kept rock house. There was a Raptor four-wheeler with a gun attached. Antlers were are all over the walls—Patagonian hunting trophies of guanaco, twelve-point deer, and ñandús. His house was clean and ready for the unexpected visitor. This was not the house of a gaucho. He had a big deep freezer filled with all the animals he had shot, and he started cooking me one of his kills.

"I am a hunting guide here," he told me.

He spoke some English, though he preferred Spanish.

"Are most of your clients from Europe?" I asked him.

Nearly every Patagonian tourist I had met was from Europe.

"No, they are almost all Americans," he said.

"Really?" I asked surprised.

Then Diego leaned on his elbows that sat on the kitchen table and plainly stated, "This is all Ted's," and when he said Ted, he said Ted like there was one Ted, and like Diego's Ted was the only Ted on earth, and now I searched my mind for The Ted.

"Ted Turner!" I screamed knowing I was right.

My journey had ended on Ted's private expansive reserve, and now in my mind I was eating Ted's massive kill, and we were all sitting around a campfire, and Ted wanted to pay me to stay in Patagonia and entertain his powerful guests, but I said, "Ted, I wanna be in the dugout of a Braves game first," and then Ted liked me more, and we went to that Braves game—me and Ted did—and Ted put his arm around my shoulder like a grandpa in a dream, and Ted said, "Follow me and we will do great things."

Ted's landmass was huge, nearly one hundred kilometers long and sixty kilometers wide, from what Diego told me. Here was home to nothing but pure, wild nature. Ted will keep it wild, with Private Property signs forever.

Diego and I exchanged gifts. He gave me a canteen from his time as a drummer in the military, and I gave him an artisan bombilla from Bolson. I told him I needed to keep walking. We were supposed to meet back up, but after an hour, I put my thumb out. I skipped the three kilometers Diego had taken me in his truck, and I was not going back for them. I was done. Here was a loser, a quitter. Here was someone who turns his back on the way to Ted, someone who always had a thousand paths to choose, and wished he could take them all, and wanted none of them.

I camped under the bridge at the intersection. Some people came up later. One guy was in his fifties and full of energy. He took a hand-knitted blue sweater off his back and gave it to me; I wore it nearly every day afterward.

I started walking north again. The road climbed a steep hill, and I stopped to pee off the side. A van pulled up behind me, and I pulled my pants up quickly. It was the same van that had given me a ride the day before. They were driving through Patagonia, hawking pirated DVDs at gas stations. I rode what would have taken six days walking to Zapala. We smoked cigs the whole way.

Zapala was a dirty dustbowl town with a casino from Four Points Sheraton. I spent most of my time in the gas station, using WiFi. I wasted two days here only because I didn't want to arrive in Mendoza early. If I did, everyone would know it wasn't all walked. I knew, but it would hurt more if everyone else knew. Confessing to God for my shortcomings was easy, seeing as he already knew them. Confessing these shortcomings to my family and friends was impossible. However, they already knew them too.

I started walking toward Las Lejas, and after a couple hours, I stuck my thumb out. It took me a little while to get a lift. Las Lejas has a dinosaur museum at its entrance but not much else. Originally Las Lejas was a town of Mapuche natives known for harvesting the seeds of the Araucaria araucana. Mapuche legend says that during a famine, God, disguised as a long-bearded old man, told a boy to eat the seeds, which lay all over the ground.

"But they are poisonous," the boy responded.

"They are a gift from God," The old man said before vanishing. "Boil them, and your people will never be hungry again."

The next morning, I started walking north again. A woman and her son picked me up. The boy was thirteen and wanted to work for the oil companies. There was oil fracking fever throughout Patagonia. Big trucks, driven by big men, with the logos of Halliburton, Schlumberger, Weatherford, and Baker Hughes were everywhere.

There was nothing in Loncopue, but I had been invited to an estancia from two American women that I met in Pucan. It was near El Hueco, farther to the North. The mom was a biker in the States, and here she was cowgirl. In Pucon she flirted with me on behalf of her homely daughter. She told me her daughter would walk a few nights with me and keep me company.

"We will send horses to come pick you up," the cowgirl had said.

I hitched the last kilometers into El Hueco, and asked around town for the residence. El Hueco is a small town that had lots of woofers from Europe. Woofers are hippies who work on farms for food and lodging, and the woofers barely interacted with me. They said the estancia was in two areas, and the ex-wife owned part of the lower estancia near town. That was the part I was at. The other part was owned by the American. This is where the new wife and homely daughter were. A strong divide existed among the woofers, and when I mentioned a few names, a Swiss Indian girl told me, "Oh, well some of us don't like them."

The woofers were going off somewhere to drink box wine. The Swiss Indian was trying to get me to pay for using the Internet on my phone, and I refused. It was another two-hour walk and a six-hour horseback ride to the other estancia.

"Maria wasn't expecting you to stay here." Maria was the ex-wife.

I left nearly as soon as I arrived and headed back into town. There was a futbol game the whole town was at, and some guys my age invited me to drink beers. Time in Argentina is better spent with the locals, and I left that evening, taking a side road to Chos Malal, and slept under a bridge that night, drunk from the futbol game.

The next morning, an old truck carrying fruits stopped, and I got inside. We drove through the sparsely populated community selling buckets of fruit for five pesos. He had ice frozen in plastic bottles to keep him and his wife cool. When we got to their driveway, he let me out, and I kept walking.

It was hot, and it was steep getting out of the dry valley. Another truck stopped after a couple hours. The driver was a preacher. He lived in Chos Malal and was driving by to check on the poor families living on the barren yellow ground that gave the town its name. We stopped at a house he was building to rent out. In a couple hours, we reached the town. I went and got a hospedaje. It had a big room and a hot tub. I bought a liter and half of wine and turned on the television.

I was watching Top Gun and started filling the Jacuzzi bathtub. It was deep, and would take a long time to fill, so my body relaxed in preparation of bliss. The big bottle of malbec wine was quickly empty-ing, and now having become far too tranquilo, I woke up at one thirty that morning needing a drink of water. I stepped out of bed, and my foot got wet. The entire room was flooded. I paused, silently saying "Shit" before going to turn on the lights. They didn't work, and I looked out the window to confirm that, yes we were the only place without power. I didn't get nervous, but I knew I had to leave as soon as possible. There was no way to smile my way out of this one.

The floors were tile, and there was a drain in the bathroom. The tile cleaned up quickly. My backpack had been on the ground and was soaked. I unplugged the TV and then removed the power strip that had been lying on the floor, placing it on the counter. It had gotten wet, and had caused the loss of power. I sneaked out into the hotel lobby and over to the front desk. The owner was snoring, the door to his room open. I held my breath as I passed. At the front counter, in the registration book was my name and passport information. I ripped out the pages to protect my good name, and I left the bed-and-breakfast in darkness at 3:00 a.m. I took a cab outside of town and hitched a ride to Buta Ranquil.

I stayed there for a couple of days under the volcano Trommen and continued to feel uneasy. I kept thinking the police were going to arrest me. I wondered what that family in the hospedaje thought about me, and how they had put the pieces together, and how I was Cleveland, and now I was the reason people hated American tourists, and I was ashamed.

Eventually I left town, but immediately went down a steep canyon to the river. The ridge was precarious, and I slowly made my way down to the muddy water. I did so in order to stay off the roads and away from any potential repercussions. The next day, I walked farther along the river. It was nice being in the wilderness. I didn't want to return to the road until I was in the next province, assuming it would be safe there.

Peace could no longer be found on the road. I was a criminal, and there was too much traffic.

The turbid water required the filter to be cleaned every couple hundred milliliters. I approached an estancia, but none of the gauchos were there. This was the winter estancia for a southern herd. It was too hot for sheep now. I found a spot to lie down. The stars came out one by one. Flies were everywhere wondering how did I get here, letting the days go by.

The next morning, I woke up and followed a river in the direction of the road. I was exhausted and found a nice little place to stay in Barrancas. They had baby Araucaria trees trying to grow. I met some local teenagers who wanted to drink beer and sit in the park, so I spent the afternoon doing that. They looked a little rough to me at first, but they were just regular "bros" who loved every movie Mark Wahlberg made. One played the guitar. The other talked about a friend who grew plants. They all had laptops given to them by the Cristina Kirchner government.

I left the next day and walked into Mendoza Province. It was great with a charged cell phone. I repeatedly sang "Into the Mystic" by Van Morrison. Before the wind, and to all, I let my spirit fly, and my mind was with Sofia, and I was rocking her gypsy soul. She would be returning to Buenos Aires soon; the snow would put southern Patagonia to sleep. My last e-mail to her said, "Meet me in Mendoza; I must see you. Walk with me. Your American Boyfriend."

I had just turned off on a dirt road when an old Mercedes cargo truck started honking at me. The occupants were drinking mate, and I got in the back. The engine had problems during the whole ride, and this gave us many excuses to stop for mate. It was a family of four, and they were heading home with a new mattress.

Here is one of the most unique sections that exist on Ruta 40. The land is molten and carved out by ancient volcanic eruptions. Visions of fire and rolling lava come easily. Petrified forests are near, and we stopped by a bridge over a huge gorge. The gorge had been formed suddenly by flowing magma and was smooth like Petra walls. Just across from us was an old bridge and the old Ruta 40. The bridge was narrow, wooden, and precarious. For an *Argentino*, driving the old Ruta 40 was legendary—a badge of honor that could take two months and a dozen tires. Now it is nearly all paved.

The truck barely made it over the hills. It was frustrating because of the stopping and starting. The family would work on the engine, we would drive for five minutes, and then they would work on the engine some more. We went through Bardas Blancas. It felt strange just driving by and not walking through. In the distance there were gas flares burning on the hillsides from oil being pumped.

Night came, and we finally finished the climb. We could cruise now, and I could relax and lay down on the new plastic-wrapped mattress in the bed of the cargo truck. The Milky Way was glowing, and it moved like a kaleidoscope as we spun down the winding mountain road. Nothing had ever been so beautiful. The entire moving universe dancing inside my night-sized pupils, and in a moment it all danced for me.

I got out at Malargue and walked to the first hostel. It took a couple days to find a better one, and it was now that I started to really feel homesick. Without a current objective, the days dragged. A guy my age who sold fabrics at markets asked if I liked plants. I said of course, and he rolled some *paraguayo*. These were plants from the Paraguayan rainforest that were pressed together in brick form and full of seeds. Sometimes gasoline is used to pack it tighter, and who knows if the human spirit rises upward, but on this plant-burning occasion, it did not.

I immediately became paranoid. We walked out into the street to burn another one. Again I felt awkward doing it so publicly. There was a chain link fence next to a concrete wall covered in graffiti. The guy got up and lodged a crumpled plastic sack in the metal fence. The stick was burning, and I thought it was a setup. The sack stuffed into the fence—it was obviously filled with plants, so I walked over to inspect the contents, and he laughed.

"No hay nada," The Fabric Salesman said, and I felt bad for not realizing in Argentina people litter next to trash cans.

We met with his friend from town and burnt the paraguayo around everyone in the park. My eyes were peeled for cops, but the other two were chill. The friend had a shaved head and black Metallica shirt.

We went to the store, and they bought an asado of all the cheapest ingredients, such as brains, intestines, and lungs. We went back to Metallica's house, and his girlfriend was there. Her hair was in a ponytail, and she hopped up to start cooking. He had huge black floor speakers, and we sat around listening to metal. Wine was poured, and Metallica watched my cup the whole time, looking to see if I was drinking, and wondering why his rufie wasn't working yet. Everyone was laughing around me. The language blurred, and I wondered what evils they were plotting. I tried to switch my drink with Metallica's but failed. I tried with the Fabric Salesman.

"Che, isn't this one yours?" He said, and I poured out my drink in the toilet.

I left the next day, and the Fabric Salesman gave me four sticks to burn. I never had any reason to be paranoid. This was just a different world, and I still couldn't really get to know anyone. My Spanish was still too limited, and everyone was too friendly. This was Argentina; the culture that lives to be social.

I started walking the next day, and I started burning the gifted sticks immediately, one after another, till they were gone. I stood on the side of the road peeing, not sure if I was dreaming, or if I would wake up with wet warmth. Finally I arrived at San Rafael. I went immediately to drink the local beer. The best visit, however, was to the Bodega La Abeja. This is the oldest vineyard in town, and according to legend, the entire land was originally purchased for a dollar. Wine country was starting to take over the campo, and Malbec stained the streets like the blood of revolution.

After a few days with the locals, I went on foot again. That night, I camped next to a Gauchito Gil monument. It was my last night as a homeless man in Argentina. The next morning, I walked a little ways and was picked up by a trucker.

I rode with him into Mendoza, but he had to stop along the way to pick up vegetables. The produce was loaded, and the driver began to back up. The rear tires went into the ditch. This forced the truck to back up farther, and soon the driver had reversed into the middle of a field worked by Bolivianos, cleaving a path through the crops, and ripping potatoes from the earth. The driver made quite the mess, running over the bumper crops the family was growing to supplement their subsistence. The poor Bolivian family, the young kids, the mothers, fathers, daughters, and brothers, they would have to go back to work, and the truck driver didn't care.

18 Mendoza and the Mountains of Wine

I got settled in Mendoza and went to explore the city. Mendoza was the place I had been waiting for, and I told everyone that I had arrived here on foot from Ushuaia. Now I was in the city of wine and mountains. Here is the tallest mountain of the Americas, the second of the seven summits, Aconcagua, the Sentinel of Stone.

A long-lost friend of my mother lived in Mendoza, and recently we had made contact. Her son was the same age as me, but I wanted to get to know the city on my own first.

I began by entering the heavily treed cosmopolitan central business district—a wide-open area free of cars, only for shops and shoppers. There I sat drinking coffee. Businesspeople and pretty women were shuffling by, when on cue, three druggies approached and asked if I wanted cocaine. They had really long fingernails, their hair was shaved in strange, random places, and they had rotting teeth.

"No, pero tienes la buena planta?"

One left to make a phone call, and I chatted for a while with the two others. Here was the most obvious illegal transaction in the world. We were in the center of a town with a million people. People in suits who were looking disgustedly at the three heroin addicts and long-haired dirty gringo. I gave them twenty-five bucks, and the one who had made the phone call left. I drank beer with the other two outside a kiosco. They were picking at their scabbed faces while I purchased craft beers, but they did not appreciate the bitterness. I didn't understand much of what was going on and only wanted the situation to be over. The guy returned with a sack and sat down at the table next to me. He told me it was another twenty-five bucks. This I had expected.

I didn't expect him to want to smoke a joint right outside the kiosco in the middle of the metropolis. He broke up the brick of paraguayo on the table and started rolling it right there. The sack was now in my possession, and I was sitting there with three horse riders, burning plants in the middle of Mendoza. The dealer got up to go to the bathroom. My nerves were on edge, and out of the corner of my right eye I saw a bike coming to a stop. It was a cop. I turned to the left and got up. The fire was across from me, burning in the hand of the youngest heroin addict, his eyes coming to a realization of what was now occurring.

"I am going to get my friend. I will be right back." I said turning.

The cop had just begun to smell the situation when the bike halted, his left foot coming to rest on the sidewalk. His body weight slowly transferred off the bike with the smooth satisfaction of arrest. I never looked back, and when I got to the corner, I started running as fast as I could. My cell phone was in my hand, and I tried to make it appear that an emergency was being dealt with.

My hostel was on Avenida Arisitides, the party street of Mendoza. All the bars, and the best hostels with pools, are there. It is also next to Argentina's largest and most famous park, Parque San Martin, named for the freedom fighting opium addict of Argentina. I planned on staying in Mendoza for a month. My mom was coming to visit me and reconnect with the long-lost family friends. After a few days on Avenida Arisitides, I contacted the Martens, and they invited me to stay at their house in Godoy Cruz, a middle-class neighborhood. Their daughter was studying in Italy, and I could use her room for a week.

I met Dante, the family's oldest son, first. He came to pick me up in his car. He was my age, height, and size. His eyes were almost black, and his hair was combed over. He spoke English perfectly, was awkward, friendly, and we were both excited to meet. Our mothers had been friends when they were only twelve years of age. Dante had found my mom on the Internet recently, but the families had not spoken in over forty years.

The Martens made me feel at home and immediately loved me like a family member. The mother, who had acorn eyes and always wore lipstick, cooked three meals a day while working as a pediatrician. She made sure I saw everything the city had to offer, and I spent eight days being a regular member of the family, just hanging out. Dante liked watching *The Big Bang Theory*. Dante's brother Matias and I smoked cigs on the balcony. He was well built, with brown hair, and a good bit taller than me. He guarded his tongue to such a degree that his thoughts became of much interest to me. He would soon be a doctor.

I went to a language-learning center and took a test so they would know my Spanish level. The instructor they assigned me was a girl in her late twenties, just a little older than me. She had a huge rack and was proud of it. She was into fashion and had us translate horrible pop songs together. We went out for coffee after class. She kept wanting us to go to a *boliche* and dance, The only time I liked her was when she yelled at me for not getting an answer right. Being yelled at by a Latina was so hot.

Boliches are Argentina's version of discotheques, and they close at 5:00 a.m. One night Dante and I went to Nacho's house. Nacho was Dante's best friend and said he had the biggest dick in Argentina. He also had a pool table, and the Victoria's Secret fashion show on the big screen. There were seven of us, and we drank Fernet with cola. They call it *"previa"* in Argentina. "We call it 'pregaming' in English," I told them, but Dante already knew. He had spent a year at college in the United States.

We went to the boliche after midnight. A French guy sat in the front, and his Argentina *mina* drove us around in her new Fiat. I was jealous. We got to the boliche, and it was packed. Thousands of people were dancing to reggaeton in what were essentially enormous mansions filled with underage girls. The guys wanted me to talk to them in English.

By four in the morning, I had tried to dance with everyone in the place. I ordered one last Fernet and cola, and we started walking home. All the cabs were filled, and none were coming back. We had to walk to Nacho's house. He and Dante were helping me walk, but the Italian liquor began to have a mind of its own.

"Yo, my brothers, I can walk," I said, pushing myself free.

They were starting to piss me off by holding me so firmly. I took off running and fell flat in the middle of the street. I looked up and saw the lights of a car right in front of me. It slammed on the brakes. I rolled away, and the car swerved.

The next morning, we managed to get up and meet Dante's family for a 1:00 p.m. lunch. The dad had cooked rabbit. The Martens' daughter had just gotten back from Italy and had adventure stories to tell. Her name was Carlita. Her brown hair was straight, and she had a nicely curved figure, but Carlita was innocently young. In my mind I had wondered if destiny had brought me here to meet her. Now I knew that it had not. She was still a girl. Sofia was a woman.

The other woman, my mom, visited and we rented a car and drove in the mountains. She is a small, petite blonde, barely five foot three, with green eyes like mine. It was great to be free on the road with her. I really wanted her to enjoy Argentina. She was everything, every breath formed by her and all her mothers before, and all the the toil and the labor, the perpetual work without keeping score, and all the mothers whom history forgot, to the very first who we blame for our thoughts, and even those mothers still covered with only their eyes to see, the mothers who sacrifice all for another to be free, this mother right here; she deserved to be me.

For a few nights, the oldest Señora Marten let us stay in her apartment. She and her late husband had traveled to Bartlesville, Oklahoma, in a worker swap with Phillips Petroleum in the sixties. They had lived next door to my mother and grandparents. One year of travel had made the Marten family pro-American ever since. The apartment had a big view over the city, and a Walmart stood right below. It almost felt like home.

We drove to Tunuyan and Tupungato and explored the bodega-filled sierras. Here the sun scorches the grapes, and the air is dry and cold. The bodegas are large and the architecturally-wonderful buildings rise one after another. Malbec has evolved the country. We went to the best bodega in Mendoza, the best in all of Argentina, and thanks to a diabolical deal, the place with the greatest wine on earth. Legend says that the founder desired this so much, and that one hundred years ago, he sold his soul to the devil, but to complete the transaction, the founder had to spend a night underground in a casket, and the next morning out came Catena Zapata, and the grapes have built an Aztec pyramid. The wine is pushed up the mountains, forcing it to adapt to the harsh climate, changing its character, and making the grapes and the country evolve.

My mom never asked what I was doing and never questioned my wanderlust. I never told her about Sofia, that would have sounded too ridiculous. My mother always let me be spontaneous, and I still had not found the way. After a tearful embrace, she left; I stayed, wondering why I wasn't going with her.

My buddy I had met in Esquel—the tall, athletic Bloomberg employee from Australia—was meeting me to run a marathon. I smoked instead of running, but William was full of energy, and we went on an easy jog through Parque San Martin to prepare. Two days later, we ran the marathon. There were thousands of runners for the international event.

The gun fired. I had a La Bersuit song on repeat. La Bersuit is a famous rock band from Argentina; "Toco y Me Voy" is their best song and was the one I was listening to. An hour into the race, I was feeling good, and I jogged easily. It took an hour to get my wind. Thankfully the race was almost entirely downhill, and during the last three kilometers, I took off in a sprint. The runner's high had taken over. My legs were still rock solid from walking, and my lungs had returned. Parque San Martin was around the corner, and I was passing tons of people. It felt good. It felt like an accomplishment. I wasn't walking in Patagonia anymore, but people were cheering, and everyone was full of excitement.

Later that night I was still feeling good, and some English guys were staying in the hostel too. They had been here for two weeks. Most travelers planned to spend only a few days in Mendoza, but they always stayed longer. Every night, the guys had been buying cocaine from a group of thirteen-year-old Bolivianos on Avenida Aristides. Tonight they came to the bar outside and began to break up the white rock.

"No, no, no, no, fuck them!" A Brit screamed, "It's chalk!"

Another of the Brits, the strong man of the group, went outside to deal with the problem. None of his friends went with him, and he came back moments later with a bruised cheek.

"I told them it was chalk and that I wanted my money back. They pulled out knives and told me they would take all my money. They jumped me. I got this, though!"

He proudly held out a big sack of Charlie. This is what the Brits called cocaine. Lines were drawn, and they went out dancing. I never went to the clubs. Plants were easy enough to find, and they kept me out of trouble. The hostel manager provided them. He had lived in Houston from age seven to seventeen. After being deported from the USA for burning plants, he made his way back home to Mendoza. It had been the most difficult experience of his life, and he said it was the best thing that ever happened to him.

His name was Mauro, and since he had grown up in the United States, his dad had made sure to teach him about rock nacional. This is the classic rock music of Argentina. Mauro introduced me to the country's most famous artists: rockers of revolution like Charly Garcia, and bands like La Renga and their pinnacle song of rock nacional "La Balada del Diablo y La Muerte" He liked River Plate, the second-most-popular soccer team in Argentina—the hated rivals of Boca. It was red versus blue, good versus bad, and rich versus poor. There are three things that bring the country together: mate, Malbec, and Maradona.

The next morning, I saw the Strongman with the black eye searching the Internet. He was looking up tattoo removal. He showed me his foot, and on the Brit's big toe, and drawn by a drunk traveling tattoo artist, was a bleeding heart with "Charlie" poorly scribbled across it.

"They told me it was a fucking good idea," he said, referring to all his friends.

I was continuing to send short e-mails to Sofi. I was going to Spanish classes, hoping to have the ability to actually talk to her the next time I saw her—if there ever was a next time. She had just returned to Buenos Aires, and I didn't want to go back to the capital. I wanted to still go north. Now I would hitchhike to Columbia, this was my new plan, and I was discussing these issues with Dante and Nacho at the beer garden. We were on our second glass of red ale when the man with the self-proclaimed biggest dick in Argentina started to get angry with me.

"You don't have to work for anything; everything comes easy to you. Things just come to you. An *Argentina* is not just going to come to you," Nacho said bluntly.

He had struck me where it hurt the most, exposing my greatest fears of having grown up with a life too good to be deserved. Nacho was not reading my mind but my soul, and like a true friend, he gave me what I needed most. Nacho had talked shit to me.

The next day, I called up Sofia. A storm had blown out the power around Buenos Aires for ten days. He brother answered, and he thought it was funny that a *"yanki"* was calling his sister. She wasn't there, and I called back a few hours later. She answered the phone, and I didn't know what to say.

"Voy a llegar a Buenos Aires mañana. I want to see you."

I was nervous and excited. It was time to leave Mendoza. I had been stagnant for almost two months. The bus ride was twelve hours, and I listened to the Argentine rock nacional Mauro showed me. I had printed the lyrics and sang along, hoping to get one last bit of Spanish language practice before the real test.

19 The New Adventure Begins

The Latina in me is an ember that blazes forever.
—Sonia Sotomayor

At Retiro, the bus stopped. I was back in busy Buenos Aires. The last time I was here, I left for Ushuaia as quickly as possible. Now a new mission had unexpectedly brought me back. At the bus stop, a person working for a hostel was looking for guests. I had heard of this place from other travelers in Mendoza. It was the biggest party hostel in Buenos Aires. The name was Milhouse. The Simpsons were the most popular show in the country, in second place was Argentina's own Al Bundy.

I walked in Milhouse and got a bed in a shared room. It was in the middle of the huge city. Many levels of floors were filled with partiers, and the place was ready to explode at a moment's notice. Everyone was standing around waiting for the sun to go down. I was anxious too, as I would soon see Sofi. She told me to look for her around 5:00 p.m. It was a two-hour bus ride into the city. She lived on the outskirts, so I went to the bookstore and purchased a Spanish version of *Siddhartha*.

As I waited, I started to wonder if I would notice her or not. I had spent nearly six months thinking about her. Would this be the girl I had been imagining? I kept looking at her pictures on Facebook, but she had only a few, and all were posted by others. I was nervously smoking Philip Morris brand cigs outside and talking to the large doorman. A couple hours passed, and she walked up.

The noise of the echoing city stopped. We knew each other

immediately, and a relieved smile appeared on her face, her eyes pleasingly processing what she saw. A spark, started by chance over a thousand miles away and months before, was now breathed back to life. The lonely road had cemented her in my mind.

I felt that energetic tingle in my shoulders. A wave of confidence crashed over me. I was on my game, alert, and even witty in Spanish. I had been preparing for this moment since I left Chalten, and we never stopped talking as we sat in front of a pizza joint, drinking beer. When two people have different lives, there are many more questions to ask. Already I was in love with her. I was convinced this was not our first life together, but learning how to love this new person with the old soul was my challenge. We went from one place to the other, finally ending up at Recoleta Cemetery—the place where the legends of Argentina, the first and most famous families, are buried in aboveground vaults. It is considered one of the most beautiful cemeteries in all the world. The brewery Buller sat across from the cemetery, and we sat on the concrete benches, having a last beer, as the city began falling asleep. I leaned in to kiss her nervously and fast. It had taken six months, and I wanted to get the stressful moment over with. The next kisses would be better.

The following day, I went to the diplomat's apartment. I was happy to see Simon, his sister was back in Asia, and the mother, Mirta, insisted I stay with them for "however long you're here." Age and injury did not allow Mirta much freedom, and she wanted company. It reminded her that she was important.

The household was pretty stressed about the state of Argentina. The leader Kirchner, though she gave away much, had been perpetuating personal presidential enrichment. This was what presidents had always done, and corruption, according to Mirta, was the reason Argentina's government had failed for so many decades.

"This country is total bullshit. Liars, criminals. She is forming an army; they are attacking Lanata!"

"She" was Cristina Kirchner, Argentina's notorious president, and Lanata was the most famous reporter in the country. Lanata was famous for his use of the middle finger, which he used when talking about the government.

One day Mirta handed Simon a piece of paper. It was a secret document.

"Do you know what that says?" she asked rhetorically. "The government is trying to replace your father with farmers." The document said Kirchner was replacing diplomats with uneducated loyalists from small towns.

Mirta had devised a plan for us to deliver the secret document to Lanata. The newsman lived in one of the richest buildings in town; it was incredibly ornate and would have been comfortable in any European city. We were in the same part of town, meaning we could walk and scope out Lanata's building. This was my first test to become a CIA agent, and I was fulfilling all my childhood dreams. Mirta had Simon wear a hat and sunglasses, and told him to be smoking cigs, that Simon was *never* not to be smoking cigs, and "act like you know what you are doing," she said flustered. Mirta was sure the government was watching Lanata's residence, and if they made the connection, things would be bad.

Simon and I started walking toward the building. He was nervous but also felt the importance and adrenaline that comes with being a spy. There were traps everywhere. Someone was following us. There he was, right there on the corner, that man in the suit, he was following us, and he was looking down at the black and white photos of us that he held, and I made eye contact with him, and I would soon be arrested, interrogated, beaten, and tomorrow, tomorrow CNN will tell the world that Caspian Ray was a spy!

Simon stopped, and I went to walk a circle around the building. I studied the gated marble entrances, looked for cameras, and felt confident about delivering the secret note the next day.

When we returned, Mirta was shaken and inhaling cigs one after the other. She wanted news. I told Sofi, who told me not to get involved in a government I knew nothing about. This was true, but Americans in foreign countries have a tendency to feel invincible.

The next day, before leaving, I took one more look at the secret note. This time I looked more at the actual document. Perhaps my test was something bigger, more intuitive, perhaps I should look deeper, perhaps I should analyze the document. I googled the first sentence and got a hit. It was a regular news article.

This was a bit of a disappointment. There was no chance at being James Bond and no opportunity for a newsworthy deportation. I began to study what had happened, and my conclusion was that the diplomat was playing a trick on his wife. He liked to press her buttons, and he knew the secret document would bring her back to the days of Cold War diplomacy. He knew it would torment her, as age and illness had made her incapable of action, and after realizing this, I liked him even more. He spoke six languages and was always the smartest person in the room, except when he was home.

On my second date with Sofia, she invited me to go slacklining with her. I was open to the idea, though it would clearly make me look unco-ordinated. We went to a park filled with hippies walking the tightrope. I was the worst one and tried not to let her see how much this angered me. I could walk across Patagonia, but I could not take a single step on the slackline. I preferred to watch Sofi's hips flex and move on the line. A blond-haired guy named Bruno who had been holding my hand, helping me walk, told us about a concert that night. It was one of Sofi's favorite bands, Onda Vaga. The venue was only twenty blocks away, and we started walking with Bruno.

The concert was in Plaza Santa Fe, and we went inside a big concert hall and started drinking a beer. A cover band was playing, and we sat down against the wall. The place was beginning to fill. The youth of Argentina all were wearing Chuck Taylor Converse shoes. Next a big ten-piece band came out, and the whole place started dancing. Everyone knew the lyrics and sang along. It was a social experiment, as the au-dience and the band became one. It was like a living organism with everyone touching, allowing decentralized electricity to flow. Here is the culture of touch.

That night, we walked back to the bus station with Bruno, and I touched Sofi's hand. It was hanging down beside her, and I could sense right away that I had made the wrong move. I had overstepped my boundaries. The whole night, I had been unable to understand much of anything said by Bruno, and I was marking my territory. It was 3:00 a.m, and we all said good-bye at the bus station. I felt defeated.

Our next date came a couple days later, and we went to the park to drink mate. She had her head in my lap in the sun. We listened to music, using one earphone each, trying to explain the meanings. Hours passed as we communicated in all forms. Every word required an explanation. Every explanation led to another story. We had such different lives. Her family's history was a mirror image of her country. Her grandfather had owned a plane, and snapped pictures from his Cessna, as he flew over the massive US naval ship that had just arrived to Buenos Aires port, a ship that was carrying President Eisenhower. Her family crashed, and traveled to the places that words should not remember, but that the spirit should not forget. The family had survived and was now beginning to recover. Sofi was strong, and she said she didn't want to learn English. I had to learn Spanish. It was so refreshing.

We walked over to a restaurant and took a seat outside. People always pandered for money, and today was no different. Children would walk by and place a small valentine card on the table. They would leave and then come back after a few minutes and grab the valentine. They were hoping to look desperate enough for a dollar. The first time this happened to me, I assumed the little girl was being cute with me.

Older guys would just ask for cash. They all were addicted to paco, the Argentine version of crack. Normally I would give them a few pesos to leave me alone. Beggars, however, had never been a problem when I was so dirty. Now that I was clean shaven and trying to impress a woman, they surrounded me. A guy came to our table, and I gave him five pesos.

"*No hablas mas*," Sofi told me. I wasn't allowed to speak.

Sofi said everything about me screamed "foreigner," and she shooed them away, one after another. She was a professional at what I could never do. No matter what they needed the money for, they needed it more than me, and I could never say no. Her phone started to ring. I couldn't understand much of what she said, but I saw the look on her face turn to one of horror. Her jaw dropped, and her eyes began to visualize what she was being told. She got off the phone. Her face was white.

"Barky had a wreck on his motorcycle."

Barky was her younger brother. He stood over six feet tall and was muscular, with curly hair and Pink Floyd tattoos. She didn't know if he was okay. She didn't know how serious it was. She didn't know what hospital he was in, and she paced with incapacity before we rushed to the bus station. I offered to pay for a cab to take her home, which would be much faster than a bus, but she wouldn't let me. Sofi got on the bus and rode the two hours home.

The next day, she told me that Barky's legs were in pieces below the knee. I didn't know what to do or say. She had just decided to travel the north of Argentina with me. She wanted to work in Cafayate, and I wanted to see Bolivia and Peru.

"You should just go without me. I don't know when I will be able to go," she said, prepared to stay with her brother forever.

She was at his side for days, but anytime she needed me, I was there. Her behavior in this situation deepened my love for her, but I was also sleeping at Simon's, which was much better than being homeless on the side of the road. I would not let Sofi slip through my fingers. I was getting fat on good food.

I spent two weeks longer in Buenos Aires than I had planned. Simon, thanks to my encouragement, started liking plants with frequency. We would walk to the roof of his apartment building and light fires. Afterward we always explored the capital, and never stopped laughing. These were some of my favorite moments of the trip. Simon and I became great friends.

I had to cross the border to get my passport stamped again. This time I planned on going to Uruguay. There was a boat that ferried tourists across the border to the quiet town of Colonia. The boats were filled with Argentinos trying to get money out of the country. The government heavily restricted the purchasing and selling of US dollars, and the greenback was the only way for people to save their earnings. The peso was depreciating at 10 percent a month, and the exchange rate was entirely artificial. The black market was called the "blue market" and was reported on daily in the news. If people had dollars, they had to get them out; the government was known for robbing their private pensions. Sofi had shown me the locations where I could exchange money on the blue market.

In Colonia, there were little novelty shops and small, old stone churches. There were places to drink coffee and to paint. All the cars stopped for pedestrians, and it amazed people from Buenos Aires.

"And the cars still stop?" everyone asked me when I got back, believing the old days would be gone completely at any moment. The world changed so fast.

In Colonia, old cars had stopped for so long that trees grew out of them. The streets were old, with uneven stones. Here was a nice place to grow old and die, but I returned to Argentina the next day.

After almost a month in Buenos Aires, I boarded a bus west for Mendoza. I needed to get everything ready for the trip. Sofi was coming in a week. Barky was recuperating slowly after multiple surgeries.

I called Sofi every day from Mendoza. I loved talking to her. Listening to her Spanish was like honey. Argentinos say they speak Castellano and not Spanish. Many old slang words exist in their Spanish dialect, called *lunfardos*. These are words and phrases that are completely unintelligible to most, and this was the intention; lunfardos were created by prisoners so they could speak openly among the guards.

Sofi called to say she would show up a few days late. A surgery had just been postponed. The doctors couldn't remember what type of screw they had put in during an earlier surgery. Now they weren't sure whether to use the flat-head or Phillips. Barky spent over forty days in the hospital and paid less than $3,000. In Argentina an injury doesn't kill you financially.

The day Sofi arrived in Mendoza, I waited anxiously during the twelve hours she was on the bus. We hardly knew each other, and now we were going to be living in a tent together. She trusted me, and I had responsibilities.

She came carrying a huge backpack, and I was full of energy. She was too. The twelve-hour bus trip hadn't caught up with her. We dropped off the backpack and headed to Parque San Martin to climb up the hill at the far end of the park. Here was the best view of the city, as well as a surprisingly cool national monument honoring Jose San Martin, the leader of independence. It was an hour and a half walk to get there. We arrived at the top and started to drink mate. Her mind seemed distant, and I wondered what she was thinking, while she wondered what she was doing. We sat there looking over the city in relative silence. Our free will and destiny were crashing together, and it made us anxious.

We rented bikes and did a wine-and-olive tour. Sofi prided herself on knowing everything the guides and connoisseurs were talking about. The smell of grape floods all of Mendoza, but in the bodegas it is suffocating, and the farther into the wine ocean we biked, the drunker we became. Cops were there to help drunk bikers get to the next island bodega so more money could be spent. We didn't need a police escort. Sofi liked racing me, and we ended up at the beer garden—the place where Nacho had encouraged me to go get this Latina.

The next day, we took a bus to Uspallata. Here we planned to trek the roads north to Salta. We got off the bus and walked down the road to the camping spot. I was so happy to finally get an opportunity to show Sofi the skills I had learned in Patagonia. I set up the tent and quickly built a one-match fire. Her long hair had static electricity running through it and stuck to the tent's walls. We fought because I belched inside our humble abode. This was everything I wanted. We were the only people in the world. Here was our first night in the tent—a chilly winter night in July, and I snuggled in my Feathered Friends sleeping bag and spooned against her.

The next day, we walked for a few kilometers and sat down for a rest. The strength of Patagonia was gone, and now I was now carrying a huge backpack with all the extra things women can't live without.

We had been trying to hitch a ride, but most of the traffic was local. I was trying to use Sofi as bait, and the first English phrase she truly understood was "Get it!" I yelled this at her any time a car was near and encouraged a her to make a sexy pose. She wouldn't, but her blushing cheeks told me she liked it. We sat down on the side of the road and started playing truco, the card game that is a must-know for any traveler wanting to fit in with locals.

A truck pulled over, and we got inside. We drove for a couple hours through the desert, and got out at the small town of Barreal. Every house had multiple beehives. There was a place for camping, and we went in that direction. A man and woman approached us, and I began to inquire about the camping. They wanted twenty-five bucks from us, so I looked at Sofi questioningly. They had noticed my accent and applied the gringo tax.

We kept walking and came upon a hospedaje. We asked the lady if we could camp in her yard. She seemed excited to have company, and she not only allowed us to camp for free but also convinced us to go on a walk with her. She wanted to show us around Barreal, and she never stopped talking. She was short, with frizzy brown hair and a fleece sweater. Her name was Linda.

We began to walk around town with the short, lonely woman. Linda had a plot of land she wanted to show us. It had a beautiful view, we were told, but after wandering for an hour, we arrived at a small plot of land with the same mountain in the distance that we had been staring at from the start. Sofi was beginning to get upset with the woman for leading us around so long. I kept trying to be nice. We were sleeping on Linda's property, and I was nervous about our bags currently inside her house. Did Linda take us on a walk so one of her friends could rob us?

Finally we made it back to town, where we began looking for a *carniceria*. Linda wanted to have an asado with us. The first two places were closed, and the town had only one more. Sofi and I both were tired, but we had the barbecue with the lady.

That night we were in the tent, and we were finally having fun rolling around in the sleeping bags. This was the new adventure—exploring our bodies. Soon after we stopped, there was a noise outside the tent. Someone was moving, making me nervous, and I cursed myself for being the male. Outside the tent I saw a man knocking on Linda's door. Earlier she had told us she was married to a professor in Mendoza. Tonight her loneliness had gotten the best of her. Together they rescued each other from the boredom of Barreal.

We left the next morning and walked to the bus station. The stop was in the park, and we waited with a bunch of other kids on their way to afternoon school.

We got off at the small town of Calingasta, and Sofia set up her slackline in the park. Some people stopped and watched her with me. The dry mountains were behind her, the yellow slackline under her toes and shaking in the wind. Sofi was balancing on the line, not thinking about anything else in the world. Watching her focus was beautiful, and we almost missed the bus to San Juan; I had to run a few blocks to buy the ticket, and when I got back, she told me I ran like a girl.

"Hey, I was just jogging. That's why I walk places!" I said, smiling. My running abilities had always made people laugh.

The bus arrived, and in a couple hours we were in San Juan. Now it was nighttime in a big city, and we didn't want to walk around the dark streets looking for a place to sleep. A hotel was right next to the bus station, so we decided to go there first. Inside, the lobby had a few old couches and bronze fixtures. The receptionist was wrinkled, and coughing, but the woman gave us our key. I opened the door, and the smell of a thousand cigarettes escaped the small room. It was claustrophobic, with just enough space for the queen-size bed and small table next to it. The view out the window was blocked by garbage piled high above it, and we mentally braced ourselves for a horrible night. I went to use the restroom. There the conditions were even worse, and I walked out gasping for breath.

"*El bano?*" Sofi asked me.

"*Horible.*" I muttered.

Then the Latina flipped a switch, the switch that only a Latina has, and the Latina told me to immediately get the bags ready. She stormed out of the room and was thundering back in less than a minute, furious.

"Vamos!" the Latina ordered. An atomic bomb had erupted, and the fire was raging, and it was the hottest fire, the center of the sun, a black-hole causing explosion, a black-hole that must be fed. Here is the Latina.

Sofi got the money back and told the receptionist the hotel was disgusting. We walked eight blocks to another hostel. The whole way, I was revolving around her, dishing out compliments of how awesome she was. That night we slept in a clean room with a clean shower.

We got a bus to Salta, and when we arrived, a nice-looking middle-aged man was waiting. He asked if we needed a hostel, and he paid for a cab to take us there. It was nice and cheap, so we got a private room.

The next morning, we headed straight for Cerro San Bernardo, which overlooked the town. It was a good trek and many people were jogging up the path to stay in shape. At the top was a restaurant, and we drank beer on their patio while admiring the view of half a million people below. The mountains stood in the distance with mummies inside. This was not the land of Mapuches, but the southern reaches of the Inca. On our way back to the hostel, we passed through the market. The cultural change from the south of Argentina to the north is striking. In Salta exists old blood and customs. One tent sold small, jarred peppers. They were really spicy, and this was more proof we were getting closer to Bolivia.

There was still more of northern Argentina left to see. We took a bus out of Salta and went a couple hours north to Purmamarca—a small pueblo tucked away under a mountain famous for the seven colors of rock that run through it. It is a geological wonder a thousand feet tall with distinct lines of colors, making each epoch vibrantly unique.

We found a place to camp, both feeling great. The town gave us spirit and begged for us to explore the steep, narrow streets. It was a unique world, and the first thing I noticed at the market was the coca leaves. I bought a couple bags and filled my cheeks with them. Sofi chewed the leaves too. I liked how they made my throat numb and my mind alert. Chewing coca leaf is like chewing coffee beans, and it is definitely not a criminal activity. A tea made with coca leaves soothes a sore throat.

The next day, we hiked a short trail to get a better view of the rock with seven colors. The mountains were covered in cacti. We climbed to the top and looked down on the resting pueblo. The wind was blowing pretty hard, and a dog that had followed us was crying. He wanted to continue the adventure, but we were already at the summit. In town we made a fire and cooked food. The mash boy's days were over, but polenta was still a staple of our diet. The next day, we left to hitch a ride to the next small pueblo to the north.

Here it was harder to walk. The elevation was over ten thousand feet in some places, and we got tired fast. I kept the coca leaves lodged in my cheeks, and we kept our thumbs out.

"Get it, Sofi! Get it!" I kept yelling at her, and we kept hitching until we had arrived at the border.

The town of La Quiaca marks the northern limit of Ruta 40.

20 Bolivia and Lake Titicaca

The whole impression was one of biological chaos, a
riotous mosaic of irrepressible plants and animals, thriving
in the richly organic microenvironment of the fields.
—Alan Kolata

Bolivia charged me $160 to enter the country. This was the reparations tax that South American governments can't live without. They all charge this fee because this is what it costs their citizens to get a tourist visa for the USA. "This is fair!" the governments all proclaimed. However, tourist visas to South America don't require two interviews and a fingerprint, as does a visa to the States. Unlike the fees paid by visitors to the USA, the reparation fees charged by South American governments go straight to the deep pockets of corruption. It was $160 that I wouldn't be able to spend at a small local business.

Street markets and coca leaves were everywhere. The strangest spices were carried in fifty-gallon sacks on the backs of the hard-working indigenous women. The men never carried anything. I hadn't been here in seven years—not since Evo Morales, the first indigenous president of Latin America, was elected. At that time, I was traveling alone, and with forged press documents, to see his inauguration. He was crowned the king of the Aymaras on the historic site of Tiwanaku. Tiwanaku is an incredible place made famous by shows like *Ancient Aliens*. My fake press pass got me to the front row, standing next to the BBC. The forty thousand indigenous Bolivians behind me were waving the colorful checkered indigenous flag, the *waphala*. If the rainbow flag of the LGBT movement were checkered, it would be the waphala. Oppressed people often live the most colorful lives.

In altiplano Bolivia, everyone was short and the woman were round. There was tremendous competition among vendors of alpaca fur and coca leaves. Farther in town was a small park. It had the only grass for miles. The dry altiplano had only cacti, sand, and shrubs. We walked around looking for a place to sleep, but each hotel was more depressing than the last. One room had beds with pee-stained children's sheets on them. The nicest hotel in town was still a twelve-story dump, but it was the only feasible option.

We set our bags down and went out to explore. Street food was everywhere, and I was eager to try it all. The tamales were fresh, and there were a thousand varieties of potatoes, corn of every color. There was a ball of fried mashed potatoes with an egg inside. There were Andean cure-alls, such as *maca*, and weird body parts from strange animals. There were dozens of pastas and dried organ powders. I tried to ask about a few of the spices, but I never could understand anything the little women said. Sofi had trouble too. They often spoke while looking at the ground. Like the gaucho in Patagonia had said, "The Bolivians won't look you in the eyes."

For nearly a thousand years, these short, round Bolivian ladies had been looked down upon, whether by the invading Incas from Peru or the invading whites from Europe. The Bolivian Aymara indigenous people have been second-class citizens in their own country since before time. The Aymara slaved at the largest silver mine in the history of the world—a mine whose influence created currency-trading in China, a mine from which the Bolivian natives did not receive even a copper cent, and a mine where they died by the millions in the mercury-filled hell of Potosi—the world's largest graveyard. No, the oppressed were not keen on making eye contact. They had learned not to, and for countless generations, Bolivian children have looked up to parents who looked down.

One lady did look up, and was squeezing juice on the corner. After a moment, she started making a special drink with bees in it. We stayed, drinking and chatting with her. When we finished, she turned to her friends. "She is going to be pregnant now!" the happy Bolivian professed.

This made Sofi blush. I wanted to scream yes, but I just shook my head and smiled.

The next morning, Sofi wanted to slackline in the park, so I decided to find a bus to take us to the next town—Tupiza. There were plenty of microbuses leaving every fifteen minutes, but they charged more. Everyone was selling something. Here was the free market of poverty.

I came back when I had the tickets. Sofi was pissed and was taking down the slackline. The park sweeper, a short old Bolivian woman, was complaining that Sofi was going to hurt the grass. People were walking by saying, "poor trees," as if the slackline would pull them to the ground.

"I asked two policemen if I could slackline here, and they said it was fine!" she told me.

With Sofi, the trip became a series of adventures that I would never have had on my own. We were both along for the ride, and destiny was driving. The bus started, and we began to venture into Bolivia's interior. I drank three beers on the ride, and because of the added elevation, I was pretty well toasted when we arrived through a narrow gorge.

Tupiza is where some legends say Butch Cassidy and the Sundance Kid, after leaving Patagonia, were finally caught and killed. Tupiza is also the starting ground for epic weeklong adventures across the altiplano. Unbeaten paths are everywhere. A girl was at the bus stop looking for travelers, and she told us how great and cheap her hostel was. Sofi thought the Bolivian girl liked me, and I liked the jealousy.

The hostel was big, with a courtyard in the middle and two levels of balconies. The walls were painted with various nature themes. One room had a huge mural of a mountain, and I wanted to sleep here. Tupiza had a good vibe, and we were in a cheap, clean room. I was throwing coca leaves in the air. It felt like a time to celebrate. I did not, like the Bolivian shamans, read how the leafs had fallen.

We went and explored the city and ate more street food. Then we headed off in the direction of a hiking trail. The rugged mountains were a deep crimson red, and covered with cacti. After a couple hours admiring ripped-apart rock sections hundreds of feet tall, we went off the trail and explored the mountains. There was a summit in the distance, and we headed to the top. Sofi got scared a couple times, but I was there to help her across. I laughed at her for being a girl, so rarely did she not act tough. We rested at the peak with a giant cactus who had long, curved needles like the hairs of an old man's beard.

On our way back, we went to an unfinished restaurant on the outskirts of town. There was a sign that said "Chicha," and I wanted to try it. Chicha is a drink made from indigenous women who chew corn and then spit the masticated mass into a vat. The mixture is left to ferment until alcohol has formed. They brought a big ceramic pitcher with matching ceramic glasses, and a sweet desert wine. The chicha here was grape and was not made from the spit of indigenous women. I was incredibly disappointed.

A middle-aged guy, the only other patron, was drunk and disheveled. He came over to talk to us, and he couldn't take his eyes off Sofia. They spoke of violence and made the situation quite tense. I tried to be friendly with him and drank the fake chicha fast.

On the way back, Sofi began feeling sick, and by the time we got back to the room, her condition had worsened significantly. The Bolivian street food had poisoned Sofi, and her insides were wrenching around with salmonella microbes. I told her it was punishment for all the racist things her country says about Bolivians. Bolivia is to Argentina what Mexico is to the United States, if Mexico was El Salvador.

Racism exists everywhere, and in Argentina, it is ingrained in their language. One of the most common insults is *"negro de mierda."* The commonality of phrases like "black of shit" speak to this inherent racism. All other nations in Latin America joke about the pretentious nature of the Argentino. Behind closed doors, many Argentinos said to me, with painful regret, that their country was a third-world nation. I said all countries had places that were third-world, but nothing hurt the Argentino more than the condition of his country. Here was a country that should be a rock star, but instead was a country that got worse each day.

"If it wasn't for those negros de mierda!" they'd say angrily in search of someone to blame, and the same people were always blamed. The "blacks of shit" were the violent *villeros* robbing everyone, and the "blacks of shit" were the corrupt politicians robbing everyone. I agreed both were bad, but decided that the country had at least three problems.

Sofi, now clearly food poisoned, was too embarrassed to use our private bathroom, and she forced herself to go outside in the cold Bolivian night, across the courtyard, and to the other bathroom. She spent more time on the toilet than in bed. I tried not to laugh but was entirely unsuccessful. She moaned.

The next day, I left Sofi alone in the room. She could at least use our bathroom now. A few hours later, when I returned, she was gone. There wasn't a note, so I went around worriedly looking for her. When I found her, she was walking like a corpse, looking for the town's *farmacia* with a prescription in her right hand and appearing lost. We bought cortisone at the farmacia and went back to the hospital to have the nurse inject the medicine. The *enfermera* encouraged Sofi to spend the night in the hospital. Sofi refused, and the nurse shoved the needle into her arm and forced the medicine inside quickly and without remorse.

We stayed in the hostel a few more days, letting her rest. When she was feeling better, we took a bus to the flattest place on earth. This is a place where the elevation changes less than a foot for over five hundred square kilometers. The size is incomprehensible. All of this flatness occurs at an altitude of over eleven thousand feet. This is the heart of the Bolivian altiplano, a dried-up lake bed covered in salt. Here is the Salar de Uyuni.

It took us a little while to find a hotel. The town of Uyuni isn't much, but the amount of Toyota Land Cruisers said there was money to be made. There were overpriced restaurants catering to the Europeans, and we unfortunately ate at one of them. Sofi was refusing to eat any more street food. That night, the hotel was very cold, and the water in our bottles froze.

In the middle of the salt flat, there is an island that the Land Cruisers take tourists to. A bus also goes there for much cheaper. With the bus, however, the ride back was not guaranteed. On the island were tables made of salt, and a hiking trail. We canoodled around; the white salt sea was endless like our passion. We found a spot where no one would see us, but anyone could if they tried. No one did see, and now I was proudly pulling thorns from my butt. Soon after our cacti coitus we got rides off the island, and headed north for La Paz.

Most things are of low quality in Bolivia, and the bus that took us to La Paz was up to par. Under the bus were bags of rotting produce, and keeping our packs clean was impossible. It was cold. The road was narrow, and the mountains tall. Everyone was crowded in the eternal casket of doom.

It was going to be nearly a twelve-hour bus ride. When we started, the scenery was incredible, and I stayed alert at all times, ready to jump out the window once the bus fell off the mountain. The driver was chewing coca leaves and driving too fast. He never used the brake until the last moment. Then, just before the blind corner, he would slam on the horn to alert the other vehicles that death was imminent. His green teeth grinned around the corners. There were old cars that had been left at the bottom of the mountains. Crosses marking wrecks were everywhere. Here the road monuments marked death; in Argentina, they marked folk heroes.

The whole bus ride was cold, but at night it was severe. We needed extra clothes and blankets, and we had to stay close to keep warm. Sofi slept, and I watched her, wondering if our journey together was going to end in a few days as planned. The next morning, we arrived at the same time as the rising sun. It was beautiful seeing La Paz wake up in the morning.

Usually we did not find hotels in advance, but La Paz was big. We had the address of a hosteria, and we took a cab there. Inside, the prices were a bit more expensive than what the Internet said, so we decided to keep looking.

In La Paz, everything is built on the steepest inclines, and the air is thin. We were soon exhausted, but each hotel in our price range was the opposite of romantic. We walked around for nearly three hours and took cabs to more dirty places. We finally went back to the first hotel, paid the extra money, and slept with beautiful blue mosaic tiles on the walls.

We were planning on going to Tiwanaku and Lake Titicaca, but we wanted to explore the city first. A bus took us down and out of the mouth of La Paz until we reached the unimpressive mansions of the country with one of the highest Gini coefficients in the world. Bolivia does not have a middle class. We walked down to the park. I was carrying Sofi's jacket in my right hand. It was a nice purple Mountain Hardwear jacket.

"Don't lose my jacket," she told me.

"I don't lose *cosas importantes*," I told her.

We sat down on benches just outside the private park, drank Sprite, and smoked a couple of puchos. Then we walked around to the park entrance on the other side. Her jacket was no longer in my hands, and I ran back to where we were sitting. It was gone, and she wouldn't let me buy her a new one. She had worked a long time to save money for that jacket. For me to just buy another with my dollars was insulting. Not only are wages lower in Argentina, but import taxes on items like this made a $200 jacket often cost $400. The right to buy a Mountain Hardwear jacket in Argentina was expensive. Argentina could make their own jackets, and they do, and they are called Montagne. Economists call this 'import substitution' and it equals easy money for corrupt governments: easy money that Cristina was handing out to all her friends, so much easy money that Cristina's bribed government friends didn't know what to do with it; so many fat stacks that they had no way to spend it; so much plata that when the next president took over, these servants of Argentina were throwing their bribes over the walls of a convent. The nuns could have it all, and the bags of cash were always for you holy mama, and *oh I am not worthy mama, por favor mama I am just a poor public works official, and oh mama, oh fuck mama how am I going to spend eight million dollars and not get caught?*

This tithe would be paid in the future though. Today, Sofi stayed in the hotel. I had just reached the Witches' Market and was asking a Bolivian hippie for directions to a camping supply store. He pointed me in the direction, but as I was walking off, he asked, "Cocaina?"

"No, no," I said shaking my head while smiling. *"El verde?"* I responded.

He went to a pay phone, and in only a few minutes we were walking through the crowds at the Witches' Market. Old women were walking with old bags and carrying old prayers. We passed one of these women, and he turned to me.

"Okay, give me the money," he said.

Soon he came back, and we started walking side by side nonchalantly. He handed me a sack, and I could tell by the softness that it wasn't paraguayo. These were high-quality plants. I took some out of the sack and gave him a nugget. Then I left the scene quickly. When I made it back to the room, I looked at Sofi and said, "Surprise!"

I had gotten nearly an ounce of plants for twenty dollars. The room had a balcony, and I started lighting fires. Now that I was elevated, I immediately went back to the Witches' Market, this time with Sofi. The market was a collection of exotic Aymara cultural traditions that have blended with the saints of Catholicism quite well. Dried llama fetuses were everywhere. These are put under a building's cornerstone for protection. There were also many catholic candles, strange potions, and a cactus—the San Pedro cactus, a cactus which contains the magical mescaline.

Various forms of the cactus were for sale. The powdered form is the easiest to use, and so that is what I bought. That way it wouldn't take eight hours to prepare and wouldn't make the entire hotel stink. Inside the long and narrow witch's shop, the *bruja* sat in the back on a stool, packaging clear green plastic sacks of coca leaves. Her body was curled under three alpaca ponchos, the outer one red. She stopped us from leaving, walked over to a shelf, and gave us two figurines. Sofi's goddess was going to bring her fertility. The ladies of Bolivia wanted a baby, and I walked out with a sack of magic.

We went back and prepared the tea. I wanted to drink Pedro in nature the first time, but I was too excited. Sofi had never done anything crazy like this before, and I wasn't sure how crazy it was going to be. The San Pedro cactus, the indigenous believe, is the key to the gates of heaven. That was why they named it St. Peter when the Spanish arrived. Here the catholic saint lives in the veins of their vision-inducing cactus.

We bought some oranges to help mask the flavor, but nothing could prepare me for the horrible taste of Pedro. The bitterness was like eating handfuls of wormwood leaves, and it was nearly impossible not to vomit. My stomach churned for an hour, not sure if the substance would be digested or purged. I had done a lot of research on the Internet and knew the peak of adventure should arrive near the fourth hour.

"Sientes algo?" She asked.

"No, do you feel anything?"

"Maybe."

"Yeah?"

We decided to go explore the city. I was excited at not knowing how intense things would be, but I was worried about getting lost in La Paz. We were laughing at everything, and I was noticing the geometric shapes of the buildings and the angles of the land. Sofi gave her half-finished Sprite to a homeless person. Everything was peaceful, when suddenly Ghengis appeared and destroyed it all. It was the guy I had climbed the volcano with in Chile.

At this moment, I didn't want to be making small talk with a Turkish engineer, and I tried to be intelligible so he would not know that I was tripping. Sofi was in her own world, not understanding a word of the English spoken between Ghengis and me. The Turk needed to get his camera fixed. The lens had sand in it from the Atacama Desert. He went into the store, and Sofi and I sat down outside. There were small squares of grass nearby. Sofi sat next to them, leaning over and touching the grass softly. She put her cheek on the grass and then put her nose between the short green blades. Sofi began to smell the grass.

"Pasto! Oh, el pasto!"

Sofi was fully Pedro'd now, and I was soon able to escape Ghengis, promising we would meet up later, while knowing it would be the last time I ever saw him. These random repeat encounters happen when traveling for extended periods. Jobless travelers all seeing the same places, with nothing to do but walk.

Sofi and I went back to the hotel, and I was frustrated. The saint did not allow me to see flying alpacas or anything else divine. I needed to make another tea, and the room again filled with the bitter odor. The taste had not dulled, and was still shockingly offensive. How this cactus was discovered, at least twenty-five hundred years ago, to have the spirit of a catholic priest, I will never believe was the result of hunger. After a few gulps, the Pedro began to overwhelm my stomach. I tried to run to the bathroom, but green slime was already on its way out. Sofi was in bed laughing at me.

We decided to get a bus to Copacabana, the border town on Lago Titicaca next to the Laguna del Sol. This was the ancient Andean home-land—the spot where legends say the indigenous peoples of South America were born.

The bus ride took us out of the city, and we passed the adobe houses and subsistence farmers. Titicaca is enormous—an ocean at the top of the world. We arrived at Copacabana and found a decent-looking hostel down the hill near the shore. We had Inca beer and respectfully poured the first sip to the dirt for *Pachamama*, the Incan Mother Earth. We were free to explore the Titicaca shores for hours. Here the creation of South American culture began millennia ago with the cult of Yaya-Mama and their ability to make the dead land fertile. The altiplano—the lifeless, inhospitable wasteland—was once the garden of Eden. The greatest gardens the world has ever seen began on the shores of Titicaca. The remains of the world's first and greatest raised-bed aquaculture are here and can be seen on Google Earth.

We made it back to the hotel, and I decided to take it up a notch. I went to the roof of the hostel and started making more Pedro. This time I used six of the doses the old indigenous bruja had sold me. I stomached the green goo and waited for the saint and his keys to heaven. Sofi came to the roof with me, and we began to dance tango. Tango is the key to Argentina, and turning that key feels like sex, and the moment we stopped the door opened, and there was Pedro. My surroundings blurred and blended together. I thought about nothing; I only opened my eyes and smiled.

We strolled to the shore and out onto a decomposing dock. It was long, creaking, and many planks were missing, so I kept my focus on Sofi. She was the sober one, and I didn't want to fall in. Then I sat down and became a part of what's bigger. I could feel the earth breathing. Frogs croaked and insects buzzed, and water splashed and kids laughed, and the boats bobbed and the wind whispered, while the sun reflected the entire world in drops falling from the beaks of the bathing birds. I was in a Monet painting, and I had no tangential thoughts.

Here was eternity, and in that eternal instant, my world shattered. A dark-skinned shoe shiner was approaching. He wasn't as young as the shoe shiners in La Paz. The shoes he used were generational and barely stayed together. His clothes were fully tattered wool. His eyes had deep rings under them, and his face appeared to be on the verge of tears. He asked to shine my shoes. I was wearing running shoes, and he looked down and shook his head in sadness.

"A friend told me there was work here, but all the tourists have shoes like yours. I left my family in Peru to make money for my four younger brothers."

Sofi had black Reeboks that were faux leather, and she removed them from her feet. I felt precarious with the Peruvian between us and the shore. He stayed squatted, scrubbing and cleaning the Reeboks like no man has ever shined a shoe. He spoke while he shined, looking down, focusing on his job. The water below reflected the clouds above.

"I have spent the last four nights sleeping in the streets. It is cold. I just want to go home. We grow papas and quinoa. We are a family. I just want to go home" His voice was tired, and quaked. I wasn't sure how many times he had repeated this story, and I wasn't sure what to do. Here was a person that produced a sickness in my stomach because seeing him made it so hard to believe in God. The Peruvian was reality, and the spirit seemed to be just a hallucination. Sofi gave him a few pesos for cleaning her shoes, and he left.

The feeling of despair took over me, and Sofi immediately felt regret. The sadness of his face was etched in my mind. I got twenty-five bucks out of my wallet, and Sofi got two hundred pesos, which was the equivalent of nearly fifty bucks at the time. She went off running. He had gone a long ways, and now I couldn't see either of them.

Here I was, sitting alone on the dock with Pedro reverberating through every cell in my body. Sofi was off running after the poor boy who had holes through every piece of clothing on his body, and leaving me to wonder if I was ever going to get through heaven's gates. Sofi found him, but my mind knew that my soul had failed the Peruvian Jesus, and that day, the Catholic saint living inside a cactus told me that I would only get through God's gates with the Latina. Sofi was my key; we had to go together.

After all that, we went to Tiwanaku—the first true city of the Americas. No one can explain the stonework of the ancient city. It is so detailed, so perfect, and so old. The original inhabitants worshipped the water, and they constructed temples to imitate its flow from the mountains to the lakes and to the depths below. The ancient raised bed aquaculture of Tiwanaku supported hundreds of thousands of people. The farmers of Bolivia's distant past lived substantially better lives than do current Bolivian farmers. Miles and miles of raised beds created entire ecosystems of life. The long forgotten mystic fog of the past has just returned to protect the crops of the freezing altiplano, where farmers today, near the Titicacan shores, have reestablished the first hectares of the massive two-thousand-year-old farms. The spirit of Bolivians is under their feet, and she is Pachamama, and they must bring back her gardens.

Sofi's eyes looked distantly and took in the landscape. She walked with her hands on the massive stone walls. She could feel the energy. She said the place had power. Tiwanaku was known for having the greatest parties in the world; everyone was drunk and having sex. Drugs were brought from the Amazon to snort, and chicha was made locally to drink. A hundred-year drought, the worst South America has ever seen since human occupation, ended the party, eliminating old trade routes and setting the stage for the Inca.

The next day, we sat on a park bench back in La Paz. Sofi started to cry.

"I knew this was going to happen. I didn't want this." She said.

The day that was always in the future now had a name, and it was tomorrow. We had not planned on being together after, and I hadn't yet told her that I planned on being with her forever. She wouldn't go to Peru with me, and I had never been to Peru—the heart of the Andes. I had studied all the pueblos and the distances between them. I wanted to continue exploring, but the walk was over. The mission, the path, my way, it had all changed, and it had all changed the day I met her in Chalten, and I was in another place where love and adventure had blended, and where solitude seemed so bad, and where now the risk felt real.

I felt her hand, and I thought about the girl crying for me. How strong she was, and how soft she was. How smart and how silly. How obsessive and how chill. How we loved and how we fought. How she challenged me. How she would fight for me. We were partners, and I would go with her this time.

"I can look for a job in Cafayate with you."

She didn't want me to give up on my adventure, but I told her that it was time for another one. Inside I was scared of regretting my decision. Peru was a sure thing, and a relationship never is.

21 Back to Argentina

Who can find a virtuous woman? for her price is far above rubies.
—King Solomon Proverbs 31:10 KJV

Cafayate is where the best Torrontés wine is produced, and at over a mile above sea level. Torrontés is a heavily aromatic white wine and is a treat. In Cafayate, we found a hostel with camping, and Sofi asked about jobs. The next day, we walked around town to see if someone was hiring. It was a pretty little wine town. The Andes mountains were in the background. Vineyards surrounded the town and went up into the hills. It was quiet, and it didn't take long to realize we wouldn't be satisfied in Cafayate. Still, we decided to spend some time. Anywhere I was with Sofia was where I needed to be.

So, the next day, we went to a good hiking spot a couple miles outside of town. The valleys around Cafayate are one of the main tourist attractions, and the air was dry as we approached the start of the Andes called the *precordillera*. In the park, we hiked for a few miles along a creek. There was a little cabin, and a dog started following us. This one was small and white, and soon we came to a narrow footbridge about eight feet over the water.

"Sofi, watch this!" I said after seeing how deep the water was below.

I grabbed the dog and threw her off the bridge into the pool. The dog got out and came right back to me. She was wagging her tail, happier than before.

"You want some more, huh?"

I threw the dog off the bridge three times before we kept walking. We found a secluded spot behind a huge bolder the size of a grand piano, and we leaned against it. The sun was shining on Sofi's long neck and olive shoulders. There was no one around except for the dog. The waterfall was cascading in the background. The birds were calling from all directions. They were bird calls I had never heard before, and in fact, the Argentinos do not say "chirp chirp" but "pio pio." On the other side of the creek, up the steepest rock ledge, was a herd of mountain goats. The babies were crying in terror, unsure of their next move, but more worried about being left behind.

I put my hands on Sofi's hips and pulled her to me. Lifting up her shirt to her giggles, and then rapidly we began to remove all garments in the middle of the clear blue sky of the precordillera. We were hidden in the mountains, animals free to the world, and I began to kiss her. The cold rock was against my back, and her warm body was against my front. It was tantric. With all the world's stimulus surrounding me, I was able to control myself like never before. No longer was I running a hundred-yard dash. Today was a marathon, and was proof that the most natural act is best done in the most natural places.

The dog was fifteen feet away, enjoying the show, and her ears perked up at the sounds of feet on rocks. I looked over the bolder down below, and my eyes made contact with a group of teenagers who minded their own business and let us finish ours.

The next day, there was a festival in town, and Sofi put out the slackline in the park. People started to crowd around, and I ran back to the hostel to grab my hat. When I returned, I set the hat down in front of her, hoping to get it filled with pesos. Kids always came up to her when she was on the line. Sofi would hold them as they walked across. I loved watching her play with kids, and we collected twenty-two pesos—just over five bucks at the time. We went to a restaurant, sat around a small table, and enjoyed the empanadas we had just earned by being hippies.

Then, after weeks of her pestering me to get a haircut, I conceded and walked to the barbershop. Afterward, I shaved to complete the transformation, and I was ready for a job interview, but when Sofi saw me she went hysterical.

"You are not you … you are not you!" She was shaking her head and putting her hands on my cheeks. Her eyes were frightened and tearful. "Don't ever change for me again," she kept repeating as she cried. The more she cried, the harder it was not to laugh, and today I became certain that I would never understand women. What did it matter if we spoke different languages?

Soon we were back in Buenos Aires, and life was different. It felt more like a home. Sofi and I were a team. We thought only of being together, and her family didn't look at me like the foreigner who had come to impregnate their daughter and leave. Her brother was walking around on crutches and showing glimpses of the old Barky. Two months of pain and immobility had hurt his spirit.

For a few days, we stayed at Barky's house while Sofi and I looked for apartments on the Internet. I had fifty days left, and I wanted to spend them all with her. Every moment we spent together had departure's inevitability ingrained within it. The end was always near.

She found me an apartment, called the real estate agent, and talked down the price. Sofi excelled in all the areas in which I struggled. The apartment was a small studio. It was furnished with two mattresses on the floor that acted as the bed and couch. It was on the fourth floor and had a small *balconcito*. We were in the district of Palermo, one of the highest-priced places to live in Argentina. A small studio apartment cost me $1,200 for forty-five days, and I had to sell a few items to pay for it.

When we got there, Sofi cleaned everything obsessively. The real estate woman normally lived here, and all her purses, underwear, diaries, and self-help books, were stuffed into drawers, and according to her writings, the real-estate agent dreamed of living on the beach in Mar del Plata, and suffered low self esteem.

Sofi and I spent most of our days locked in that small apartment. There was no cable, and we constantly had to move the antenna to get a signal. We cooked together, showered together, and practiced languages in the nude. We had a few books written with Spanish on one side and English on the other. She would read the English out loud, and then I would read the Spanish.

If she pronounced a word wrong, I would pinch her butt. If I pronounced a word right, I would pinch her butt, and I found learning Spanish was so much easier with her naked. I was a baby, and my mind was a sponge. Learning Spanish had nearly been impossible for me. Now the doors to Argentine culture were opened completely. Finally I had a woman who demanded her language of me, and after nearly a decade of trying, I finally had the disease. Spanish, Jackson had always told me, is a language that is sexually transmitted.

Sofi loved me now, and we started the process of applying for a tourist visa. Traveling to the United States is a big ordeal, and it is nearly impossible if you don't have a job or any assets. The United States wants the traveler to have a reason to return. Tourist visas are responsible for the lion's share of illegal immigration, and is nothing a wall will ever stop. I helped Sofi fill out all the forms. We had to answer yes or no questions like "Have you ever been involved in human trafficking?"

Sofi had her first immigration meeting on Calle Santa Fe, a short subway ride from our apartment. The line was out the door. Hundreds of people were ready to give their fingerprints over to the US government.

Sofi had her body catalogued, and we left. She would have her second meeting soon.

Afterward we went to the park to drink mate and slackline. This is how we spent many afternoons. Drinking mate in the park is what the country does instead of working. President Cristina Kirchner had increased the number of holidays exponentially by extending the week-ends around them. A Thursday holiday therefore meant the Friday was a holiday as well.

The trash piles were stacked high on the street corners, and the sub-ways would frequently stop running because of strikes—a conundrum that seems to have no solution. Nearly 40 percent of the workforce belong to trade unions, and in Argentina, it is so expensive to fire an employee that workers must behave horrendously in order to force ter-mination and collect a heavily increased paycheck. The unions are the government's little sister in corruption, and their bosses have summer homes around the world.

We were pretty close to Simon and the diplomat's residence, so I frequently walked to his apartment. Mirta liked having me and always had lunch ready. Sofi started giving her Pilates classes, and I brought gifts back from Bolivia for the family. I always brought Mirta flowers, but to the diplomat I gave an interesting rock I had found at the top of a mountain near Tupiza. A thick mineral vein cut across it. The diplomat stood in his apartment, surrounded by hundreds of valuable gifts from the world's most important people, and the diplomat took the rock, admiring it and making me believe it was the best present he had ever received. Here was a man deserving of all the gifts he had received, and he rushed back to work with the rock in his hand.

Simon was burning plants with regularity. He always wanted to burn them on his balcony. He assumed his mother, the woman who spoke a dozen languages, wouldn't realize it. I encouraged him to burn all the plants on the roof, and over lunch Mirta began to tell us a story about the Middle East. There she had servants who went and smoked hookah after dinner.

"I think they put hashish in it, because it smelled funny and they were always laughing!" she said while reading our expressions. Simon never made the connection. His eyes had a glaze over them.

Mirta loved to talk, and I loved to listen. Her opinions were strong. She liked the news. It made her mad.

"You know the problem here? It is the men. They think they are all macho. Pussies—every one of them." She hated machismo, but she hated Kirchner more. "There is no respect in this country. Cristina wants foreigners and sixteen-year-olds to vote! I tell you, she is a criminal. Into the drugs! The people here just let it happen. The peso will get devalued. All the money is leaving the country."

Earlier, while hitchhiking, I had heard a rumor in Calafate that Cristina Kirchner had killed her husband, the former president, as he retained too much influence over the government after her election. This excited me immensely, and I asked everyone I could about it, and here is the last and the newest of the Patagonian legends.

"Yes, there was a closed casket. It wasn't a heart attack! He was murdered!" one would say.

"No, no, no, the casket was empty. He is living in a mansion in Patagonia!" another would respond.

In fact, not a single person I asked believed the reported story. The most interesting version of the death of President Nestor Kirchner came from a man in his early fifties I met while sitting alone in Cafe Tortoni, the legendary hangout of Buenos Aires. He was across from me and was reading the *Economist*. I went over and introduced myself in English, and soon I had a seat next to his. He said he worked for the government. His Ray-Bans were on the table in their case, and his suit was long and supple. I never felt bad about asking questions. People loved that I knew enough to do so, but when I asked him about Nestor, the mood changed. His eyes looked around without his head moving. He inhaled and then began to speak sternly, but only to me. He leaned over and said, "I will tell you what happened." He paused to whisper with silent anger. "She was sleeping around like always, *una puta*. Nestor did too, of course, but one day he confronted her about it angrily. She was no longer attempting to conceal her indiscretions. She was *haciendo cuernos* while Nestor was in the house! They got into a big shouting match. The son approached Nestor, high on cocaine, and shot his dad in the face. That is why there was a closed casket. They never have closed caskets in Argentina. That is why the maids and other workers that were there have had to flee. They escaped to Chile and other countries. Their families were killed to silence them." As he was finishing, the words became quicker, more pointed, and angry. He had loved Nestor.

I told the story to Mirta, and her face turned pale.

"Don't ever repeat that in Argentina again!" She made me promise I would not. She said I would end up like Nisman, and it didn't end good for Nisman.

The longer I was here, the more confusing Argentina was becoming. It was so beautiful, big, productive, and corrupt. How could a country go from a global economic powerhouse to an embarrassment? Here was the Argentine economic paradox. On the blue market, I was exchanging dollars for nine pesos. Banks were allowed to give me only five.

Here is a country where the government, only a few decades prior, sedated its own citizens and then threw them out of planes. The bodies landed in the ocean and were never recovered. The mothers of the disappeared youths still march on the streets, lest anyone forget such a dirty war. Argentina is a country where corrupt infrastructure investments have led to huge public transportation problems. Trains taking workers into the city are filled like chicken trucks, and they crash frequently. The lack of institutions to help facilitate and alleviate the good and bad from immigration breeds populism. The Argentine car industry, with models like the Patagonia-roaming Estanciera, produced with help from Willys Jeep, is now entirely gone or foreign owned. Nepotists, military juntas, and drunken politicians took the greatest country in South America and kept it for themselves. Regardless of party affiliation, Argentine leaders have historically used the office for personal financial gain. Cristina Kirchner continued this policy and left office with a net worth, according to some estimates, of nearly a billion dollars. When her husband took power, it was seven million.

Now, it was time for Sofi's second immigration appointment. This was the interview part of the appointment, and Sofi was nervous. We went over possible questions she might get asked. I told her to never lie. She needed to always tell them the truth. Barky thought this was hilarious and began to yell, *"Nunca mentir!"* He was walking around on crutches now, and his spirits were almost back entirely.

Sofi and I went to the US Embassy. It was a powerful megalithic building with Cold War architecture. A big iron fence surrounded it. She was trembling and felt certain the visa would get declined. We waited in line, and then she walked through the metal detector alone and entered the embassy. I crossed the street to sit on the bench outside.

An 18-wheeler pulling the biggest John Deere tractor I had ever seen drove in front of me and the tall iron gates of the embassy. I laughed and assumed the truck drove circles around the building to show off American dominance in farming. Sofi returned an hour later with a reserved smile. She sat down. Her hands were still shaking. A red stress rash was forming at the bottom of her neck, near her collar bone. The adrenaline of reality was starting to hit her. She was going to the United States—something that had never crossed her mind until she met me.

Now she started to worry about her English. She never had before, and like most, the English she learned in school was British. However, nearly everyone's true vocabulary came from American movies and shows. In a short time she would be in a small corner of the Ozarks—the land of Walmart and the Razorbacks, and she would need to say y'all.

We went back to the apartment and celebrated with beer. I googled photos of the Ozarks, and all my other favorite places, such as Crestone Needle, Colorado, and Toroweap, Grand Canyon. Showing the United States to her made me feel proud. I couldn't wait for her to see my country. I was going home first, and Sofi was coming the month after. I was leaving so soon; we always seemed to be rushing. A break seemed responsible.

I went over to Simon's to tell the family the good news. Mirta was delighted, and Simon and I went to the roof to make a fire. When we got there, he started asking me questions.

"Do you love this chick, man?"

I couldn't control the slight twinge in my lips, and I looked at my shifting feet.

"You fucking love her, man. Oh shit … shit. You're fucked, dude. You love an Argentina. You are really fucked."

"Yeah, man, I am fucked."

It was a week till my plane took off. Earlier I had bought a return ticket when I was in Mendoza, and I was going home without Sofi. She would come soon after, but now I began to question leaving Sofi alone. Would she actually pack her bags and get on the plane without me? Could she make it through customs alone? I wanted to be by her side.

We had been together for only a few months. The most intense months. Nearly every night was spent together in a tent, a tiny roomed hostel, or our tiny studio apartment. I loved her from day one in Chalten, and I had searched my mind for the way without ending. I'd be damned if I was going to leave Argentina without her. That was not the way.

"*Quieres volver conmigo?*" I asked abruptly four days before departure.

"Friday?" she asked, surprised and excited.

"*Por que no?*" my grin was huge. She was going to say yes.

Then she began to panic. There were so many things she needed to do in so little time. We went to tell Barky the news. He was excited, but I could see sadness exiled to the back of his eyes. He was losing his favorite sister. She was the only person who had stayed beside him day and night in the hospital. Now he was using only one crutch.

Sofi's dad came over, and he liked to talk. His name was Flavio, but everyone called him Machet, like "machete," so I did too. Happiness came to Machet while he removed tree branches with one swing of the long blade, and he had many theories and ideas, but none of them really interested me. Nor could I understand any of them. He used lunfardos, the old slang of Capital—a language where "scratching an egg" referred to boring days.

"What did you do today?"

"*Me rasque un huevo.*"

Machet knew his insights to life fell on deaf ears. He was disappointed, unable to tell me all the things a father wants to say in these moments. I was not.

Carla, Sofi's friend, came over to say good-bye. They had met in Chalten while working seasonal jobs. Carla's parents owned an organic bakery in the capital, and she brought bread. I was sitting on the futon, watching the two of them talk. I saw the way Sofi moved and how she expressed herself—the way her eyes reacted and changed with emotion. I witnessed her spirit overflowing. She was a Latina in love. Nothing was more beautiful than her being herself. One million years of evolution had produced a billion neurons firing in this precisely exquisite form, and here was the work of God.

It was too much—this woman, this country, this adventure. I had to go out on the balcony and smoke. I was staring through the glass at her. I couldn't hear the chaotic city below. Our true love was pure luck—a thousand unlikely events leading to now. It was pure destiny. She was the reason my soul had always taken me to Latin America. She was the fulfillment of every previous event in my life. I was in control of nothing. I would have never met her if Devin had not encouraged us to go see Patagonia's most famous mountain. Destiny is not random, but life is, and thank you God that it is what it is.

We had our last Argentine asado, and I covered everything in chimichurri. The smell of freshly made chimi mixed with the aroma of mate permeates every Argentine home. There was always cumbia music coming from somewhere, encouraging people to dance. Everyone wanted to give friendly kisses, and my brain was on overload. The whole adventure was ending, and I was using all of my senses to take in each and every bit of Argentina before it was too late.

Barky drove us to the airport. We parked in the handicapped/pregnancy spot, and Barky carried his sister's bags. *"Esta embarazada,"* he yelled, and it was hard for her to say good-bye. Even though I hated to admit it, I was ready to go home. Much time had passed. I missed my family, my dogs, and my language, and I was proud of who was coming with me.

22 USA

I have made more friends for American culture than the State Department. Certainly I have made fewer enemies, but that isn't very difficult.
—Arthur Miller

When we landed in Houston, Sofi and I had to get in separate lines. Mine was shorter and went faster. It was for US citizens. It took Sofi a long time, and I was beginning to get worried about her. She looked somewhat flustered after she made it through.

"Babe, what happened? Are you okay?"

"He asked me why I was getting angry, and I told him it was because he kept asking me the same questions."

"You got mad at a customs official?!"

She never stopped amazing me, and I felt like a modern conquistador coming back home with the booty. The reason for adventure in the Americas is no longer for God, gold, and glory, but to live, to learn, and to love. When we landed in Arkansas, I had done all three, and now I couldn't wait to show Sofi my country. Never had I felt so much pride in the United States.

"You see; there is no trash anywhere!" I said, pointing along the sides of the road.

My family was waiting for us. Everyone wanted to see "the girl." I knew my mom was intimidated, but only I could tell. There was a new woman in my life, and this time she was different. My mom was small, blonde, and reserved. Sofi was long, with athletic legs and arms. Sofi was a Latina. They could barely communicate, and I was the only one who knew how similar they were.

The family went over to my grandparents and had coffee. Everyone was chatting and wanting to hear the legendary love story. Sofi had been repeating it in Spanish over the last few weeks, and now she was hearing the same story for the first time in English.

Soon we got settled in a routine, but something had changed in me. I could focus better. The days of solitude while stuck on Ruta 40 had detoxified my mind. I had spent months in a mental prison, surrounded by unreachable beauty, parched with thirst, and beaten down by the sandy wind. Through all that, my mind sheltered me by eliminating the unnecessary. I could be happy anywhere.

It wasn't all good, though. My country's flaws became more apparent as I witnessed someone trying to adapt. People here, because she spoke Spanish, assumed she was from Mexico, and they looked down on her like the Argentinos do the Bolivianos. The social awkwardness of North Americans is painful after a life in Argentina. The United States is country lacking physical touch. Here we compete with our neighbors, take antidepressants, and two weeks vacation a year. The rhesus monkey will always choose Argentina.

We fought. We had big fights. Sofi was an explosion. She was uncontrollable, honest, and homesick. She was the smoothness of a feather at the end of an arrow.

We sat down on some rocks under a bridge at a lake.

"What if you don't love me anymore? What if we try and it doesn't work?" she said.

"Then we make it work."

"But what if it doesn't?"

These words terrorized me. The idea of having a failed marriage like both our parents made me nauseated, and anything can fail if it is allowed to.

The challenge is loving someone through different situations and experiences. Often I would remember her from the studio apartment in Buenos Aires, her body leaning over the counter as she talked to her friend Carla. I remembered seeing her personality and her spirit flowing out of her. That was the real Sofi. That was the Sofi with unforced smiles—the girl who was comfortable in her own skin and speaking her own language. That Sofi was fading away.

I didn't know when to translate. During the conversation, if I translated too much, it made her look and feel dumb. If I didn't translate enough, then she looked and felt dumb. We couldn't play chess anymore; she always won.

What did I have to offer her but my spirit and love for life? All I had was passion and energy. She demanded so much from me. She knew what I was thinking before I even thought it. When my mind was wandering or when I wasn't in the best mood, she did not accept it. She wanted my best at all times, and we fought when I didn't achieve it. More importantly, though, she wanted me to be good, and she loved me because she thought I was. Sofia satisfied all my needs. She was the new everything.

The tourist visa was coming to an end. We had to make a decision. The new year had started. It was 2013, and Patagonia was gone. Sofi would have followed me anywhere. She had faith in me and said that we could do anything. Her support was unwavering. She was a lioness. I knew what Saint Pedro had told me: Sofi made me the man I wanted to be.

My mom had the ring of my great-grandmother. Her name was Juanita Wise. She and Pa used to drive on the train tracks from Oklahoma to California. This is one of the few things I know about them. The adventure part of life becomes the fairy tales, becomes the wind, an invisible presence. Adventure becomes the only part of life that does not die.

"I told grandpa when y'all got here, 'I think he found his wife,'" my mom said.

She was smiling and trying not to cry. She was full of nervous excitement. She wanted to help plan a wedding and was eager to walk me down the aisle. Now that I had the ring, I couldn't wait a second longer. Sofi was home, and I drove there fast, and I had always known the way, and it was to be spontaneous.

She was standing inside the kitchen when suddenly everything slowed down. The reality of my decision had hit me the second I walked in the door. With dazed, wide eyes, I gave her a hug and kissed her cheek. She was standing by the sink, against the kitchen counter. She wore my white T-shirt which was exposing her angular collarbones and long neck. I chuckled nervously. My knees got weak, and I gave in to them, feeling drunk and lightheaded.

"Babe," I said while dropping my right knee on the ground and regaining my senses.

I could see in her eyes that reality had just hit her as well. Infinite emotions in a blank stare. Her lips started to quiver. She wondered whether to laugh or cry, attempting both simultaneously. I was ready.

"Will you marry me?"

Update on the Mythical Characters

Manuel has built a greenhouse and has thousands of different plants—perhaps the greatest collection of species in all of Tierra del Fuego.

Jackson has started a Patagonian honey business that is *not* called Patagonia Bee Products.

Devin is teaching, investing, studying, and traveling.

Manny is back with his true love; they are engaged.

Caspian and Sofia have a baby.

Argentina has elected Mauricio Macri; his name was found in the Panama Papers.

The USA has elected Donald Trump, and decades from now brilliant economists will call the way a paradox.

Contributors to the Legend:

Kathy	Nicolas
Robert	Roger
Beverly	DrewBear
Sarah	Carol
Justin	P-Diddy
The Burdette Family	The Fontarum Family
Stephen	Shay
Joey	Bill
Brandon	Beau
Dylan	The Fugitt Family
Watford	Mikal
Katwei	Amanda
Maria	Maximus
Shorter	Angela
Chesley	Martin
The Massey Family	Rebekah
Booth	Joe
Christopher	Mark
Micsak	Finch
Farrar	Amy
Myrlinda	Gracey
Vicky	Robbie
The Burg	Benjamin
Yong—a goose-heart eater	The Ozanne Family
Phoenix	Meesh
Schmidt	Jan de Roos
Javier	Nacho

Made in the USA
Middletown, DE
03 February 2020